MARKETING

JONATHAN GROUCUTT

TEACHING FELLOW AND CONSULTANT

CHERYL HOPKINS

MARKETING CONSULTANT

First published 2016 by
PALGRAVE

Palgrave in the UK is an imprint of Macmillan Publishers Limited, registered in England, company number 785998, of 4 Crinan Street, London, N1 9XW.

Palgrave Macmillan in the US is a division of St Martin's Press LLC, 175 Fifth Avenue, New York, NY 10010.

Palgrave is a global imprint of the above companies and is represented throughout the world.

Palgrave® and Macmillan® are registered trademarks in the United States, the United Kingdom, Europe and other countries.

ISBN 978–1–137–34824–1

This book is printed on paper suitable for recycling and made from fully managed and sustained forest sources. Logging, pulping and manufacturing processes are expected to conform to the environmental regulations of the country of origin.

A catalogue record for this book is available from the British Library.

Library of Congress Cataloging-in-Publication Data
Groucutt, Jon, author.
Marketing / Jonathan Groucutt, Cheryl Hopkins.
pages cm — (Palgrave business briefing)
Includes bibliographical references and index.
ISBN 978–1–137–34824–1 (paperback)
1. Marketing. I. Hopkins, Cheryl, author.   II. Title.
HF5415.G7659 2015
658.8—dc23   2015026708

Typeset by MPS Limited, Chennai, India.

Printed in China

CONTENTS

LIST OF FIGURES

LIST OF TABLES

PREFACE

Our overall aim has been to write a text that will help you to explore, in easily accessible language, some of the basic principles, concepts and frameworks used in contemporary marketing. We suggest that this text will be ideal for students new to the subject area and others who might find some of the larger textbooks available particularly challenging.

This book is not intended to provide you with a detailed, comprehensive and in-depth examination of the subject. It is a companion to more detailed texts such as *Principles of Marketing: A Value-Based Approached* edited by Ayantunji Gdadamosi, Ian Bathgate and Sonny Nwankwo or *Foundations of Marketing* by Jonathan Groucutt, both published by Palgrave.

In order to provide such an introductory overview we have had to be selective in our approach. Some areas may be discussed more fully than others. However, these areas will be key to your knowledge, understanding and appreciation of how marketing affects, to a greater or lesser extent, each and every one of us.

Throughout this text we have generally used the term 'organisation' rather than company or firm. This is because it is not just companies that engage in marketing – charities, government departments, political parties, non-governmental organisations (NGOs) and others – all use marketing to promote themselves and their services.

We have also sought to add as many examples as possible throughout the text so that you can see how the theories/concepts link to the real world.

At the end of each chapter we have provided the following:

- A brief bullet-point summary of the key points of each chapter.
- A series of questions to help you explore the subject further. Although the vast majority of these can be undertaken individually, you might

want to work with your colleagues in teams so that you can compare and contrast your various points of view and solutions.

- Sources for further investigation and reading so that you can explore both marketing (in the wider context) and specific subject areas in more detail. The additional material comprises books, journal articles and a couple of conference papers. The academic level of these resources ranges from foundation through to advanced.

The text is written in the first person as we are seeking to have a conversation with you, to engage you in a discussion about marketing. We hope that this text provides you with the incentive to explore the subject further, not only through reading but also by going into different retail outlets, navigating online and looking at how you, your family and friends participate in marketing.

We hope that you find the text a valuable aid to your overall understanding of this subject.

Jonathan Groucutt
Cheryl Hopkins

ACKNOWLEDGEMENTS

The authors wish to thank Jenny Hindley, Holly Rutter and the production team.

1

Marketing, Markets, Competition and Co-operation

OBJECTIVES

By the end of this chapter you should be able to:

- Define marketing in its broadest terms.
- Relate marketing to your own experiences.
- Explain what is meant by the term 'marketing mix'.
- Discuss how marketing begins to fit within the wider business context.
- Explain how the macro (or external) environment can influence / impact upon marketing activities.
- Explain the differences between competition and co-operation within a contemporary business environment.

INTRODUCTION

Marketing is one of those subjects that we can all relate to as it influences our daily lives. Whether a theme park, a cinema, supermarket or, even, a museum, all illustrate the essence of marketing. As we progress through this text we will explore with you a range of examples, some that you may be familiar with and others perhaps not. However, all will show how marketing interrelates and, some readers may even say, underpins our lives.

WHAT IS A MARKET?

As we will see later in this chapter, marketing is engaged in 'exchanges', usually a product or service for a form of payment. Many villages and towns across the world still retain the traditional market place – often located as a focal point for local people to congregate. It could be argued that large supermarkets have, in many locations, replaced the traditional markets that sold items ranging from fresh food through to clothing and household appliances. Moreover, in the UK, for instance, we have seen the supermarket, both online and in-store, significantly increase the range of products and services on offer, from food through to finance and mobile phone agreements.

However, these are not the only markets that exist. In essence a market is any place (real or virtual) that trading can take place. In the City of London, for instance, there is the London Metal Exchange, where companies trade precious metals. This is a market like any other.

Whilst the shape, size and scope of everyday family markets may have changed in many countries, the basis of their existence remains – a place for purchasing a product or service.

Mini Case: Tesco Supermarket

Tesco is one of the UK's leading supermarkets that has expanded internationally. Originally a supermarket selling a selection of fresh food and vegetables, it now sells a vast range of products and services both in-store and online. These products and services include mobile phones, banking/finance, insurance, clothing, furniture and electronics.

Tesco operates in 12 countries, including China, Hungary, India, Malaysia and Poland (Tesco, 2014).

Mini Case: London Metal Exchange

This illustrates an example of a Business to Business (B2B) marketplace. The London Metal Exchange (LME) is the world's centre for the trade in 11 industrial metals, comprising (1) non-ferrous, including aluminium and tin; (2) steel billet; (3) minor metals including cobalt; and (4) precious metals, gold and silver (LME, 2014).

Over 80% of non-ferrous metals are traded on the LME, and in 2013 this equated to $US 14.6 trillion (LME, 2014).

This regulated exchange allows producers and customers of metals to come together within a physical market. Buyers can take their financial risks on the futures market through hedging. This means the buyers are purchasing future metal stock at today's price, thus hedging their risk against future price fluctuations.

HOW DO WE DEFINE MARKETING?

There are numerous definitions of marketing, a collection of which would indeed be enough for a book. For this text, however, we will focus on two American Academy of Marketing (AMA) definitions. We feel that they provide well-rounded explanations that encompass both the individual consumer and organisations. We start with the most recent, then look back to the 1960s (AMA, 2014a).

> *Marketing is the activity, set of institutions, and processes for creating, communicating, delivering, and exchanging offerings that have value for customers, clients, partners, and society at large.* (AMA, Approved July 2013)

> *Marketing is the process of planning and executing the conception, pricing, promotion and distribution of ideas, goods and services to create exchanges that satisfy individual and organisational objectives.* (AMA, 1960s)

Moreover, these definitions provide a foundation for this text. By dissecting their meaning we can begin to gain a better understanding of marketing.

Process of Planning: Marketing doesn't happen by accident. Companies often make significant financial investments, not only in creating a variety of products or services but in bringing them to the marketplace. With efficient and effective planning companies seek to maximise their return on that financial investment with sales-generated revenues. Whether it is an everyday item, such as bread, or a 'high-ticket' (expensive) item, such as a luxury sports car, both require a planned approach to bring the product to the appropriate marketplace.

Executing (the plan): It is one thing having a plan, it is something quite different executing or operating that plan. It is taking something written down and translating that into an action that will benefit both the company and their customers. An organisation must have the flexibility to modify plans in order to meet their own expectations, those of their customers and the influences of the macro environment.

Pricing, Promotion (Communication), Distribution (Placement): These are three elements of what is known as the 4Ps (Product being the other one) of the marketing mix. Price is determined by a combination of the cost of creating and producing the product or service, the return on investment and the value placed upon it by the purchaser. As we will see later within this chapter, we live and work within a highly competitive globalised world, as such today's companies need to find effective ways of promoting their products and services to their potential buyers. Both products and services have to reach the potential buyers, and this can only be achieved through effective distribution systems. Originally food was brought to a local market by those who either grew or manufactured it. Today food items may be shipped in through a combination of sea, air, rail and road to reach manufacturers, distributors and retailers prior to landing in your shopping basket. The elements that comprise the marketing mix will be explored in more detail later within the text.

Exchanging Ideas, Goods and Services: Often the definitions only refer to goods and services. However, ideas have to be marketed as well, whether it is an idea for a new movie (*Star Wars* was a concept in the mind of producer/director George Lucas), a new concept in vacuum cleaner design and operation (James Dyson) or a portable digital device to store and listen to music on the go – iTunes and iPod (Steve Jobs at Apple). Of course, the challenge is taking the idea and being able to turn it into a viable business operation. In the case of the three ideas above, all have become a reality, creating innovative and financially successful businesses.

Customers, Clients, Partners and Society at Large: This phrase helps us to place marketing within the wider context of stakeholders. It is not just about seller and buyer, as many more of us are engaged in a wider 'marketing experience', whether developing the ideas behind a promotional campaign or suggesting to our friends to read a particular book or see a particular movie. Moreover, there are the ethical issues of, for instance, consumerism and how they affect society as a whole (see Chapter 11).

As stated above, definitions often refer to 'goods' rather than products. Goods can refer to a range of items, from raw materials (for example, iron ore, copper, cotton fibre and unrefined sugar) to finished items (such as smartphones and computer software), which we tend to call products. However, it should be noted that the word 'product' is often used to encapsulate both raw materials and finished items.

We perhaps only think of 'new products', yet many of the products that we consider purchasing have been developments of existing products. Think, for instance, of the forerunners to the iPhone 6s developed by Apple. The iPhone 6s was developed (with enhancements) out of the previous smartphones. Of course, there was the original founding product, which, as in the case of the iPhone, was a breakthrough product for both the company and the sector.

Services have become increasingly important to the discussion of marketing. However what do we really mean by the term 'services'? As we will explore in Chapter 7, a service tends to be intangible and is consumed as we experience it – at the point of delivery. For example take the service provided by the company supplying electricity to our home. The outcome or consumption of that electricity supply may be translated into light and warmth, but we do not have direct involvement with the supply itself, for obvious reasons. We pay the supply company, and for that payment we gain access to light, heat, cooking facilities and the power to operate a range of devices from washing machines to computers.

The increased examination of 'service provision' led to the refinement of the marketing mix with the inclusions of an additional 3Ps: People, Physical evidence and Process (see Figure 1.1). Customer service

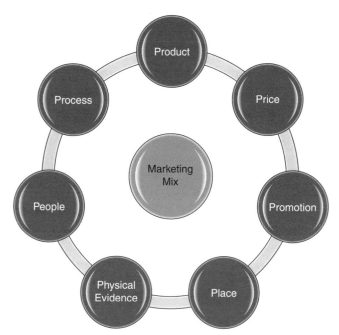

Figure 1.1 The 7Ps of the marketing mix

is delivered by 'people', whether they are the person serving you at the checkout section of a store or delivering your post in the morning. What is critical in the service delivery is that the person has been appropriately trained to deliver the service and motivated to do so.

Good examples of 'physical evidence' or 'physicality' are clothing stores, supermarkets and restaurants in terms of their design and layouts. Are they 'inviting'? Does the décor encourage customers to enter?

It may not be the prices on the menu in a restaurant that discourages customers but the way it looks inside. A restaurant's customer may not just look at the relationship between how appetising the food was and the price. They may also consider whether or not the décor and people (waiting staff and chef) added value to the overall experience of dining in that particular restaurant. These combining factors may determine whether or not that customer dines there again.

'Process' can be considered as the means of delivering a particular service. There may be particular situations where numerous processes are involved in order to deliver a service.

Mini Case: The London Underground Network

A customer using the London Underground train network can use an Oyster Card (a plastic smart payment card that holds an amount of credit that can be 'topped up'). The card is swiped over a reader and is updated with the payment made, then the barrier opens. Equally, the customer can use a contactless-enabled credit or debit card instead. This process provides for the quicker movement of customers through the barriers either entering or exiting the station. Additionally, there has been over the years (through the use of new technologies) an enhanced number of trains following in succession. Normally, there is only one/two minute's separation between trains on most of the London Underground lines. These developments in 'process' contribute to the London Underground's transportation service, which moves 1.265 billion people each year in and around London (Tfl, 2015).

Later within this text we will discuss the various components, in more detail, that comprise the 7Ps of the marketing mix. What is important to understand is that the various elements that comprise the marketing mix should not be viewed in isolation. The appropriate combination of the marketing mix components can add significantly to the real and perceived value of a product and/or service.

Creating Exchanges: As indicated earlier in this chapter, markets are a place of exchange of products or service for some form of payment, usually a recognised currency. However, in some situations that exchange may be one product for another considered of equal value.

Individual and Organisational Objectives: There are two main groups who engage in the marketing relationship: us as individuals, and organisations (companies, charities, non-governmental organisations and indeed, government departments). For us as individuals our objectives will revolve around normally personal choices, for example, what type of present to buy for a friend's birthday or what groceries to buy this week. What we buy may be determined by what's available, what might be on special offer, how much money we have available (via cash, debit and credit cards) and any time pressures. For organisations their objectives will often be very different from ours. For example, they are likely to be buying in bulk where they will seek discounts, and the delivery methods will mirror the size of the order.

The elements that comprise the AMA definitions will be explored in greater detail as we work through this text.

MARKETING AND OTHER ORGANISATIONAL FUNCTIONS

Marketing is only one component of an organisation, and it cannot operate in isolation. There needs to be both direction and structure within any organisation, and this direction normally emanates from a corporate strategy. This articulates a series of questions, which normally includes (but not limited to):

- What business are we in?
- What business should we be in?
- Where do we want to be as a business?
- How are we going to get there?
- What capabilities (resources and competences) do we need?
- What is the time frame to achieve these goals?

In order to achieve the corporate strategy, each functional unit of the organisation (marketing, operations, human resource management, finance, research and development) must also develop a strategy (see Figure 1.2). In order to achieve the marketing strategy, tactics will be deployed. These tactics (as we will see later within this text) will include pricing, promotion and distribution activities.

In order to achieve their own strategy each of the functional units must work with each other. For marketing to achieve its strategy it must work with finance (to gain a budget), human resource management (hiring the right staff to fulfil the marketing objectives) and operations (the facilities

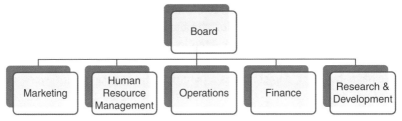

Figure 1.2 A stereotypical structure of the functional areas of a medium to large-sized organisation

to provide the products or services in the right quantities, at the right cost, quality and in the right place at the right time).

TYPES OF CUSTOMERS

This is an area that we will explore further in Chapter 2, however it is important that we gain a basic understanding of the different types of customers.

Traditionally there have been two broad categories – Business to Business (B2B) and Business to Customer (or Consumer) (B2C). The latter category is the one that we all experience every time we enter a store or shop online. More recent categories that have come to prominence are Consumer to Consumer (C2C) and Peer to Peer (P2P).

From Transactions to Relationships

We will explore Relationship Marketing in greater depth in Chapter 11. However, it is important that we consider the links between transactions and relationships. When we purchase a product, whether in-store or online, we are engaged in a transaction. We may purchase the product once or we may become repeat buyers. Companies who track our purchase either online or through in-store loyalty cards may seek to build a longer-term relationship with us. As part of our loyalty, they may offer us discounts, other special offers and loyalty (or bonus) points.

As a loyal customer we may become advocates, that is, individuals who share our positive experiences of the brand/company with others. This level of engagement is often depicted in a loyalty ladder, with the rungs of the ladder highlighting our position in relation to the brand/company. We have, however, depicted it as a pyramid. This is because not everyone becomes an advocate for a brand/company (see Figure 1.3). As discussed in Chapter 10, the more we spend on the brand, the more profitable it is for the brand/company.

> Advocate: This is a customer who in addition to being a repeat customer champions a particular product, service or retailer. They share their positive experiences with friends and family. As discussed further in Chapter 2, an Advocate may not necessarily always be a customer.
>
> Repeat Purchaser: This is a customer who regularly purchases a particular product or service or shops at a particular store.
>
> First-Time Customer: This is an individual who purchases a product, service or shops at a particular store for the first time.
>
> Prospects: A segmented group who are targeted with information on a product or service. This information may be used as part of their decision to purchase the product or service. Equally, they can use this information to decide against making such a purchase.

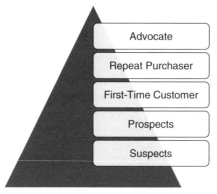

Figure 1.3 Levels of engagement and loyalty

Suspects: This is the broader population. On seeing either promotional material or the product itself (in-store and/or online) they may become a prospect.

THE MICRO AND MACRO ENVIRONMENTS

The micro environment normally refers to that environment within the organisation and over which that organisation exerts some control. This will include employees, production, operations, customer service and to some extent the relationship with stakeholders.

Then there is the sector/industry in which the organisation operates and its customer base.

At the outer edge of our diagram is the macro environment (see Figure 1.4). This generally refers to the wider world and which, generally, the organisation has little or no control over.

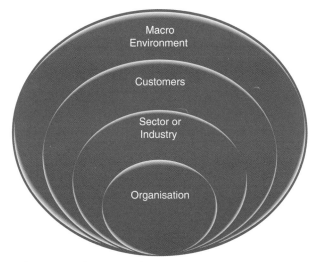

Figure 1.4 The micro and macro environments

The micro environment encapsulates the organisation. Then there will be the sector in which it operates and their customers. The macro environment (also called External/Pestel Factors) operates around these categories.

The macro environment is usually examined through the Pestel framework – Political, Economic, Societal, Technological, Environmental (natural) and Legal factors (see Figure 1.5).

Political: The plans and actions undertaken by governments. This can include agreements that open up and enhance trading relationships between nations, which influences the ability to market products and services overseas. Equally, it could mean sanctions and embargoes that can prevent or restrict the marketing of products into a region or country.

Economic: At times of economic growth the average citizen may have more disposable income, thus being able to spend more on products and services. This is in turn beneficial for the continued growth of the

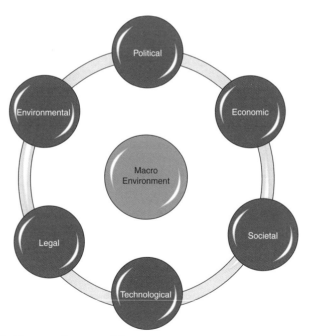

Figure 1.5 Macro environmental factors

economy. Equally the reverse is true, and if the country is entering recession the average level of disposable income declines. The reduced level of spending can push an economy further into depression, leading to closures of businesses and austerity measures being imposed by government.

Societal: This includes changing cultural perspectives and how society perceives different types of businesses. This can result in either a growth in a business sector (for example, organic food) or a decline (for example, certain types of tobacco products). Increasingly our view of the world is communicated 24/7 via social media.

Technological: These can be developments that occur within different business sectors yet impact upon a particular sector. For example, the development of computer processors and memory chips had a direct impact upon the future of typewriters. As computers became accessible to most people during the 1980s/1990s so the need for typewriters declined. Simply, the producers of typewriters could not compete with this fast-developing market. Today, computing power has led the way in the development of smartphones and tablets.

Legal: Consumer rights have been championed in many regions (for example, the European Union), with countries protecting consumers from faulty products, dishonest marketing promotions, pressure selling techniques and dangerous goods. What may be legal in certain countries may not be in others. For example, certain ingredients for Chinese medicines may be perfectly legal to use in China, but not in other countries such as the UK. This may be for several reasons, including (1) that the ingredients originate from an endangered species, thus making it illegal to import into the UK; (2) concerns regarding the toxicity of the ingredient; and (3) the overall health benefits of the final product and how it is marketed to the population.

Environmental (considered as the natural environment): The physical world in which we live impacts upon our everyday activities. A hot summer in the UK usually witnesses a rise in the sales of ice creams, equally a wet colder summer can result in the opposite. Sudden rain can result in impulse buying of umbrellas.

Environmental disasters such as earthquakes and tsunamis not only wreak physical devastation but also severely affect the operations of businesses and society. Iceland's volcanoes have intermittently released ash into the atmosphere, disrupting not only European but also international air traffic (BBC, 2014a). The difficulty here is that fine ash particles can potentially damage a jet's engines, posing a risk to the flight. The regulators responsible for European air safety decide, in such circumstances, to ground all aircraft flights across Europe as a precaution. This not only affects flights from within Europe but also those entering European airspace to either land (for instance, at London's Heathrow airport) or fly across the territory. This impacts upon airlines in terms of the positioning of both aircraft and flight crews and their customers waiting to travel either for leisure or business.

The spread of contagious diseases such as SARS and Ebola affects communities, restricting access to raw materials, goods and services. They equally, increase the demand for vaccines, equipment and specialist medical treatment services.

Macro Factors: Integration

An important point to remember is that the various macro factors can operate both in isolation and collectively. For example, in 2012 and 2013 the Greek government imposed a series of stringent austerity measures to gain European Union (EU) finance to stabilise a failing economy. The near economic collapse brought hardships to Greek society as reflected in the level of disposable income available to the vast majority of the population. The reduction in disposable income impacted upon the sale of products and services within Greece. While some of these products were produced within Greece, others will have been imported from, for instance, neighbouring countries. The reduced level of disposable income will also have had an impact (to a greater or lesser extent depending upon the type of product) on imported products. Thus the political and economic issues of Greece will have an impact upon companies in other countries.

An important point to remember here is that we cannot view the macro factors purely from our own country's perspective. Due to global interconnectivity we have to consider the interrelationship of the macro factors across nations.

MARKET LEADERSHIP

Within highly competitive environments it is important to understand which company holds the greatest share of the market and those who might challenge that position. Equally, companies or organisations can operate in very specialist or niche markets (see Figure 1.6).

Market Leader: This is the company that holds the largest share of the market. A company that operates, for instance, within several overseas markets may be a market leader in some and a market challenger in others. In order to protect their position the market leader may deploy several different tactics:

> They could expand the market for their brand through promoting new uses for their product. For instance, a breakfast cereal could be marketed as an all-day healthy snack food. This may create a first-mover advantage, however challengers could also use similar types of promotions.

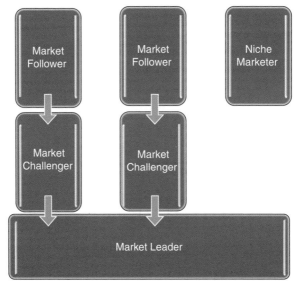

Figure 1.6 Market positions

The company seeks to protect and defend its market position through the use of marketing communications and the development of brand extensions. Such tactics maintains the brand positioning in the customer's mind (see Chapter 4), however these tactics often require significant long-term investment in resources. In many cases only major competitors will have the resources to match those of the market leader.

The company could seek the acquisition (either friendly or aggressively) of a competitor. The acquisition would provide scope for increasing market share. However, in many countries there are anti-trust/anti-competition regulations that do not permit domination of a particular market (this links to the 'political' and 'legal' aspects of the Pestel factors). These regulations are enforced so that the customer has freedom of choice within the market.

Market Challenger(s): There may be one or more companies that have the resources to challenge the market leader. A challenger has to operate on two levels: (1) it has to watch the actions of the Market Leader, especially if it is seeking to challenge that position; (2) a Market Follower may decide to no longer follow the Market Challenger but to challenge. Therefore Market Challengers can be 'sandwiched' between two moving forces. The Market Challenger can deploy a range of tactics if they decide to mount a real challenge to the Market Leader:

Frontal Attack: This is where the challenger deploys its resources to directly challenge the leader within the marketplace. The tactics can include matching advertising spend, price competition (price matching and/or price reductions), or launching a brand extension or new product. The challenger can also seek to acquire another company so that their combined capabilities (resources and competences) can be used to challenge the leader directly. Depending upon the Market Leader's capabilities, they may decide to deploy their forces directly against the challenger on the basis that they can continue the momentum whereas the challenger may not be able to sustain their actions.

Flanking Attack: This is not a broad direct challenge as in a Frontal Attack. A Flanking Attack is where the Market Challenger seeks out any weaknesses within the Market Leader's position. For instance, there may be one/two market segments where the Market Leader's position is not as strong as others. The challenger can then deploy their capabilities to gain some of the market within these segments. The Market Leader may react in several ways: (a) They could allow some loss of share within those markets, so that they can concentrate their capabilities in maintaining the larger proportion of the market. (b) They could counter the challenger's actions, especially if they were planning to develop those particular segments further over the medium to longer term.

Encirclement: This is a longer-term tactic and builds upon the concept of the flanking movement. The challenger establishes itself within the leader's vulnerable segment and seeks to develop a strong market position. Eventually over time the challenger expands outwards from the segment, seeking to encroach into other segments within the leader's market. The ultimate aim is to gain significant market share to overwhelm the leader's position. Such an action requires considerable capabilities and assumes, to some degree, that the leader will not be aware of the challenger's actions.

By-Pass: This is where the challenger seeks to diversify into other markets and business interests where it has a greater possibility of gaining market share and increasing its own capabilities. The challenger can enter an unrelated segment/market through acquisition of another company. At a later stage when the challenger has the necessary capabilities it may mount a challenge against the leader in the original market.

Guerrilla Attack: This is where the challenger mounts often unpredictable, short-term actions against the Market Leader. These can include special promotions, significant price reductions (perhaps for a limited period) and interest-free credit. These can be used both individually and collectively. While such actions may gain some additional market share, it may only be a short-term benefit for the challenger. Once, for instance, the special promotions come to an end, customers may return to the Market Leader's products and/or services.

Market Followers: These are companies that may tackle either the main Market Challengers and/or the Market Leader. However generally they tend not to mount challenges as they realise that they may not have the capabilities to be successful in their challenge. Instead they seek to imitate, where possible, the Market Leader in terms of products, services and operations, without breaching copyrights, trademarks and patents.

Consider the range of household cleaning products that are available in supermarkets and discount stores. Some of the brand names you might be very familiar with are produced by multinational companies such as Procter & Gamble (P&G), SC Johnson and Unilever. However, there are other medium to large companies that produce both own-label products for supermarkets and manufacture and market their own particular brands. An example of this is the UK-based company McBride.

Niche Marketer: This is a specialist market which is sufficient in size to provide growth and profitability often for more than one company. The market can be large enough for several companies to operate profitably. As Niche Marketers develop and expand they can eventually become challengers to Market Leaders.

The UK-based natural ethical beauty brand The Body Shop started business in 1976 as a small niche marketer in a single store in Littlehampton in Southern England (The Body Shop, 2014). In 1984 the company was launched on the London Stock Exchange, and in 2006 it was acquired by the French-based company L'Oréal for £652 million (The Body Shop, 2014). As of October 2014, The Body Shop had 2,500 retail outlets in over 60 markets (The Body Shop, 2014). The company caught the UK consumer's imagination through the active campaigning of the store's founder Anita Roddick. Over time, Roddick transformed the company from a niche player to a major challenger within the cosmetics market.

A company can also operate within multiple niche markets. For example, Halo Foods (a Raisio Group company), is UK-based and operates within several niche markets: as supplier of nuts and crisps to leading hotel chains, fruit and cereal snacks and confectionery ingredients.

COMPETITION AND CO-OPERATION

We now live within a globalised world where companies often trade internationally. A key point to remember is that today companies are not bound by their size and geographical location, and even small companies through the use of the Internet can trade beyond their local geographical environment. This opens up the opportunity for a greater level of competition within the marketplace. In theory this presents the consumer with a wider range of choice.

Types of Competition

Broadly we can establish that there are two types of competition:

Direct: This is where a customer, for instance, makes the choice between two virtually identical products. For example, making a choice between two chocolate bars of similar size and price made by two rival companies.

Equally, imagine a couple who want to travel from London to a hotel in the Highlands of Scotland for a vacation, an approximate distance of 900 km. They will have various options, which could include:

1. Driving in their own car from London to the hotel in the Highlands.
2. Being chauffeur-driven from London direct to their hotel in the Highlands.
3. Taking a daytime train from London's King's Cross rail station to Inverness rail station and then hiring a car to their hotel. They could also hire a taxi.
4. Taking an overnight sleeper train from London's Euston rail station, arriving early next morning in Inverness. As in the previous example, they could either hire a car or a taxi for the drive to the hotel.
5. Flying from an airport near London to Inverness and then either hiring a car or a taxi to their hotel.
6. Taking a coach from London's Victoria Coach Station to Inverness and then either hiring a car or taxi to their hotel.

As you can see, there are various options. The couple will make their decision based upon certain interconnected factors. These will include:

Price: What are the relative costs involved in travelling from London to Inverness. Some modes of travel may be far more expensive than others, for instance, being chauffeur-driven compared to self-driving. Equally, the price charged for the mode of transport may vary depending upon when it is booked. A flight booked one month in advance may be considerably less expensive than one booked the day before the intended travel – that is, assuming that there are seats available.

Flexibility: Prices may be lower on certain days of the week than others. This can include the price for the hotel as well.

The level of comfort required: Even with two people sharing the driving, 900 km is a very long drive even if there are stopovers for rest and meals.

Ease of journey: Flying from London to Inverness normally takes 85 minutes. Compare that to train, coach and car journeys, all of which will be relatively longer. Driving may well require a stopover for the night, which will incur more expense.

Stopovers: Whether (if driving) the couple want to stop somewhere overnight. This may be necessary for reasons of driving safely, especially when fatigued. Equally, a stopover may be part of the journey – to see another part of the country for a day.

Time commitments: Depends how quickly the couple need to reach their destination in order to enjoy the full value of their vacation.

These are the types of decision-making factors that we will also explore in the next chapter.

Indirect: Having reviewed the costs and time factors, our couple may decide not to travel to the Scottish Highlands for a vacation but remain at home in London. Instead of the vacation, they may decide to undertake DIY to enhance the overall look of their home. Therefore some of their vacation budget will be allocated to the cost of the materials (for example, paint, tools and other essentials) for the refurbishment.

This is an example where customers seek substituted products or services. Competitors are aware that the customer has a wide range of choices, therefore they need to focus their marketing effort to build brand recognition and promote the products/services' features and benefits (a point that we will return to in Chapter 12: Marketing Planning & Strategy).

However, it would be easy to imagine – sometimes supported by the vibrant promotion of products and services – that only competition exists. This is not always the case; companies do collaborate and co-operate across both sectors and industries. Bluetooth is a very good example of where major manufacturers competing in similar markets sought co-operation. They understood that such co-operation provided both mutual and individual advantages (see Mini Case: Bluetooth).

Mini Case: Bluetooth

Bluetooth is a unifying technology and brings together promoter companies or members to share technologies that allow many of our everyday devices – smartphones, computers, household appliances – to communicate with each other. It is these technologies that allow us, for instance, to access emails via smartphones.

KEY POINTS

In this chapter we have considered the following:

1. We asked what defines a market both in consumer and business terms? The concept of the market has, in many countries, changed over the centuries. In developed nations the traditional market has been largely replaced by supermarkets and hyper markets, and vast shopping outlets. Businesses engage in markets, whether for cocoa, orange juice, oil or precious metals. Markets have also moved from the physical world of bricks and mortar to that of the virtual. It could be argued that the online retailer Amazon is a vast market where we can shop 24/7.

2. We offered a definition of marketing, but it should be stated that this is only one definition of marketing. As you explore the subject further, it will become clear that many marketing organisations and writers have, over the years, either adapted or created their own definitions. This approach is good for marketing as it helps to challenge and reinvigorate the subject.

3. We saw how marketing must operate with other functional units inside an organisation in order to create and operate a meaningful strategy.

4. We highlighted the structure and interrelationship of the 7Ps of the marketing mix.

5. We looked at the role of competition within a contemporary setting and how co-operation, even among competitors, has a value for both the companies concerned and their customers.

6. We examined how the external or macro environment can influence and change how business operate and products/services are marketed.

QUESTIONS

Here are a series of questions and activities for you to undertake to aid your knowledge and understanding of the points made in this chapter.

1. Review the key elements of the American Marketing Association's definition of marketing. Then reflect upon your own marketing experiences, for example, shopping in your local supermarket. What can you match from the definition to that experience?

2. Explain the difference, using examples, between the micro and macro environments.

3. Explain, using different examples, the role of markets within a contemporary business setting.

4. Explain, including examples, why marketing, as a function of business, cannot operate in isolation.

5. Outline why it is important for an organisation to develop a marketing strategy that links into the overall corporate strategy of that organisation.

6. Normally after we complete our supermarket shopping we store away the various items and dispose of the itemised receipt. If you have completed a shop for a relatively large basket of groceries, review the receipt and reflect upon why you made those purchases. Note down your reasons. As well as adding to your understanding of what defines marketing, it will also help set the scene for the following chapter on buyer behaviour.

FURTHER STUDY

The following are additional resources that can help you in your wider exploration of marketing.

Civi, E. (2013) Marketing strategies to survive in a recession. *International Journal of Business and Emerging Markets*. Vol 5 No 3. pp: 254–267.

Day, G.S. and Malcolm, R. (2012) The CMO and the future of marketing. *Marketing Management*. Vol 21 No 1. pp: 34–43.

Kotler, P. (2011) Reinventing marketing to manage the environmental imperative. *Journal of Marketing*. Vol 75 No 4. pp: 132–135.

Lee, B. (2012) Marketing is dead. *HBR Blog Network. Harvard Business Review*. June.

There are many different types of organisations and institutions that support the ongoing development of marketing. This is just a brief selection of some of the different member-based organisations:

Academy of Indian Marketing: www.aoim.in

American Marketing Association: www.ama.org

Arts Marketing Association: www.a-m-a.co.uk

Australian Marketing Institute: www.ami.org.au

Chartered Institute of Marketing (UK): www.cim.co.uk

Direct Marketing Association (UK): www.dma.org.uk

French Marketing Association: www.afm-marketing.org

Hong Kong Institute of Marketing: www.hkim.org.hk

Institute of Direct and Digital Marketing (UK): www.theidm.com

Institute of Marketing Malaysia: www.imm.org.my

Marketing Association of Australia and New Zealand: www.marketing.org.au

Marketing Institute of Singapore: www.mis.org.sg

2

Understanding the Customer

OBJECTIVES

By the end of this chapter you should be able to:

- Compare and contrast business customers with individual consumers.
- Analyse the factors influencing both business and consumer purchasing decisions.
- Explain the consumer buying process.
- Be able to explain some of your own purchasing behaviour.

INTRODUCTION

This chapter examines why people buy products or services, specifically the factors that influence such purchases. Moreover, we seek to compare and contrast Business to Business (B2B) with the Business to Consumer (B2C), Consumer to Consumer (C2C) and Peer to Peer (P2P).

As we work through this chapter, consider the types of buying decisions that you make and what influences you to make those particular decisions. This will assist your understanding of marketing and the processes that are undertaken to influence people to make buying commitments.

WHO ARE THE BUYERS AND SELLERS?

As indicated in Chapter 1, traditionally the relationship between buyers and sellers was broadly described as Business to Business (B2B) and

Business to Consumer (B2C). It has also long been the case where individuals would sell directly to other individuals, what we could describe as Consumer to Consumer (C2C). For example, the classified advertising section of newspapers and some magazines would have 'for sale' sections where people could sell their unwanted goods, such as musical instruments and cars.

The development of the Internet and websites such as eBay and the UK-based Gumtree.com have more broadly established this Consumer to Consumer (C2C) category. Today with C2C, individuals can advertise personal products (anything from rare CDs through to watches) for sale via the eBay portal to which individuals can, depending upon how they are advertised, offer to pay the price shown or bid for the item. This additional category has, in many ways, changed the traditional landscape, in the process turning an initial limited portal into a multi-billion dollar business.

In addition, in the UK there is a new platform being developed, namely Peer to Peer (P2P). This is a different way of marketing financial support for businesses beyond the traditional commercial and high street banks. In this case funding is provided by either an individual and/or business (through a funding organisation) directly to a borrower. So several individuals may be providing the funding for a new entrepreneurial business or for an already established business that seeks to, for instance, enhance its capabilities (resources and competences).

In 2014, for example, approximately £1 billion of funding was provided in the UK in this format (P2PFA, 2014). In the UK P2P funding is regulated through the Financial Conduct Authority (FCA), the same as any other financial company. It provides another channel for the provision of funding and competition in relation to the more established lenders. This is likely to be a business area that could grow significantly over the next few years.

Figure 2.1 broadly illustrates the types of potential buyers. We discuss these in more detail in Chapter 10, but it is important that we gain an overview here.

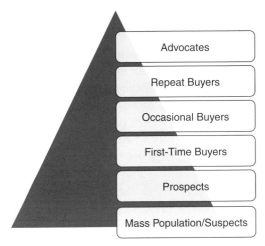

Figure 2.1 Potential and actual buyers

Advocates: These are individuals who champion the product and/or service to their friends, family and even to strangers through the use of social media, such as Twitter, Facebook, Google + and Pinterest. Traditionally Advocates are considered to be loyal regular/repeat buyers. However, is this always the case? Advocates can be individuals who, whilst not always customers (regular or otherwise), passionately believe in the product and/or service that a particular organisation may be providing. They might not be purchasers for various reasons:

1. The Advocate is an independent journalist writing about a particular product and/or service, for instance, a motoring journalist who has test-driven a new sports car. Although the journalist may not own one (perhaps too expensive), nonetheless they may write a favourable review about the car – style, performance, comfort, road holding, fuel efficiency and so on. They may even believe that this is the best car they have driven for some time. They may even keep referring to it, using it as a benchmark to compare and contrast with other

similar types of cars. So in this case the Advocate is independent of the company providing positive public relations (see Chapter 9).

2. In a similar manner to the above an individual may not be able to afford a particular product and/or service but may be passionate about certain aspects of it. For instance, continuing with our sports car analogy, the individual may be very vocal about the styling and the beauty of the car. They not only tell their friends (who perhaps equally cannot afford the car) but they also use social media to alert others. It is through this networking that they can emphasise their passion for the styling of the car, which in turn can lead to people (who can afford the car) to take a look. Moreover, it should not be about 'instant' sales as Advocates are an important contributor to building a positive image about a brand and/or an organisation. People then connect to this brand.

Repeat Buyers: These are individuals who normally purchase the product and/or service on a regular basis. Repeat Buyers may, over time, become Advocates for the product and/or service.

Occasional Buyers: As the name suggests, these are individuals who purchase the product and/or service on an infrequent basis.

First-time Buyers: This is an individual who has made their first purchase of this product and/or service. This may be the only time that they make such a purchase, however, they could also become Occasional and then Repeat Buyers.

Prospects: These are individuals who have not made a purchase, however are most likely to at some stage in the future.

Mass Population – Suspects: This is the wider population, some of whom will/could purchase the product and/or service at some stage in the future.

[Here it is important to note that an organisation would seek to find the most appropriate groups of people to whom they would market their products/services. We explore this in more detail in Chapter 4, when we examine Segmentation, Targeting and Positioning (STP).]

THE CUSTOMER'S PERSPECTIVE

Lauterborn (1990) suggested that companies needed to see the marketing mix (7Ps) from the customer's point of view. This became the 4Cs:

Customer: What can the product or service deliver in terms of the customer's needs and wants? Organisations therefore aim to provide features and benefits that seek to meet these needs and wants. We must bear in mind that these needs and wants will vary over time. Equally, the needs and wants of one group of customers in one part of the world may vary to those in another.

Cost: As we will see in later chapters, the price that a customer will pay depends upon the value that they derive from the product or service. Equally, as indicated in Chapter 1, the macro factors, especially economics, also determines the price that customers are prepared to pay for a product or service.

Consider, for example, these two positions: (1) A customer in a developing nation will not be able to afford to pay the same price for a fast-food meal as a customer in a highly developed nation. Whilst the meal may have the same name and similar ingredients, the ability to pay is different. (2) Even in highly developed nations recessionary movements within the economic cycle will normally impact upon individual levels of disposable income. Companies, therefore, may have to revise their pricing structures (possibly reducing margins) to maintain sales levels.

Convenience: From a customer perspective it is the convenience associated with how the product and/or service is delivered. This can be viewed from both a place/placement and a process perspective. Broadly speaking, Place, within a marketing mix context, refers to location and distribution. Traditionally we would view this in terms of bricks and mortar – physical structures. These remain vital to the delivery of products, whether it is our local convenience grocery store or a warehouse from which a company organises delivery to a customer's home.

Both the Internet and smartphone apps have enhanced our approaches to 'convenience'. Consider the following examples: (1) Through online banking we can pay general bills, transfer money (both in our home country and overseas), apply for loans, create new savings accounts and arrange standing orders. We can conduct these transactions on a 24/7 basis, and no longer need to wait till the physical branch opens the next working day. (2) Via sites such as Amazon and Apple we can search for our favourite music tracks, pay and download them within a matter of a few minutes. Again, we can do this 24/7. (3) We can order groceries online and have them delivered (normally for a charge) at a time that is reasonably convenient for us. In parts of the UK some supermarkets will deliver 08.00 to 23.00 Monday to Sunday. Subject to future demand it is always possible that these times could be extended further. (4) Donations can be made 24/7 to the charity websites, especially when there are major disaster appeals for financial support.

In addition to the delivery mechanisms, organisations have sought, without comprising online security, to reduce the processes involved in purchasing products/services online. This includes the storage of address and credit card details (normally excluding security number) to reduce the number of 'clicks' between the online basket and completion of the transaction.

Communication: The means of communicating with customers has, with the aid of technology, changed dramatically over a relatively short historical time frame. Technological developments will continue to enhance and change how organisations communicate with their customers. As illustrated in Chapter 9, there are a range of tactics and techniques that can be used to promote products and/or services to customers. In addition to the broad approaches, for instance, television advertising, there are more 'personalised' means of communication. These can also be linked to the idea of 'convenience' as stated above.

Organisations can communicate with their customers via normal postal services, telephone calls (can be linked to telemarketing), email and text messaging. Equally, technologies such as email and texting allows generally easier contact between the customer and the organisation.

Consider the following examples: (1) A customer can alert their credit card company either by text or email that they are travelling overseas and will use their card abroad. This means that the card company can note that there may be a valid change in the use of their card within a particular time period. (2) A customer can be tracked (through the use of cookies) as they navigate a website. As they browse the website (for instance, a holiday company) an icon may appear asking if they want to engage in an online real-time chat with a sales representative to help them with any queries. If the browsing is outside the times where a 'real-time chat' is feasible, then a call-back option might be available to the potential customer. Here a sales representative will call the potential customer back at a mutually convenient time. There is no cost to the customer. (3) An individual may purchase concert tickets online (although the actual tickets might be sent by normal post), and they receive an auto-response email addressed to them stating what has been purchased and an estimation of when they might receive the tickets.

BUYING DECISION PROCESS

Engel, Blackwell and Miniard (1990) outlined six steps that we normally undertake when making a purchase, a process that remains generally valid today. We have also provided additional comments at the end of this section in relation to online activity and loyalty.

These authors' six steps in the buying decision process are:

1. Recognition of an unsatisfied need or want.
2. Search for information.
3. Evaluation of alternatives.
4. Purchase.
5. Consumption.
6. Post-purchase evaluation.

1. Recognition of an Unsatisfied Need or Want

This is where we recognise a particular need or want and seek ways of satisfying it. The amount of time we invest in recognising this want or need will depend upon the specific nature of the need. In Chapter 1 we referred to a sudden downpour of rain may lead to the increase sales of umbrellas. This becomes an impulse purchase because the need is immediate – our aim to keep dry! Equally, it may take us longer to recognise an unsatisfied need, for example, purchasing a new overcoat that we feel looks good, suits our style and will keep us warm in winter.

2. Search for information

The search for information leads to consideration of the level of involvement we invest in the process. The level of involvement is a measure of how much time and effort we are going to invest in satisfying the recognised need. It is usually subdivided into high and low involvement.

High Involvement

High involvement is where the buyer seeks more information on the product or service prior to making their final decision. Usually this is the case where the buyer is purchasing a relatively expensive item such as a HD-enabled touch-screen, voice-activated television. The buyer will research the various features and benefits promoted by the manufacturers, the price, payment terms as advertised by the retailers (for example, instalments, interest free credit for 12 months), consider the various delivery options (for example, same or next day delivery), the guarantees available and the overall reliability of the product. Increasingly both manufacturers and retailers display customer ratings and feedback online (the UK retailer Argos is an example of this practice). Additionally social media may contain comments on the various products on the market.

Also with an item, such as a television, the whole family may be engaged in the discussions prior to the actual purchase. In such a case, various members of the family may have their own particular needs and wants in terms of what the television can offer them. For instance, can it be linked to a games console? What size should it be? What is the sound quality? Can it be linked to wireless speaker systems? Are there special offers, especially if it is a particularly expensive model? As you can see from this brief list, the questions and issues discussed by a family can be many and varied.

Equally, the customer may go to a 'bricks and mortar' retailer and look at a selection of televisions in operation and discuss with the sales representative the various needs of the family. Another example is buying a new car. It is a normal practice at car dealerships to be able to take the car for a 'test drive' to check out comfort, road handling abilities and performance. This we can consider as 'trialling' or 'testing' the product before we make a purchase.

There may be other circumstances when we 'trial' or 'test out' a product or service before we make long-term commitments. For instance, we may decide to sample a new frozen meal that we have seen advertised on television. We seek this out during our visit to the supermarket, checking the label for ingredients and the various levels of fats, sugars, salts and so on. Perhaps we purchase one to see if we (and the family) like it or not. If it creates a positive response then it can become a long-term purchase on our supermarket shopping list.

Low Involvement

With low involvement the buyer already believes that they have sufficient information to make the purchase. They may be purchasing a product that they have regularly purchased over a period of time and thus are satisfied with the value, quality and pricing. An example could be a brand of orange juice from the supermarket. Equally, it may be an impulse purchase. Earlier we used the example of a sudden downpour of rain and the increase in sales of umbrellas. To prevent getting wet a buyer may just seek to purchase, in reason, any umbrella that is available from a nearby store. They may not even be interested in the colour – as long as it keeps them dry.

3.   Evaluation of Alternatives

Continuing our example of purchasing a new television, the buyer will examine the various brands available and the various features and benefits that they provide. This is closely aligned with a high level of involvement.

Taking some or all of the points stated above, the customer will compare and contrast the various features and benefits available. In the UK several online retailers (such as Argos) provide facilities where a customer can choose a number of brands to compare and contrast their various features and benefits side by side. This provides the customer with easily accessible information that can help them to make an informed choice. This is closely aligned with a high level of involvement.

4. Purchasing Decision

The buyer takes the decision and purchases the television, thus entering into an exchange – the product for the payment.

5. Consumption

This is the period of using the purchased product and forming an opinion on it.

6. Post-Purchase Behaviour or Reaction – Cognitive Dissonance

It is normal for us to have doubts regarding our purchases and to, perhaps, seek reassurance either from other people and/or from within. This behaviour is known as Cognitive Dissonance. The level of dissonance may vary depending upon a range of personal circumstances. For instance, a billionaire will probably feel less dissonance when buying a new car (even a significantly expensive one) than someone on an average national income who may have to take out a loan (either through their bank or a finance company).

Equally, many of us will experience dissonance in terms of whether or not we actually 'need' to make this purchase. We may even indicate to ourselves a concern that 'we may come to regret the purchase'. That is not necessarily a reflection on the quality of the product/service we are seeking to purchase, rather it is about our own decision making.

In our example, the buyer has invested in a HD touch-screen voice-activated television costing £700. This is a significant investment and there is likely to be a degree of post-purchase dissonance. Although, as stated in our mini discussions above, the buyer has sought to compare and contrast various brands (both online and in-store) and discussed the family's requirements, they may have lingering doubts regarding the purchase.

Most people subconsciously seek reassurance that they have made the right decision. In our example of purchasing a new television, the buyer may seek:

- Additional information on the brand regarding its features/benefits and reliability. This will help to reinforce their choice of brand especially if it meets all (or the majority) of family requirements. Equally, if the brand has received positive reviews in terms of reliability, the buyer may well consider that they and their family will gain a long-term series of benefits from the television.

- Additional information on the price of this brand in relation to others currently on the market. This helps to reinforce the choice of the brand in relation to price and value for money. When linked to reliability, as mentioned above, the buyer may think that over the longer term the cost of purchase will actually be relatively small. For instance, the buyer may think that the television will last at least seven years before being replaced. In relation to the cost of purchase, that is £100 per year. Of course there is also a licence fee and the cost of electricity to pay annually, however the mind of the buyer is focused on whether or not they have made the right decision to purchase this particular brand.

- Reassurance from family members that they have made the right decision. This could be in the form of direct questions, for instance, 'What do you think of the choice?' Or a more indirect approach such as saying 'Just look at the sharpness of the picture quality ... those colours really stand out....' Here the buyer is seeking an acknowledgement, an agreement. When they receive such an agreement they may feel reassured.

- In many countries, for example, the UK, the television will be under various product and legal consumer guarantees whereby if not satisfied the buyer can return the product (undamaged) within a certain time frame. This can provide the buyer with the reassurance that if it does not meet, for instance, the family's 'overwhelming' support, they can have it replaced. Of course, such guarantees and consumer rights do not apply to all products and indeed to all countries.

- In addition to standard guarantees (usually 12 months), the buyer may decide to purchase an extended warranty agreement, which they renew on an annual basis. Such warranty agreements normally cover replacement components and labour charges.

[Marketers will, through various forms of marketing communications, seek to reduce our levels of cognitive dissonance. This may be through stating the reliability and performance of the brand and emphasising 'non-contested money-back guarantees'.]

Additional Steps

There are three further steps or areas for possible consideration. Additionally, we can consider these as also linked to the theory of cognitive dissonance in that they can be used by the buyer as reassurance of their purchase.

Additional steps in the buying behaviour process linking to online and other activities are:

1. Support Mechanisms.
2. Updating – Upselling.
3. Loyalty – Advocates.

1.   Support Mechanisms

Let's assume that you have purchased new software for your laptop. You would normally receive this either via a CD (in-store or through the postal service) or as an online download directly from the manufacturer. In this instance, we will focus on the downloading of the software. This generally is a smooth operation; however, there will be cases of problems – connection speeds, interruptions and so on. Major companies seek to provide support mechanism (via both email and telephone) so that such downloading is as easy as possible. While we might 'take this for granted' such support and the quality of that support is value added. In other words, it can mean the difference between retaining a customer (thus more purchasing opportunities) and losing one.

2.   Updating – Upselling

Staying with our software example, companies often provide free updating (including security patch fixes) and extras (such as Microsoft with PowerPoint templates). Equally, companies will offer, usually at a discount to registered users, the next generation of the software. The company promotes the new features and benefits of the new version. This is known as upselling to an existing customer.

3.   Loyalty – Advocates

The overall aim, as stated in both Chapter 1 and this chapter, is to build loyalty and create Advocates. As indicated above with our software example, the company is providing free additional material, as well as the option to pay for upgrades at a discount. This is a means of building such loyalty, as long as the product (and service follow through) is of an appropriate standard in the mind of the buyer.

We can link the work of Engel, Blackwell and Miniard (1990) to that of Rogers and his work on the Theory of Adoption (Rogers, 1983). In Figure 2.2 we have used the example of an individual seeking to purchase a new car and the steps that they may undertake.

Adoption can be viewed as a series or sequence of events. However, this sequencing may take place over different timescales, depending upon the product and the circumstances surrounding the potential purpose.

The other significant area of research undertaken by Rogers (1983) and others is our pattern of adoption (see Figure 2.2). Rogers (1983) suggests that people fit into five broad categories (Innovators, Early Adopters, Early Majority, Late Majority and Laggards) when we look at new products and/or services entering a market.

Awareness	• The potential customer (prospect) is made aware of the product and/or service via different forms of marketing communication, including social media. Although there may be marketing communications visible to them, they may have sought to find a solution to a particular need. This need may be a new family car.
Knowledge	• The prospect seeks more information on the product and/or service. This may be through reading articles (both on and offline), navigating the brand's website, discussing with friends and family, and asking for comments and information via social media.
Evaluation	• This can be in the form of comparing and contrasting material that they have gathered on different car models. Amongst the factors that they may compare and contrast are overall cost, financial arrangements, fuel efficiency (kms per litre/hybrid systems), safety features, level of comfort for both driver and passengers and the length of warranty.
Trial	• Having selected a range of car models the prospect visits various dealerships to test drive different models. This also provides the prospect with an opportunity to discuss, with the sales people, the various pieces of information that they have gathered on the vehicles. Equally, the sales people have an opportunity to discuss the possible promotions that are currently on offer.
Adoption	• The prospect makes a decision. This decision may be either their own or with others, for instance, family members. In Engel et al. (1990), they refer to post-purchase reactions. These can vary depending upon the level of satisfaction experienced by the buyer. In this particular example, it may not just be that of the prospect but their family as well. As we have stated above, there may be moments of cognitive dissonance.

Figure 2.2 Sequence of adoption

Innovators: These are the individuals who we might consider are at the 'cutting edge'; they want to be the first to either own a new product or experience a new service. They are the people who will queue, perhaps overnight, in order to be there when the store doors open and a new version of a smartphone is available to purchase. For some pre-ordering it online does not have 'the buzz' – that feeling to hold a new product in your hand at the time that it has been released to the market. For many it is about being the first, and companies realise this and through marketing communications seek to cater for this group.

We should not underestimate the value (both in terms of finance and media coverage) of such events. In 2012 Apple sold five million iPhone 5s in the first three days of trading (US, Australia, Canada, France, Germany,

Hong Kong, Japan, Singapore and the UK), two million of which were pre-ordered (Apple, 2012a; Rushe, 2012). Overall this was one million more than the iPhone 4s sold within the same time frame and resulted in Apple selling out of its initial stock of iPhone 5s (Rushe, 2012). When the iPhone 5 went on sale in China in December 2012, over two million units were sold in the first three days of trading (Apple, 2012b). Since these launches Apple have broken their own sales records.

Early Adopters: These are individuals who may wait and see, for a relatively short period, if the new product and/or service on offer is of relevance to them and of value. However, they will still be among the first to purchase the product.

Early Majority: These are individuals who perhaps comprise the bulk of the buyers. They will normally wait and collect information before committing themselves to the purchase.

Late Majority: These are individuals who perhaps comprise, along with Early Majority, the bulk of the buyers. However, they have taken longer to acquire the product and/or service.

Laggards: These will be the last to make a purchase, if at all. We could look at this not only from the perspective of, for instance, an individual make of smartphone but whether or not the individual seeks to own a smartphone or not. There remains in some international markets various basic mobile phones as well as landlines. Perhaps not everyone has a need or a desire for a smartphone?

ORGANISATIONAL BUYERS

Many of the products purchased by an organisation are the same as those purchased by individuals. An example of this can be cleaning products and detergents. These are usually manufactured by major companies such as P&G and Unilever, however the difference is where we buy one or two products at a time, a company will purchase in both larger sizes and quantities. Often the manufacturers will create a brand name specifically for these industrial/commercial products.

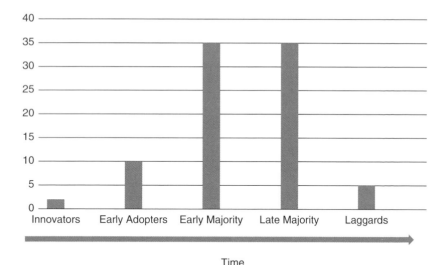

Time

Figure 2.3 A diagrammatic representation of adoption theory. This illustrates a generalised pattern of adoption. In a specific analysis the vertical axis figures would represent a particular value, for instance sales with the horizontal axis representing time, perhaps a five-year period. The numbers in Figure 2.3 are just for illustration and do not represent any specific values

It is worth considering the size of organisations and their relative demand for products and services. The following were the world's largest employers (as of 2012).

1. US Department of Defense: Employees 3.2 million.

2. People's Liberation Army, China: Employees 2.3 million.

3. Walmart: Employees 2.1 million.

4. McDonald's: Employees: 1.9 million (this figure includes franchises).

5. UK National Health Service: Employees: 1.7 million.

6. China National Petroleum Corporation: Employees 1.6 million.

7. State Grid Corporation of China: Employees 1.5 million.

8. Indian Railways: Employees 1.4 million.

9. Indian Armed Forces: Employees 1.3 million.

10. Hon Hai Precision Industry (Foxconn): Employees 1.2 million.

(Alexander, 2012)

[The information is provided by the BBC and was derived from many different sources, which can be seen on the BBC's website. As the BBC team point out, exact data may, in some cases, may not be readily available. However, from our perspective we want to convey overall scope.]

The levels of employment provide a sense of scale for these organisations. It also helps us to understand the scale of facilities and equipment that these organisations will require in order to function. They, in one form or another, are engaged in transactions. In some cases buying and selling produce, for example, Walmart and, in others purchasing supplies, for example, the US Department of Defense. They will all, to a greater or lesser extent, also be engaged in Public Relations (see Chapter 9).

In addition to bulk purchasing there are other factors that differentiate organisational buying from that of the individual. Some of these factors are explored below.

Product or Service Type

Some products or services can be bought by an individual and a company, for example, a BIC ballpoint pen or a personal insurance policy. The difference is the scale of the purchase. However, where a company is concerned the products or services required may be on a larger scale (an airline ordering a fleet of Airbus aircraft) or one-off projects (the building of a new steel mill).

Procurement Departments

Large organisations, such as government departments, have their own procurement departments which are organised to make purchases on behalf of the organisation. The scale of the purchasing can range from stationery products through to large-scale projects such as the building of a new ship. See Mini Case: *HMS Queen Elizabeth*.

Purchasing Expertise

Organisations will usually employ teams who have the expertise in bulk buying and negotiating with suppliers and manufacturers on such purchases. Depending upon the scale and scope of the procurement, the team may be the final decision makers. In other cases, the decision may have to be referred to other managers/directors in more senior roles.

Time Horizons

The delivery of the order can range from a few hours (a stationery order in London) through to several years (the building of a ship).

Tenders

Depending upon the size and complexity of the project, the buying organisation may engage in a tendering process. The organisation informs possible suppliers that tenders are open for a particular project/service. Those companies interested respond to the brief by a set deadline. The buying organisation will have a set number of criteria, which they will match with the response to the tender. These may include level of experience, reliability especially in relation to delivering to budget and on schedule, approach to working with customers, health and safety record, and overall reputation.

Tenders are competitive, and the final decision may not always be a question of price. Organisations generally will be seeking value for money, especially if quality/delivery are paramount to the awarding organisation.

In the UK, government contracts are often selected through a tendering process. The UK government's procurement service is part of the Crown Commercial Services, which is an executive agency of government. Their remit is to 'work with both department and organisations across the whole of the public sector to ensure maximum value is extracted for every commercial relationship and improve the quality of service delivery' (CCS, 2014). UK government procurement can range from language services, vehicle purchasing through to travel service and linen supplies and laundry services (CCS, 2014).

Contractual Terms & Conditions

Depending upon the size and scope of the order, the procurement department will seek to negotiate the terms and conditions of the agreement prior to signing the contract for the order. Where large projects are concerned, such as the building of a new cruise ship, the shipping line will seek penalty clauses for the late delivery of the ship from the builders. The shipbuilders, on the other hand, will not only purchase special insurance to cover such a possible event, they will also build in such penalty clauses to their various suppliers. Shipyards with a reputation for on-time delivery are the ones that often gain numerous repeat orders from the major cruise lines.

Pricing & Price Flexibility

Price, whether for an individual or a company, can have an effect on the decision to purchase. A procurement department will seek discounts on bulk orders of stationery. Equally a company may not actually purchase a product but lease it from the supplier. Photocopier machines, for instance, are rarely purchased but leased. This allows the company to upgrade the machines in the future without having to make a new purchase; it will be an extension of the lease agreement. There are benefits in undertaking such leases – no large initial payment, as with a full purchase; part of the monthly lease payment is based upon the number of photocopies produced; and the lease allows for upgrading of the machine within the agreement based upon company requirements and call-out for copier malfunctions and repairs. For companies that require numerous photocopiers (such as a university or a bank) this can be financially advantageous (see Chapter 6: Delivering Value and Pricing).

Mini Case: *HMS Queen Elizabeth*

In 2007 the contract was signed to deliver two new aircraft carriers for the Royal Navy – *HMS Queen Elizabeth* and *HMS Prince of Wales*. As of 2014 the cost of the project was £6.2 billion (Whyatt, 2014). In August 2014 the first of the two ships, *HMS Queen Elizabeth*, was launched. At 65,000 tonnes she is the largest warship ever to be built for the Royal Navy and is longer than the Houses of Parliament (Whyatt, 2014). Although officially launched she will not be handed over to the UK's Ministry of Defence (MoD) until 2016 and then into service in 2020 (BBC, 2014b). This is due to the significant amount of 'fitting out' or completion work that today's highly sophisticated ships require.

The Aircraft Carrier Alliance (ACA) was formed comprising of the aerospace and defence firms BAE Systems and Thales UK, along with the engineering group Babcock (ACA, 2014). The UK's Ministry of Defence, as well as a member of the alliance, is also the customer, as the government's representative for implementing defence policy. Although, these are the major contractors for this project, there are hundreds of SMEs, across the UK, who are providing everything from wiring through to navigation systems and catering equipment.

As highlighted earlier, there may be many suppliers, including niche product or service providers, who are engaged in such long-term projects. Many of these companies will have had to tender for the project work, thus demonstrating their capabilities (see Chapter 12) to manage and complete the project.

INDIVIDUAL CONSUMERS

In order to develop effective marketing we should understand what drives us to buy specific products or services. The American humanistic psychologist Abraham Maslow (1908–1970) proposed a hierarchy of five human needs – see Figure 2.4 (Maslow, 1943). Whilst the hierarchy was created in relation to research on motivation, it has clear implications for buyer behaviour. Maslow was seeking to establish a set of 'needs' where fulfilment is sought at each level. So we would seek to fulfil our basic physiological needs prior to meeting our safety needs and so on. Maslow's hierarchy is briefly outlined below:

Level 1: Physiological Needs

These are the basic human needs that require fulfilment: food, drink, shelter, sexual satisfaction and other physical needs. In many societies, especially the most affluent, we take many of these most notably food and drink, for granted. However, these are basic to our survival but not readily available to all people in all societies.

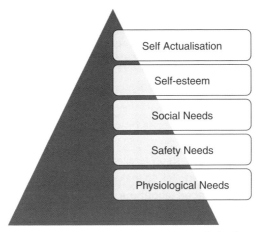

Figure 2.4 A standard diagrammatic representation of the hierarchy of needs theory as developed by Maslow (1943)

From a contemporary marketing perspective, major supermarket chains promote their range of food products. The food market in the UK has become highly competitive. Even traditional staple foods such as bread, potatoes and milk have become products that are significantly discounted as supermarkets compete for market share.

Level 2: Safety Needs

These cover the needs for order, security and protection from physical and emotional harm, as well as assurance that physical needs will continue to be met.

In a marketing context this may result in the purchasing of additional locks for our homes, shutters for windows, alarm systems (for cars, home and personal use) and health and accident insurance policies.

Level 3: Social Needs

This is where we seek affection, belonging, acceptance and friendship. From a marketing perspective we can consider the growing range of dating and friendship agencies. While modern dating and friendship agencies have been in existence for many years, today, through the use of the Internet and computer software, these have greatly expanded. They are often supported by significant marketing budgets.

Level 4: Self-esteem

Self-esteem covers the need for self-respect, reputation, achievement and status. Many organisations can engage in marketing from a 'self-esteem' perspective. For instance, fashion retailers, cosmetic companies and dieting product manufacturers can seek to make us want to 'look and feel good'.

Equally we can 'feel good' about ourselves when we donate to charities and NGOs, especially during disaster relief emergencies.

Level 5: Self Actualisation

This is where we seek self-fulfilment and the achievement of our personal potential. Organisations, through marketing, may seek to provide us with the means to achieve our personal potential. Consider, for instance, how universities may promote their various courses and programmes. The marketing may not only be about the programme content but also the possible end goals, with examples of the successes of previous students.

Equally, many authors and publishers have marketed a range of self-help guides to possibly assist us in reaching our long-term potential and ambitions. It is for individuals to decide to what extent such guides/approaches have helped them achieve their goals. However, it is also a measure of how marketing can be used to promote ideas and concepts.

We can link all of Maslow's Hierarchy of Needs, to a greater or lesser extent, to the products or services that we purchase within our lifetimes.

Table 2.1 reflects the various factors that can influence individual buyer behaviour. There are clear links to Maslow's Hierarchy of Needs, for instance in personal lifestyles. Equally, characteristics (in this case we have used Social status) can apply to different overarching factors.

These factors are not static. An individual's situation will normally change, to a greater or lesser degree, over time. For instance, a person seeks a better job, perhaps within another culture where their salary has

Table 2.1 Factors influencing buyer behaviour

Culture	Social	Personal	Psychological
Social status	Family	Age	Motivation
Heritage	Friends	Career/	Perception
Religion (also worth noting that in	Work colleagues	occupation	Cognition
certain countries the political system,	Role models	Health	Beliefs
religion and law are integrated)		Lifestyle	
		Social status	

a high level of disposability – thus they have greater spending power. They may be influenced by local cultural traditions and thus seek out local stores and traditional foods.

Below we examine some of the factors or issues illustrated by Table 2.1 so that we can better understand some of the reasons for our purchasing behaviours. Additionally, we should look at individual buyer behaviour in a dynamic rather than in a static context.

PERCEPTION

Schiffman, Kanuk and Hansen (2012) describe perception as 'the process by which an individual selects, organises and interprets stimuli into meaningful and coherent picture of the world'.

We can consider physical or Sensory Stimuli as:

- Sight
- Sounds
- Smell
- Touch

We encounter these through different **Levels of Exposure**. For instance, as we enter a coffee shop we may hear the sounds of jazz or classical music playing in the background.

We order a cappuccino coffee. We see it being made by the barista, and it is poured into a branded takeaway carton, which we can feel and through which we can also sense the warmth of the coffee. We remove the lid of the carton and we can smell the richness of the coffee that we have purchased.

In this particular case we experience all four sensory stimuli. However, our level of exposure to these stimuli will vary depending upon the circumstances in which we encounter them.

Our **Degree of Reaction** to the sensory stimuli will also depend upon certain factors. These could include:

- Our preference for certain sounds and smells: For example, we may prefer certain types of perfumes or music over another. Some of us may prefer going into a coffee shop that plays jazz or classical music whereas others may prefer house music.

- Our age: As we grow older our sight, sense of smell and hearing may change, in some cases dramatically. Thus we lose the ability to sense and interpret certain stimuli.

- Our gender: Research indicates that women have a much more acute sense of smell than men, thus may appreciate certain smells or odours (for example, perfumes) than men.

The combination of Sensory Stimuli, Levels of Exposure and Degree of Reaction leads us to the **Point of Acquisition or Rejection**. This is where we react either positively or negatively to the sensory stimuli and what they represent. The result could be either a purchase or avoidance.

Marketers will use different types of stimuli to promote a product or service. Much of the information that we receive and process comes via sight, what we see. In terms of marketing that could be through advertising (both still and moving images) and packaging. Lindstrom (2005), cited in Schiffman, Kanuk and Hansen (2012), suggests that smell has become the second most important stimulus after sight, although this is probably open to debate. Could smell be higher rated than sounds, as sounds accompany so much of what we witness in terms of television and radio advertising, the discussions with sales and customer service staff and shared experiences with friends and family? What too does music contribute in terms of our emotions within a marketing context?

Immediate Family

As indicated above in the example of the purchase of the television, the whole family may, to a greater or lesser extent, be involved in the product/brand choice. This will not happen across all ethnic groups, where in some cultures the male will make the final decisions.

In very close-knit family groups various members of the family might have some influence over purchasing decisions. In traditional West Indian families, for instance, the grandmother, due to seniority, could influence how her children and grandchildren live their lives.

We are, to a greater or lesser extent, influenced by our family traditions and lifestyles. Our experiences as children might have a lasting impression upon our purchasing habits. If we were brought up in austere surroundings then, no matter how successful we become, we review our purchases in terms of price/value. Even if we could afford the best tomato juice on the market we might still opt for the low-cost own label brand because we return to our heritage, our roots, and the need not to 'waste' money.

Close-knit families within various communities will also have 'connections' within those communities. These 'connections' can be very important influencers; for instance, a person may go to one particular store because the owner is a friend of their relative. As such there is a loyalty to the community, even if the buyer could purchase the product at a lower price elsewhere.

Friends

Our friends can influence us in several ways:

- Through conversations they may recommend anything from a good book, to a movie or a new club.
- By trusting them, perhaps for a good restaurant in a particular area of town.
- By asking for their recommendations.
- By buying us a gift such as a book.

From reading that book we become engrossed in the world the author has created and seek to purchase others in the series. A particularly good example could be the Harry Potter books by author JK Rowling.

Fashion

We are often influenced by the fashion of the times we live in. That fashion can be promoted by celebrities, a style of music (Punk in the 1970s and Grunge in the 1980s/1990s) and the media. However, other factors can contribute. Once the style of the fashion catwalks of London, Paris and Milan were beyond the disposable incomes of most people. New production and distribution techniques have allowed clothing retailers to remain in tune with styles, if not lead them. Fast Fashion, as it has become known, allows retailers to mirror the high-fashion catwalk styles but at affordable prices (Hines and Bruce, 2007).

Production is often off-shored to countries such as Bangladesh where production costs are significantly lower than in the UK, the US and many European countries. Even with transportation costs, many clothing retailers can reduce prices, while still attaining profit, thus making the clothes affordable to a wider customer base.

Media Recommendations

The views of critics, journalists and specialists who either write for the media or are interviewed by them can influence everything from the movies we see to the food we eat.

An important element is the level of 'trust' we imbue the writer/interviewee. There are many movie critics, for instance, who are highly respected. Their columns, blogs, TV and radio programmes are often eagerly awaited by the movie-going audiences. Clearly, film distributors and production companies equally realise the importance of such comments, adding key words, phrases and star ratings to their advertising (posters, newspaper and magazine adverts).

Culture and Religion

This also links to the section on family as some religions play an important role in our buying habits. Islam and Judaism, for instance, have strict dietary laws, which cover the preparation of food and the types of foods that cannot be consumed.

Social Media

Increasingly, social media has become an integral part of many people's lives. While Facebook may comprise many friends, platforms such as Blogs and Twitter comprise followers who are unlikely to have met each other. However, the comments made within such media can influence an individual's beliefs and ideas.

Customer Feedback Sites

As stated earlier in this chapter, various online retailers include customer feedback (user-generated content) on various items. Many of these feedback sites are independent of the retailer sites, providing feedback on a range of different types of products and services. Several major feedback sites have developed since the early 2000s. These include TripAdvisor and Reevoo. TripAdvisor Media Group owns 24 travel brands and states that it is now the world's largest travel site, operating in some 45 countries with more than 170 million reviews and more than 60 million emailable members worldwide (TripAdvisor, 2014). Reevoo is a UK-based review and ratings business that collects, collates and publishes comments from people who have made verifiable purchases (Reevoo, 2014).

Recommendations on Retailer Websites

Online retailers such as Amazon provide recommendations based upon either purchases made on the site or already owned and rated (1–5 star). For example, the purchase of the US crime drama series *Law & Order: Criminal Intent* may lead to the recommendation of, for example, the UK spy series *Spooks* (broadcast in many other countries with the title *MI-5*).

Health Concerns

Since the 1980s there has been growing interest in health foods and fitness (Smithers, 2014; Soil Association, 2014; Leisure Database, 2015). This has been reflected through media coverage, specialist magazines and a variety of television programmes.

There have been various discussions and debates on health-related matters including types of food products, the levels of obesity in children and young adults, the use of sun creams to protect from the sun's rays, use of vitamin supplements and the relative value of fitness training and exercise.

Equally, there has been a rise in the use of health and accident insurance policies in various countries, such as China (Yao, 2015).

Loyalty Cards & Rewards

Since the 1990s there has been a steady growth in loyalty cards, ranging from airlines through to chemists and supermarkets. We may seek out an airline for a particular flight due to the level of rewards that we receive. Equally our weekly grocery shop (whether online or at the supermarket) may be determined, not by price/products/value alone but by the number of loyalty points we can collect. Moreover, some loyalty cards provide the opportunity for customers to redeem points against other company's products and services. For example, loyalty points collected on some supermarket cards can be exchanged for air miles with various airlines.

Ethical & Environmental Concerns

(Also refer to Chapter 11 on marketing and ethics.)

Since the 1980s there has been increased media coverage regarding the ethical and environmental issues associated with various products and services. Initially, it was just a few companies that focused on ethical products and services, for instance, the cosmetics company The Body Shop, the supermarket chain The Co-operative with organic farming, and a few investment companies who did not invest in certain industries such as weapons manufacturing.

There were concerns expressed about the natural environment in the 1970s, specifically in relation to CFC gases and potential damage to the earth's atmosphere. Since those early days there has been a much broader approach to ethical and environmentally friendly purchasing that goes beyond testing on animals and the source of food production.

Contemporary issues and approaches include:

1. Where are garments manufactured? Do the workers who produce the garments for the UK high street earn a living wage? Are those employed within the overseas garment industry above a certain age?
2. Are the various paper-based products that we purchase from supermarkets sourced from renewable or recycled supplies?
3. Containers that are either recyclable and/or biodegradable so that the need for landfills containing waste products is reduced.
4. Development of biodegradable containers.
5. Reduction in the amount of packaging required.
6. Reduction of the carbon footprint for the manufacturing and transportation of goods. Many suppliers, including airlines, provide a note on the extent of the carbon footprint for a particular product or service.
7. Supporting companies – through product purchase – that seek to reduce the impact of greenhouse gases.

Distress Purchasing

Earlier in this chapter we considered the purchasing of an umbrella during a rain storm as an impulse buy. A distress purchase normally has wider consequences.

Imagine it's a Sunday afternoon and suddenly water flows from the upstairs bathroom. You find the leak, which is getting larger by the minute; you try and fix it but find that you do not have the appropriate tools or fittings to make the repair.

The only solution is to call out an emergency plumber, which is going to be more expensive because it is 'last minute' and on a Sunday. Whilst many plumbing businesses may state that they are 24/7 operations, out of what could be called 'normal working hours' will result in premium charges. As the leak worsens there is the risk of damage to the ceiling and the electrics (potentially no power or even, a fire), and therefore a plumber needs to be contacted. Depending upon the legal clauses within the household insurance policy, the cost of an emergency plumber's labour and the ensuing repairs may be covered.

Ease of Purchase

The ease by which we can purchase a product or service can influence our decisions. The vast majority of physical retail stores have an online presence. Where physical stores normally have limited opening times, although there are a few exceptions, the online version is open 24/7. This means that customers can select and order their shopping at any time day or night and, in fact, from virtually any location using computers and smartphones.

Increasingly we are seeing a 'one click' action to purchase at online retailers, especially if we have already stored our address and credit details with the retailer. We will return to this point in Chapter 7: Delivering Service.

Price

Although Chapter 6 is devoted to value and price, it is useful to briefly discuss the pricing factors that influence our purchasing decisions.

We are influenced by price in relation to value in several ways:

1. If an individual is price sensitive (normally meaning that they have very limited cash available to them) they will seek the lowest-priced product on offer. Many supermarkets, for instance, will display a range of own-label products with varying prices depending upon the perceived/real quality of the product. Customers who are price sensitive may seek out the supermarket's own-label products due to the lower prices.

2. Whether the product is on sale and for how long.

3. Special Offers – Buy One Get One Free (known as a Bogof), Buy One Get Two Free, Buy Three Get the Cheapest Product Free.

4. People are influenced by psychological pricing. This includes the £3.99 price tag where the potential buyer looks at the '3' rather than the price being one penny below £4.00. Additionally, in the UK, stores that charge either 99 pence or £1.00 for products have been very successful.

   Buyers see a set price and believe that they are getting a 'bargain'. However, this may not always be the case, especially, within an increasingly competitive marketplace. For instance, a generic medicated hand wash may be cheaper in a supermarket (if only by a few pennies) than in a discount retailer. While a 'few pennies' may not be significant to an average consumer within an affluent area, it will be to a consumer who is on a low income and thus particularly price sensitive.

5. It is not always the cheapest or the special offers that influence our buying habits. A buyer may be seeking exclusivity. This could be purchasing either a luxury product, perhaps a sports car, or a collector's item (this could range from an antique clock through to a die-cast toy car).

Reputation

Reputation associated with a product, service, manufacturer and/or retailer can influence not only what we buy but also where we buy it. The reputation of companies may be long established and thus create their own form of loyalty. This can be seen in anything from novels (a particular author) through to boutique hotels and specialist food shops.

Mini Case – Novelists

Why do some novels become bestsellers and others seem to disappear without trace? There may be many reasons including the quality of the story itself. However, there is also the marketing of the novel; does it meet the needs of a particular segment of the population (for instance, the different genres – crime, spy thriller, adventure, fantasy, sci-fi or romance)? What is the reputation of the author? Since establishing themselves as a novelist what genre have they focused upon? What have been their sales? What do the critics think? (although that is not always a good indicator of success). What do others think? Thus the link to social media, where even the author might engage in discussions regarding their own work.

Many authors have gained a successful international reputation for their work – for instance Tom Clancy, John Grisham, Dean Koontz and J.K. Rowling, based upon figures obtained from various sources, have sold an estimated 1 billion books between them. These novels will be in various formats and languages.

An author's reputation and their readership following provides a strong indicator of the future success of their next novel. Their reputation for delivering a good story to their target audience becomes a powerful marketing tool.

No Choices Available

There are situations where only a monopoly exists. This may be the case where there is only one utility provider (normally State-owned), for example providing electricity. In such cases the customer has only one supplier and thus no choice. Increasingly monopolies are rare, and most governments have introduced regulations that encourage several suppliers thus providing customers with choice.

The Thrill of the Adventure

Bungee jumping, extreme sports and rollercoaster rides are examples of an 'experience' – the thrill of adventure. The popularity of these activities and the investment in more G-force-pushing coasters demonstrates that people are seeking 'edge of the seat' physical thrills. The demand for these adrenaline-rush activities results in entertainment companies providing significant investments in utilising the latest technologies for both indoor and outdoor thrill rides.

KEY POINTS

In this chapter we have considered the following:

1. How Maslow's Hierarchy of Needs illustrates five levels of needs that we seek to fulfil during our lifetime.
2. The various models that illustrate buyer behaviour patterns.
3. The key factors that differentiate organisational buyer behaviour from that of the individual buyer.
4. The various factors that influence why (and when) we buy certain products and services.

QUESTIONS

Here is a series of questions and activities for you to undertake to aid your knowledge and understanding of the points made in this chapter.

1. After reviewing this chapter, reflect upon why you buy the products and services that you do. Consider what factors listed in this chapter apply to you and to what extent.

2. By using one example, explain three of the factors that can influence an individual to buy a particular product or service.

3. Critically evaluate the consumer buying process.

4. Undertake research into a major business project, for example, a new railway project or a new skyscraper building. What organisational buying factors do you think will be taken into consideration?

5. You are the Marketing Director of a leading European-based luxury fashion retailer (J&G). The company manufactures and retails clothing for men and women. You have been asked by the Board of Directors to produce a report on consumer buying behaviour. The company is currently known for retailing clothing for the 40+ age group. However, the Board is interested in the possibility of launching ranges for a younger market, specifically the 25–30 age group, which they believe could be a profitable market segment.

   Prepare a coherent and evaluative report to explain the possible buyer behaviour attitudes of this group. You can focus on either men's or women's fashion.

   We suggest that you look at stores that fit these 'profiles'. This might be helpful in understanding the target market.

FURTHER READING

Apple (2012a) iPhone 5 First Weekend Sales Top Five Million. Apple Press Release 24 September 2012.

Apple (2012b) iPhone 5 First Weekend Sales in China Top Two Million. Apple Press Release 17 December 2012.

Barden, P. (2013) *Decided: The Science behind Why We Buy*. Oxford: John Wiley & Sons.

Cialdini, R. (2007) *Influence: The Psychology of Persuasion*. New York: HarperBusiness.

Ries, A. and Trout. J. (2001) *Positioning: The Battle for Your Mind*. New York: McGraw-Hill.

Underhill, P. (2008) *Why We Buy: The Science of Shopping*. London: Simon & Schuster.

3

Marketing Research

By the end of this chapter you should be able to:

- Understand the importance of marketing research in relation to the marketing planning process.
- Understand the difference between market and marketing research.
- Explain the different types of research that marketing teams can undertake and how they choose them.
- Explain the differences between primary and secondary data collection.

INTRODUCTION

There are two main areas of research in relation to marketing.

Market Research: This focuses on an individual market (for example, the market for shampoo) and an investigation into customer behaviours, the size and scope of the market, profile of the typical customer and consumption patterns.

Marketing Research: The approach here is much wider. Whilst it takes into consideration the characteristics of the 'market', it also considers the organisation itself, the competition and the macro environment in which it operates. In the case of the macro environment this can include the influence/impact of economic and societal changes.

WHY UNDERTAKE RESEARCH?

Organisations undertake research to better understand their customers and the marketing environment in which they operate. Such an approach enables organisations to:

- Make better-informed decisions regarding product/service launches and relaunches.
- Better understand the financial viability of products/services over the longer term.
- Help determine whether or not a company should cease production of a particular product.
- Gauge reaction to possible rebranding of a product or service.
- Gauge what the 'market wants', thus seeking out opportunities. These can include new services, new pricing structures or implementing new distribution methods (for instance, traditional newspaper companies making content available via digital formats such as tablets).
- Understand developing trends, perhaps in fashion, and how these may influence other business operations.
- Identify problems. These might be in the product/service itself or how they are priced and delivered to the customer.
- Monitor and evaluate marketing communication campaigns.

However, in order to have the right outputs (the decisions) an organisation has to have the right inputs (data and analysis). As stated elsewhere in this text, many organisations develop, either in-house or through outsourcing, data warehouses of information. These can then be data-mined to provide the organisation with information to debate and then implement decisions. This information can originate from a variety of sources, including marketing research.

How and when information is gathered will normally depend upon the type of organisation and its requirements. For instance, whilst both a university faculty and a hotel will be seeking feedback on 'satisfaction', they will ask very different questions and in different ways about 'satisfaction'. However, both may take action to seek to enhance overall satisfaction levels.

WHY IS THE ORGANISATION CONSIDERING MARKETING RESEARCH?

As with any type of research there needs to be a clear focus on the following questions:

- What is being researched? For instance, consumer preferences for hand-wash liquids.

- Why is it being researched? For instance, a company is considering developing and manufacturing a range of fragranced antiseptic hand-wash gels. There is growing concern in the media and wider society of the spread of various bacteria, especially associated with food preparation at home and eating food in the workplace. This may be a developing market if the company better understands customers' concerns. As this could require a substantial development budget the company, understandably, wants to make as sure as possible that they have a financially viable product range.

- How will this research be undertaken? This focuses on what methods (qualitative – quantitative – primary – secondary) could be used, with a rationale for each one chosen.

- When and how will the marketing research plan be implemented? This will be the scheduling of the actions to undertake the research.

- What methods will be used to analyse the information collected?

- When will the findings be published internally? The information gathered from both the primary and secondary data collections is analysed.

From this analysis findings are produced and these findings can be used by the client organisation to plot future courses of action. In the example cited above this may be developing a particular fragrance for the hand-wash gels as this was rated highly by those questioned in the survey.

MARKETING RESEARCH PROCESS & PROTOCOLS

This provides an outline of the direction of the research process and begins with seeking to understand why the research may be necessary. There is no defined timeline for each of these steps as it will depend upon the original purpose of the research and the objectives to be met. In some cases there may be an urgency, perhaps in relation to a crisis or a proposed government policy that may impact upon the sales of a particular product or service. For instance, the proposed levying of a new tax on a product and how that may impact upon purchasing habits.

In Figure 3.1 we have sought to briefly outline the ten key steps in developing a marketing research process. We have devised it as a step formation, however, as you will see from the notes, there are interrelationships between the steps that also need to be considered.

Additionally, the researchers need to establish a set of 'protocols' or procedures. Some of these are indicated within our ten-step procedures. Protocols would include:

- Rationale for the research.

- How the project will be managed. This will include budget responsibility.

- The approach to quality assurance and how that approach will be managed.

- Ethical considerations. What are the potential ethical considerations and how these will be managed (for example, the use of consent forms)? (Ethical issues in marketing are discussed in Chapter 11.)

- How the final report will be structured.

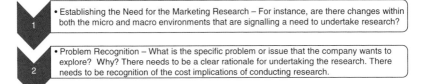

1 • Establishing the Need for the Marketing Research – For instance, are there changes within both the micro and macro environments that are signalling a need to undertake research?

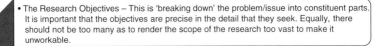

2 • Problem Recognition – What is the specific problem or issue that the company wants to explore? Why? There needs to be a clear rationale for undertaking the research. There needs to be recognition of the cost implications of conducting research.

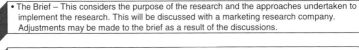

3 • The Research Objectives – This is 'breaking down' the problem/issue into constituent parts. It is important that the objectives are precise in the detail that they seek. Equally, there should not be too many as to render the scope of the research too vast to make it unworkable.

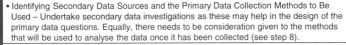

4 • The Brief – This considers the purpose of the research and the approaches undertaken to implement the research. This will be discussed with a marketing research company. Adjustments may be made to the brief as a result of the discussions.

5 • Identifying Secondary Data Sources and the Primary Data Collection Methods to Be Used – Undertake secondary data investigations as these may help in the design of the primary data questions. Equally, there needs to be consideration given to the methods that will be used to analyse the data once it has been collected (see step 8).

6 • Questionnaire Design – This would also include 'testing' the questions for understanding and accuracy.

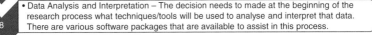

7 • Data Collection – This can be secondary (desk research) and primary (interviews, questionnaires, focus groups).

8 • Data Analysis and Interpretation – The decision needs to made at the beginning of the research process what techniques/tools will be used to analyse and interpret that data. There are various software packages that are available to assist in this process.

9 • Final Research Report – This is a professional document that can be presented to Department Heads and possibly other members of the Senior Management Team.

10 • Department Heads and other members of the Senior Management Team review the report and decide upon actions.

Figure 3.1 The ten steps of the marketing research process

- Methodologies used.
- Approach to data management and analysis.
- The dissemination of the report. This will include who will be the recipients of the report.

TYPES OF RESEARCH

Research can be subdivided into several different, yet often interrelated groupings.

Qualitative and Quantitative

Qualitative can be described as the words that convey thoughts, emotions, ideas, motives, attitudes and feelings.

Quantitative can be described as the 'numbers' part of research, the statistical data that can be gathered and then analysed. For instance, the number of people who buy a particular brand of washing liquid in a particular part of the country. Technology allows marketing teams to gather large volumes of statistical data which can then be analysed for trends.

Secondary Data Collection

Secondary data can be described as information that already exists as it has been collected for another purpose. This information can be both internal and external to the organisation.

Internal Data: This is information held within the organisation. It can include previous surveys, marketing and sales reports, customer feedback, financial projections, details of customers and their purchasing habits (consider the amount of data available through loyalty card schemes).

External Data: This is information available from other organisations.

This data can include information from:

Companies with Stock Market Listings: Companies listed on a stock market normally have to provide an Annual Report and Accounts for share or stock holders. In addition to the financial information, these documents will indicate how the company performed and its objectives for the next 12 months and beyond. These and other documents (for instance, sustainability policy) are normally available via the company's investor relations website.

Government: Government departments collect statistical information both at home and internationally that can be beneficial to organisations. For instance, in the UK there is the Office of National Statistics (ONS). This is an independent government agency that collects and analyses data on economic and social trends including agriculture, crime/justice, education/skills, energy, health/social care and travel/transport. In the US similar information is provided by the Federal government Data.Gov.

Institutions: There is a potential cross-over between universities, agencies and think tanks. Specialist institutions engaged in research can provide valuable data as to future developments, for instance, in use of smartphones for ordering products and services.

International Agencies: Organisations such as the World Bank and the International Monetary Fund (IMF) and the World Tourism Organisation provide marketing and other statistical data. The vast proportion of this data is free to access via the agencies' websites.

Management Consultancies: Various management companies provide reports both on trends and the current position of market sectors.

Market Research Organisations: There are various companies that gather survey data on specific sectors and trends. Mintel, for instance, is a global market research company that collects data on consumer markets, product innovation and provides market and competitor analysis. Organisations can purchase reports from market research companies to assist their understanding of markets and possible future trends.

Media: The media comprises of television, radio, newspapers, magazines, and Internet blogs, forums and social media. The media can provide valuable data in several ways:

(a) Depending upon the source they can provide unbiased information on companies, their products and services.

(b) Information on market trends either gathered from various sources by them or through market research companies (as in the form of a press release).

(c) Through the interviewing of CEOs and other high-ranking company officials. They often discuss products/services, branding, their marketing strategies and business trends.

(d) Through commissioning their own surveys. This is most prevalent when examining the various strengths and weaknesses of political parties, particularly their marketing (and promises) to the electorate.

Think Tanks: These are organisations that examine various trends, often drawing conclusions on what will be the shape of the future. Companies either engage these organisations to provide tailored research and/or they purchase the latest trend reports.

Trade Associations: These represent the particular business sector or industry, for instance, the British Retail Consortium (BRC) represents all retail companies within the UK. The BRC provides its members with information on various aspects of retailing from economic data through to footfall (the number of shoppers who enter various types of stores within certain time frames).

Universities: Academics within higher education institutions often engage in research activities, for instance, trends analysis within certain business and industrial sectors. The data from this research may be published in various formats ranging from academic journals through to business magazines and being discussed on radio and television. Some academics and universities will make this information available free of charge to interested parties via their respective websites.

Primary Data Collection

This is where an organisation collects information (for example, through a questionnaire) for a specific purpose. A great deal of what we call 'secondary data' either started directly as primary data and/or is the result of actions taken based on the findings. For instance, the original results from previous surveys and research reports.

Samples and Populations

It is perhaps useful, prior to examining the different types of primary data collection methods, to consider 'samples and populations'. This will help us understand some of the tasks that need to be undertaken as we formulate our approach to data collection.

A 'population' in marketing research terms is the total number of people who could, for instance, use a particular product or service. Unless it was a very specific niche market, it would be difficult to contact the whole 'population'. Even contacting the narrow niche market would be a challenge. As it is difficult to contact the relevant population, researchers will seek a representative sample as a basis of their research.

Sampling provides various benefits:

- Represents a 'sample' of the relevant population.
- Reduces cost in terms of gathering data.
- Provides results with a generally known and understood accuracy, as it is a representative grouping.
- Reduces the risk of bias: however, there needs to be a careful selection of population, sample and sampling method.

There are various different types of sampling methods. Research companies will seek to use the one that best suits their particular objectives:

- Random Sampling: This is where every member of the population has a calculated opportunity of being included within the sample. For instance, all adults standing on the concourse of a major railway station could conceivably be approached and asked for their views on rail communication links in that particular city. Each person may well have an opinion, however it would be difficult to stop each and every one. Therefore a random sample of people would be approached. However, human judgement does increase the potential risk of bias in terms of who the researcher actually approaches. [It should also be noted that the first part of any questionnaire would normally have questions relating to age range and gender.]
- Systematic Sampling: With this method, human judgement and decision making do not enter into the selection of the sample. For instance, if you had a list of loyalty card holders in a particular area the researcher

could contact every tenth person on that list. This reduces any bias in choosing the sample.

- Stratified Sampling: This can be either random or systematic. The population is divided into two or more groups based on specific population characteristics.

- Cluster Sampling: Grouping together 'units or groups that display similar characteristics', for example, all major supermarkets within a particular (limited) geographical region.

- Convenience/Haphazard: The sample is chosen at the time the survey is occurring and is not pre-planned. This can be considered as 'stopping anyone in the street' to ask them the survey questions. With such an approach there is no guarantee that the individuals stopped meet the attributes of the population. Whilst this is a relatively easy method of approach, in some cases many more people need to be approached to gain a semblance of a representative sample.

- Quota: Seeking to choose a sample who possess certain characteristics that are displayed by the population. For instance, men who wear blue suits in a business district of a city on a particular day.

Primary Data Collection Methods

There are various methods that can be deployed to gather primary data from both a qualitative and quantitative perspective:

- Questionnaires/surveys – This is where an individual is asked a series of questions.

- Questionnaires/surveys can be undertaken in various environments.

  Physical: There are three possible variants:

  (a) Self-completion: where a person receives a physical copy of the questionnaire/survey. This can be via the post, hand-delivered (via their home address) or handed to them (for instance, as they pass through a railway or bus station). These normally have a pre-paid envelope for their return to the research company.

(b) A person may be called at home either on their land line or via their mobile and asked to respond to a set of survey questions. The respondents' answers can be loaded directly onto a database (data warehouse) from which findings can be generated.

(c) Where a person is stopped at a location (for instance, a café or a railway station) and asked questions. In this case the person asking the questions completes the documentation according to the responses.

Virtual: This is where the respondent completes the questionnaire online. It may be via a website or an email which has been sent to them. Various types of organisations often use this method to gain feedback on the perceived quality of their web and social media sites.

These surveys may contain questions that are Closed, Open-ended or a combination of the two.

- Closed Questions are where respondents provide one answer from a series of possible answers. For instance, ticking the box against your specific age category. This allows for the generation of quantitative data, in this example the percentage of respondents within certain age groups.

- Open-ended Questions are qualitative and provide the respondent with the opportunity to express their views more freely. For instance, an open-ended question could be: 'What do you feel about the proposed "green" tax on airline travel?'.

When setting questions the research team has to consider the following:

- Questions should be easy to understand, and need to be clear, succinct and unambiguous.

- Questions should not 'direct' the respondent towards a particular answer.

Often questionnaires/surveys are 'pilot tested' with a small sample of the designated population to check the validity of the questions. Following analysis of the 'pilot test' the research team can modify, for instance, the wording of questions, the ordering of questions and create additional questions.

Observations

There are two main types of observations: The secret/mystery shopper and electronic counting.

Secret/Mystery Shopper: A person is employed by a company to visit a store or series of stores. There are various permutations of mystery shopping:

(a) The mystery shopper may be representing the owners of the store who want to gauge, for instance, the effectiveness and efficiency of customer service.

(b) They may be representing the owners of a particular brand stocked within that store. Here they may be seeking to determine the level of brand knowledge among the staff by asking questions about the product.

Electronic Counting: This is where electronic devices record a customer's actions. For example:

(a) The number of people who enter a store during certain times of a day can be electronically recorded. This will provide the retailer with footfall data. This allows the retailer, for instance, to plan staffing levels across a typical day so that efficient and effective customer service can be delivered (such an approach may provide the retailer with a business advantage over local competitors).

(b) Electronic Point of Sales (EPOS) – This provides two broad sets of information to a company:

• For instance, the type of products being sold, when and in which stores. This is useful, especially for major supermarket chains, as they can track what is selling and what is not. The levels of sales may be due to a range of macro factors, for instance, changes in the economy leading to reduced disposal income. Whilst the sales data can be gathered electronically, the additional information regarding environmental influences would be collected and interpreted as secondary data.

- Information gathered on loyalty card owners. Every time a loyalty card is swiped computer systems record the purchases – value, type and range. The same is true when, for instance, the customer orders their groceries online for later delivery. The company can construct an overall picture of their customers through their loyalty card usage.

(c) Tracking current and potential customers as they browse and navigate a website, noting how long people pause to view certain sections of the site. This provides data that helps determine the effectiveness of the website and areas for possible development.

Focus Groups: These are normally small groups of six to twelve people who display similar attributes and characteristics, for instance, age range, shopping at particular stores, professional occupations, income levels, with children of a particular age and so on. They are brought together to discuss and debate a particular relevant topic or issue.

Focus Group sessions are normally moderated by a representative from an independent marketing agency who organises the sessions, rather than anyone from the client company. This is to reduce the risk of bias in the presentation of the topic, the moderation of the session and the summary of the findings.

Focus Group sessions can be video recorded. However, in many countries, for instance the UK, it is a legal requirement that each individual provides signed written permission for the recording to take place. Moreover, it could be judged unethical if such permission is not sought, whether a legal requirement or not.

Focus Groups can also be undertaken within a virtual environment, as well as a physical one, with the groups forming online. Opinions can also be gathered via social media. However, whilst some social media users may display certain similar characteristics or attributes, not all will, thus not providing a suitable sample of the required population. Moreover, it can be difficult to moderate such interactions.

QUESTIONNAIRE - AN EXAMPLE

The following is an example of different types of questions that could be used in a questionnaire to discover what customers need/want from a shampoo brand. Many more and different types of questions could be asked depending upon what the company is seeking to discover, especially in relation to its objectives.

Gender

Male   ☐
Female   ☐

Age range

18 – 24   ☐
25 – 34   ☐
35 – 44   ☐
45 – 54   ☐
55 and over   ☐

Annual family income

Less than £9,000   ☐
£10,000 – £14,999   ☐
£15,000 – £19,999   ☐
£20,000 – £29,999   ☐
£30,000 – £39,999   ☐
£40,000 – £49,999   ☐
£50,000 – £59,999   ☐
£60,000 +   ☐

Which of the following types of shampoo do you use?

[Please tick all that apply]
Medicated for dandruff   ☐
Medicated for a skin irritation   ☐
Medicated for another purpose   ☐

Shampoo and conditioner combined ☐
Non-perfumed shampoo ☐
Fragranced shampoo ☐
Shampoo with Tee Tree ☐
Shampoo with Apple ☐
Shampoo with Mint ☐
Other ☐
[If other, please provide details]

How often do you wash your hair with shampoo?

Every day ☐
Twice per week ☐
Three times per week ☐
Four times per week ☐
Once per week ☐
Once every fortnight ☐
Once per month ☐
Don't know ☐

Which of the following brands do you use?

[Please tick all that apply]
Brand A ☐
Brand B ☐
Brand C ☐
Brand D ☐
Other brand ☐
[If other brand, please state name]

Which of the following do you look for when purchasing a shampoo?

[Please tick all that apply]
Brand name ☐
Colour of the liquid ☐
Ingredients ☐

Not tested on animals   ☐
Price   ☐
Reputation   ☐
Shape of the bottle   ☐
Size of the bottle   ☐
[The above or similar could be rated in order of importance using a Likert Scale.]

How would you rank the following statements?

1 = Not important
5 = Very important

Which of the following do you look for when purchasing a shampoo?	1	2	3	4	5
Brand name					
Colour of the liquid					
Ingredients					
Not tested on animals					
Price					
Reputation					
Shape of bottle					
Size of bottle					

Supplementary questions could be asked regarding the rankings, such as why certain attributes were rated '5', the highest. For instance, 'price' may rank higher than any other attribute because of income or other household purchases have a greater importance. This may be a general factor or one at a time of recession within the economy when shoppers may be particularly price sensitive.

This allows the researchers to gather qualitative data, the rationale behind the purchase.

INTERNATIONAL CONSIDERATIONS

As there are significant business operations conducted trans-nationally it is important to consider the international aspects of marketing research.

- Language: If the questionnaire/survey was originally written in English then careful consideration has to be given to translations. There are various English expressions and words that do not translate well into other languages, as they can have slightly different meanings or interpretations.
- Experiences: In many countries there is significant experience in terms of undertaking marketing research. This can be from two perspectives: those developing and implementing the marketing research and those responding to, for instance, the survey. The level of experience will vary in other countries, and therefore it cannot be taken for granted that the standard of marketing research will be the same internationally.
- Samples: It may be possible to ascertain a verifiable and representative sample, for instance, via a database in one country. However, the quality of a database in another country may not be the same and thus difficult to select an appropriate sample.
- Infrastructure: The infrastructure of countries varies, sometimes significantly. One country may have an excellent communication system in terms of telephone and postal services. In such cases there are various methods of contacting members of the sample audience. However, in other countries such communication systems may be limited in their scope and efficiency. Some countries, for instance, are far more advanced with their private mobile phone systems than with the State-controlled land-line telephone systems.
- Culture: Although it could be argued that attitudes are changing, not everyone is relaxed in terms of answering questions about, for instance, themselves and their purchasing habits. This may be particularly true in countries that have emerged from a highly regulating political system into a more tolerant democratic one. Countries within the former Soviet Union that are now part of the European Union could be considered suitable examples. In these countries people tended to avoid stating too

much about themselves and their views in fear of persecution. Whilst this may remain with the older generations, the younger generations embrace the freedom to express their views and opinions.

Equally, consumer behaviour can be driven or influenced by a person's own national culture. Therefore buyer behaviour within one country may not always be replicated in another. This too can have an influence upon how individuals respond to surveys and questionnaires.

CRITICISM OF MARKETING RESEARCH

There have been various criticisms levelled against marketing research, which include:

* The data gathered and analysed cannot always be trusted as a relatively accurate reflection of the marketplace and buyer behaviour. Marketing research is unlikely to provide an absolutely accurate picture, however it can provide strong indicators that can aid the decision-making process. Having a focused approach to developing actionable objectives and the careful selection of research methods can aid the level of accuracy.

* Secondary data created for another purpose is not useful. The 'usefulness' will depend on several factors: (1) The age of the data – does it provide an insight into, for instance, current buyer behaviour? (2) How the researcher examines the secondary data. On face value it may not be relevant, however further examination may reveal, for instance, recurring patterns that could inform a new questionnaire/survey.

* Accuracy of Secondary Data: The researcher is examining published (internal or external) information which could be valuable. However, do they know how that information was gathered and analysed? In terms of research reports from leading market research companies, the methodology for collecting the data is normally stated within the report. Such companies will seek accuracy in both their data collection and analytical methods.

* However, how accurate is data from other sources, especially internally within the client company? How accurate is old data that may have

been acquired using different collection methods? To what extent has subjectivity rather than objectivity entered the analysis of the information, especially in relation to qualitative data?

- Bias also enters into our 'interpretation' of the secondary data. As we read and examine information, within various documents, we risk the 'biases' of our own interpretation. We may look at the information in a different subjective way than the original compliers of that information. This can be especially true when we examine trends over a time line. We may, for instance, look at how a market operated in a moment of time but with the knowledge of the factors that influence markets today. That may affect our understanding of why certain business decisions were taken at that original moment of time.

- Marketing research cannot be implemented trans-nationally. As stated earlier in this chapter, there are circumstances that reduce the possible effectiveness of surveys/questionnaires within a trans-national setting. Equally, the difficulties can be either overcome or their effects at least mitigated with appropriate advanced planning.

- Respondents are not always 'truthful', which impacts upon the validity of the findings: Yes, a respondent may be 'economical with the truth'. In the example questions presented earlier we asked the question 'How often do you wash your hair with shampoo?' A respondent may be absolutely truthful in their response, even when they say once per month. However, others may look upon this question as a 'hygiene' issue. Even though their name is not recorded and they will not see the questioner again, they sense embarrassment and state 'every day' whether it is accurate or not. Research companies usually build into their analysis a margin of error to cover misunderstanding of questions and levels of bias.

- Unrepresentative Samples: Whilst small sample numbers might provide some indicators, the question is whether or not they represent the wider population. Equally, does the sample represent the attributes or characteristics of the required population? If these requirements are not aligned, then the quality of the data can be questionable.

- Poor Question Setting: This is a major challenge in marketing research. Questions need to be set that do not lead the respondent in a particular direction; a direction that may, for instance, be more 'suitable' for the company. These ill-judged questions may be unintentional, however they create a bias in the findings. This can also be applicable in terms of surveys (via email or phone) after a problem has been rectified to gauge the level of customer satisfaction. It is important to reflect how the customer 'feels' at that particular time as well as perhaps as a long-term customer.

If there are inaccuracies and/or bias decisions may be made on inaccurate data that can have potentially serious financial consequences for the business. Companies that undertake developing and implementing their own surveys/questionnaires do run the risk of poor question setting if they do not have the appropriate in-house experience and expertise.

- Cost of Undertaking the Research: Undertaking quality marketing research (secondary and primary) can be expensive, and there needs to be a dedicated budget allocation. Whilst it can be relatively expensive, the returns (benefits) can often outweigh the cost of the investment.

- Marketing Research for the Sake of Marketing Research: The criticism here is that organisations (or more likely sections/departments within organisations) undertake marketing research because they need to be 'seen' undertaking it. The section/department do not believe in it but they undertake it to show senior management that they are 'doing something'. Marketing research should only be undertaken when there is a clear purpose and rationale to do so.

- Data is Collected but No Action is Taken: This partly links to the criticism above where data is collected and analysed but no action is taken after the report is delivered.

- Poor Decision Making: This refers to the quality of the decision making taken in the light of the findings of the marketing research report. This, of course, does in part depend upon the quality and presentation of the information provided to the decision makers. Equally, it can be argued that it also depends upon the knowledge and skills of those who are charged with making decisions.

KEY POINTS

In this chapter we have considered the following:

1. The reasons way organisations undertake marketing research – to better understand the markets in which they operate, as well as the needs and wants of current and prospective customers.
2. The marketing research processes from identifying a need through to implementation of the research, the analysis of findings and the decisions taken as a result of the findings.
3. The different types of marketing research – qualitative, quantitative, primary and secondary.
4. The different types of sampling methods and when you might use each one.
5. The different types of primary data collection methods, including interviews, focus groups, questionnaires and electronic forms.
6. That it is important to consider marketing research within an international context. A data collection method may work well within one country but be unsuccessful in another for cultural reasons. Therefore marketing research must be tailored to the specific needs of the research and the environment in which it is being undertaken.
7. Marketing research is not without its criticisms, for instance, the problems associated with accuracy, bias, costs and formulating appropriate questions for primary data collection.

QUESTIONS

Here are a series of questions and activities for you to undertake to aid your knowledge and understanding of the points made in this chapter.

1. Using the series of questions on shampoo as a template, develop five or six questions related to toothpaste. Once you have

formulated the questions, test them out on your friends and f
What does the collected data reveal to you?

2. Why do you think it is valuable to undertake secondary collection and analysis prior to formulating questions for prin data collection?

3. Select a particular sport. Explain how you would undertake researc at a university, to discover which students (1) like this particul, sport, (2) how frequently they go to watch it, (3) do they participat in this sport and, if so, (4) how often.

4. Discuss how marketers can use their own websites to better understand their customer's needs and wants.

5. Develop a ten-question questionnaire using a Likert Scale to find out how individuals decide on what type of chocolate to purchase and how frequently they purchase it. Once you have devised this questionnaire undertake the following: (1) test it out on your family and friends, (2) then convert the responses into a set of graphs, (3) what are your findings and your conclusion from them? (4) Once you have completed the activity reflect back upon it and consider the following: Would you keep the same questions, if not why not? Would you change the wording of any of the questions, and, if so, why? Would you change the order of the questions, and, if so, why? Would you add more questions, and, if so, why?

6. Explain how electronic (or mechanical) observation techniques could help a 'bricks and mortar' retailer better understand customer footfall.

7. Discuss the possible reasons why a marketing research campaign worked well in one country but did not in another. Seek out examples to support your discussion.

8. What are the potential problems associated with secondary data collection and analysis? Suggest ways that these problems could be either overcome or mitigated.

9. Collect three or four customer questionnaires from different hotel chains. Compare and contrast the questions that each one asks. What type of data are the hotel chains seeking to collect? Why is

4

Segmentation, Targeting and Positioning

OBJECTIVES

By the end of this chapter you should be able to:

- Outline the concepts of segmentation, targeting and positioning (STP).
- Explain why and how markets are segmented.
- Explain how customers are targeted with various products and services.
- Explain why and how products and services are positioned to reach the targeted audience.

INTRODUCTION

We have already established that a market is where products can be exchanged for a payment, and that payment may be a currency or another product. Equally, it is unlikely that everyone who visits the market wants to buy our product. Trying to sell our product to everyone who visits the market will be a waste of time and money. In order to maximise our resources and revenue potential, we need to find ways of positioning our product within the market so that we are able to target that particular segment of the population which is most likely going to buy our product.

An example of this is chocolate. Imagine that we are a chocolate company selling a mid-priced brand. Here are some of the characteristics of the market that we need to understand if we are going to be reasonably successful at selling our product. Some of these characteristics are clearly common sense:

- Not everyone likes chocolate.
- Some people cannot eat chocolate, for health reasons.
- Some people cannot eat chocolate on cultural/religious grounds.
- Some cultures may consider eating chocolate more of a feminine behaviour than one for both men and women.
- Some people will only eat certain brands of chocolate.
- Some people only want plain chocolate – not with nuts, fruit or liqueurs.
- Some people may be price sensitive to the cost of certain brands. They will not only seek out the cheapest brand but they may also consider size of the chocolate product; perhaps asking the question 'Am I getting value for money?' (This is a point that we will review in a later chapter.)
- The chocolate may be too sweet for some palates and perhaps not sweet enough for others. (A chocolate brand may have similar wrapping from one country to another – but actually taste slightly different depending upon consumer demands.)

So from this very simple example we can see that if we try and sell our chocolate brand to everyone we could well be wasting resources. By positioning our brand to the right target audience we have an improved opportunity to maximise our overall position within the marketplace. Therefore improving our opportunity to increase revenue and thus profitability.

The interrelationship between segmentation, targeting and positioning (STP) can be viewed in several different ways, for instance as a continuum. However, we prefer to look upon STP as a triangle (see Figure 4.1). In this approach we suggest that the three 'elements' support each other, linking

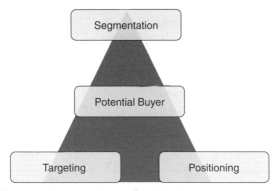

Figure 4.1 Segmentation, targeting and positioning

to the potential buyer in the centre. After all the focus needs to be on the buyer – but the right buyer for the organisation's product and/or service. When the three STP elements are 'strong' then the organisation is better placed to efficiently and effectively market their products/services to the right customer.

SEGMENTING MARKETS

The aim of a segmented market is to find people with similar 'likes' so that organisations can focus their promotional activities (see the chapter on Marketing Communications) towards this particular audience (see Figure 4.2). This links back to Chapter 3 (Marketing Research), in that companies seek, through research, like-minded people who may be interested in their products and/or services.

In some cases a segment of the population can be further subdivided into subsets. For example, referring back to our chocolate example above, we may have our segment – those who like mid-priced chocolate – but that might not be all. There may be those who prefer dark chocolate when compared to plain, and, those who prefer richer chocolate (a higher level of cocoa) than 'ordinary' chocolate. So, in theory at least, we can create a series of sub-sets to better understand our audiences.

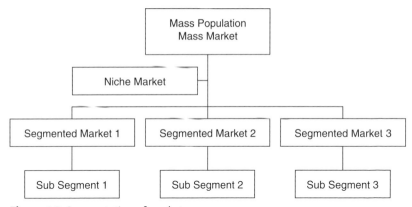

Figure 4.2 Segmentation of markets

In the above example we have segmented a population. However, this example still represents a significantly large group of people. There are cases where the target audience is already well-defined, focused and narrow in its structure – a niche market.

What is important to remember is that segmented markets do not remain static – they are prone to change or develop over time. These changes may be dependent upon many factors, including the interplay of macro factors (see Chapter 1).

How are Markets Segmented?

Technology has played an important (some observers may say 'crucial') role in providing marketers with the means to capture and analyse data to segment markets.

Buyer Behaviour

The use of technology, whether online or in-store, can help companies/ retailers track customer purchasing behaviour. For instance:

- Types of products and/services purchased.
- Product size and colours (if relevant).

- Frequency of purchase.
- Are the purchases online, in-store or both?
- The price ranges purchased.
- Methods of payment.

Companies such as Amazon collect data on an individual's purchasing history and seek to match actual purchases with 'recommended' products that are similar, such as a movie in the same genre and style.

Equally, purchasing history information is particularly useful to super-markets in providing customers with 'added value' through loyalty offers (such as money-saving coupons on certain products, coupons that redeem loyalty points or prize draws or three for two offers). These are aimed at 'influencing' the customer to remain both loyal and to purchase more of the product (or similar) products that they normally purchase.

Geodemographics

This is the combination of both geographical and demographic informa-tion. The geographical information refers to locations (neighbourhoods, towns, cities and regions) and the influence of location on behaviour. Within this context of location the regional and national cultures often have a major impact upon how people behave. Demographics refers to the individual's personal details.

These personal details can include a range of factors. However, it is important not to consider these in isolation and to reflect upon where there may be interrelationships.

Age Range: This allows organisations to understand the needs and wants of individuals in relation to age. For instance, a bank can provide differ-ent products and services dependent upon an individual age and age cycles. There could be special benefits for accounts for children as well as pension plans for young adults and retirement plans for 50+ groups.

Education: Governments tend to provide significant investment across the educational spectrum. A better-educated population tends to lead to greater prosperity for both individuals and nations. Organisations will use 'educational levels' as a criteria in segmenting a population. Generally speaking, individuals with certain types of qualifications can earn significantly more than other professions, for instance, those who have trained as lawyers and doctors. Equally, those with MBAs may have greater earning potential (and thus spending power), especially if they studied at prestigious institutions such as Harvard University or the London Business School.

Ethnicity: Diverse ethnic groups can possess both significant spending power and seek specialist types of products and services. For instance, it is estimated that the ethnic minorities in the UK have a combined spending power of approximately £300 billion, which is also expected to rise (Ogunyemi, 2014). In London, for instance, there is a significant niche market for hair care products specifically aimed at the Afro-Caribbean ethnic group. These products (as of 2014) are not usually available through major retailers but through more specialist hair and beauty stores. Ethnicity can also provide a geographical indicator as well. Some ethnic groups may focus on a particular location in order to build a strong sense of community. For instance, in parts of the UK there are strong Indian and Bangladeshi communities, whilst in the USA there are vibrant Hispanic and African-American communities.

Family Composition and Size: This information helps organisations to provide the right information that could be of benefit to both individuals and the family as a whole. For example, a leisure centre targeting families within specific neighbourhoods with special membership arrangements for families (adults and children between certain ages).

Gender: By understanding a person's gender, the organisation can target products and services that are more suited to men or women. Of course, there are occasions when the marketing communication is applicable to both men and women. For instance, while perfumes may be directly focused on the female market, there are occasions (for instance, Valentine's Day) when companies through their advertising will target men to encourage them to buy perfumes as a gift.

Sexual Orientation: In the UK the spending power of the lesbian, gay, bisexual and transgender communities (LGBT), sometimes called the 'pink pound', is worth approximately £6 billion per year (Burn-Callender, 2011). In the US it is estimated that the value is in the region of $750 billion, with a global market of $3 trillion (Antunes, 2013). (According to Hardy (2012) referring to YouGov marketing research, 60% of gay people are more likely to purchase products and services from organisations that are seen as 'gay-friendly', whilst 50% suggested that they would be encouraged to make purchases from organisations that depicted gay people in their advertising.

Income Levels: Many organisations will seek to segment their audience based upon income levels that match their products and services. For instance, people within high-income brackets that can afford luxury vacations and meet the criteria for premier banking services. Equally, organisations will segment their audiences across a range of income levels so that the most appropriate targeting can be undertaken. However, it does need to be borne in mind that during recessions and periods of austerity, middle-income earners may become more price sensitive and chose to purchase items from discounters.

Occupation and Career: This also links to levels of education and income. Organisations may use this factor to develop not only a segment but also a profile. Consider, for example, a newly established lawyer who has a promising career ahead of them. As they progress through their career so their circle of friends may increase, as does their social activities and earning potential. A bank, for instance, may be able to market to them during their career a range of products and services (bank accounts, life assurance, investment products and a mortgage). For the bank they have been able to create a life-time customer with the minimal of marketing spend.

Religion: As with ethnicity, religion can be an important factor in segmentation. There are products and services that are based upon people's religious beliefs and traditions. For instance, both the Jewish and Islamic religions have specific dietary requirements. Whilst some mainstream supermarkets do provide a selection of produce to meet these requirements, they are normally fulfilled by specialist retailers, both online and in-store.

Social Class: A person's social class can be segmented using various methodologies. For instance, the largest single study in the UK revealed seven categories (BBC, 2013). The methodology focused on both economic and social capital (income, savings, property values, activities and the type of people an individual might know) (BBC, 2013). The categories are: Elite, Established middle class, Technical middle class, New affluent workers, Traditional working class, Emergent service workers and Precariat (the poorest in society) (BBC, 2013). Organisations can use such information to target the specific social classes that are relevant to their products and services.

From this combination of information, marketers can build a profile of people (with similar traits) within an area or region. The development of technologies to capture and analyse data has greatly enhanced the accuracy of the targeting of products and services.

Psychographic Segmentation

Here segmentation is based upon a series of psychological or personality traits reflected in a person's values, attitudes and opinions. A political party, for example, could use this form of segmentation to target individuals with a similar set of attitudes or values, for instance, liberal or green values. It can be argued that the success of the Body Shop was due to the company focusing on potential customers who felt strongly against testing cosmetics on animals.

Behavioural Segmentation

Organisations segment a population based upon their behaviour towards a product or service. In relation to segmentation marketers generally consider behaviour in terms of the following variables. As stated elsewhere these variables should not be considered in isolation.

Attitude: Individuals may have differing attitudes to the same product or service. In some cases we may be highly enthusiastic, becoming advocates (see Chapter 2), and on the other hand we may be negative, even hostile towards a specific product or service. In understanding people's behaviour, organisations will focus on the enthusiasts, those with a positive attitude towards the product or service and those who are 'not sure' and indifferent.

With the 'enthusiasts' and the 'positives' there is 'relatively' small marketing investment. With the 'not sure' group, marketers will seek to explain the benefits in an attempt to persuade them that this is the product or service for them. Here there is an increased level of marketing spend, however with the potential for greater returns. Organisations will normally seek to avoid those with negative or even hostile attitudes as it will usually require a significant level of marketing investment with no guarantee of an attitudinal change.

Benefits: What are the benefits sought by the customer? Here we need to be mindful that not all buyers of a product or service derive exactly the same benefits. We, as customers, can look at benefits in very different ways. One person may seek out functionality and reliability, whilst another may want to consider whether or not the product is environmentally friendly. Equally, the focus might be on whether or not the product or service delivers time-saving benefits (this can be linked to our later discussions on process within the marketing mix).

Cost: Our behaviour may be predicated on the price of the product or service and what we feel that we can afford. This will also link to the value that we derive from the product or service and whether we feel that we are gaining 'value for money' in our purchase. As mentioned elsewhere within this text, when there are periods of recession and austerity, even financially secure groups may become price sensitive, thus seeking lower-priced products and services.

Events and Occasions: Our purchasing behaviour may be triggered by certain events and occasions. These will range from organising the annual family vacation through to birthdays, anniversaries and observing religious celebrations (this links to both ethnicity and religion as stated earlier in this chapter).

Loyalty: Marketers are interested in the level of loyalty displayed by customers. Some customers will be extremely loyal to a specific brand (links to advocacy), others partially loyal, whilst others have no loyalty to any brands. In order to maximise the value of the marketing spend, organisations will focus their attention on those that display a greater degree of loyalty behaviours. However, as Kotler and Keller (2009) suggest, loyalty can be driven by many factors not just a passion for the brand. Such factors can include being 'comfortable' with the brand and not shopping around for a better option, no real alternatives available and levels of price sensitivity (Kotler and Keller, 2009).

Usage Rates: This considers the level of usage of a product or service; this might be defined as heavy, medium and light. How these three categories are quantitatively defined will depend upon the organisation and the specific nature of the product or service. This behaviour can be tracked, for instance, via our loyalty cards (how often we purchase a particular product) and the number of times we use an online service, such as banking.

User Status: We can link this back to the loyalty pyramid in Chapter 2. There we examined different levels from the wider population through to occasional and repeat buyers. Here organisations are interested in user behaviour from the perspective of converting potential buyers into occasional, and occasional buyers into repeat buyers. In order to generate successful conversion the organisation needs to understand the behaviour underpinning the level of usage. Is it, for instance, based upon different attitudes, beliefs and level of experience (consider here groups with limited experience and understanding of using online services and their concerns over security)?

DATA WAREHOUSING AND DATA MINING

Data has been collected in one form or another for decades, but what makes data collection different today is the scale and scope. It is estimated that some 90% of all data available was created in the early 2000s (Wall, 2014). IBM suggest that some 2.5 billion gigabytes of data was generated every day in 2012 (Wall, 2014). Storing or warehousing such data is no longer an issue, and even our own computers and smartphones can store significant amounts of data. Businesses can store data either on their own mainframes or use 'cloud-based' storage facilities.

Warehousing the data is only one aspect of the process; the data has to be mined. Analytical tools have been developed to analyse what is often unstructured data sets to provide useful data for businesses and thus marketers. Google Analytics is a tool which harvests and analyses visitor traffic to particular websites. This provides the website owner with different levels of information on the current and potential customer base.

One of the difficulties associated with collecting such data is understanding who both ethically and legally owns the data. For example, a person makes a comment on their Twitter account and disperses it across the network. This action generates data – but who owns the data is often an area of debate. What is known, however, is that such data can, when analysed effectively, contribute to more efficient use of production, operation and marketing resources.

Data Collection: Impact of Social Media and Gadgets

It should be noted that the development of social media has added to the relevant data collection. Today individuals appear to be more willing to share information across networks. Moreover, the various gadgets that we use in our daily lives from smartphones, notebooks, loyalty cards through to intelligent refrigerators both store and transmit data that again can be used to create a 'picture' of our different behaviours.

This data can provide marketers with valuable insights into people's lifestyles.

BENEFITS OF SEGMENTATION

There are several benefits associated with segmentation:

• Provides organisations with the opportunity to market their products and services to those who are more likely to purchase them. This is beneficial to all organisations, whether they are for-profit companies (such as WalMart), Non-governmental organisations (NGOs, such as Unicef) or charities (such as Save the Children Fund and Médecins Sans Frontières).

• Allows organisations to allocate appropriate resources to the right markets. This will include 'fine-tuning' elements of the marketing mix (product, price, promotion, placement (distribution/supply-chain and logistics), people, physical evidence and process) to best serve the segmented market.

- Provides the opportunity to reduce resource wastage by focusing on the most appropriate markets, thus maximising the value of the marketing budget.
- Valuable for an organisation to analyse how market segments may change/develop over time. No market remains static, especially where there is viable competition or, indeed, the threat of new entrants into the marketplace (see Chapter 1).

BENEFITS OF TARGETING

There are several benefits associated with targeting:

- Whilst an organisation may know the scale and scope of their market, the real benefits come with being able to specifically target groups of customers. The most valuable will be those who are repeat customers buying the same or similar products over time (see Chapter 2). By gaining greater understanding of their customers, an organisation can deliver marketing messages (see Chapter 9) that best suit a particular group of customers.
- As stated above, market segments can change over time; equally so can targeted audiences. Customers may cease to buy a product or service for a variety of reasons (for example: changing lifestyles and moving to a different district or country). It is in this context that organisations need to monitor their targeted audience for any notable changes in purchasing habits and behaviours.

POSITIONING

This is positioning the product or service in the mind of the customer and links closely to segmentation and targeting. In essence it is stating that 'this is the right product or service for you (targeted audience)'.

Such an approach is particularly relevant in highly competitive markets where products/services may display certain similarities, for example, in the luxury car market where many of the features and benefits derived are similar. The differentiating factors may be created through branding (see Chapter 5) and value-added items such as after-sales service (for instance, types of insurance cover, warranties and servicing arrangements).

Equally this applies to when we visit the supermarket and see the scope of laundry washing powders, tablets, gels and liquids available. Many of these products are very similar in terms of chemical formulation and effectiveness.

Positioning can take place in the following areas:

- Products that are specifically eco-friendly (these may be own-label brands or major brands).

- Pricing (in addition to stocking the major brands a supermarket may have a selection of own-label products that can range in quality and value and thus price).

- Quantity (for instance, a container for one brand of laundry tablets may hold more tablets than a similar brand at the same price).

- Reputation (customers may seek out information – from independent sources – on the overall reputation of the brand).

Benefits of Positioning

The objective of positioning is to locate a product and/or service in *a clear, distinctive and desirable place in the mind of the customer relative to any competing product and/or service.* In order to achieve this action, the organisation needs to have a good understanding of the requirements of the customers within the particular segments.

Once there is agreement on the position to be achieved, then the marketing mix elements can be assembled and communicated to the target audience.

An effective product/service position can provide an organisation with several benefits:

- A clear position can act as a differentiator – emphasising what makes it different or distinctive in relation to the competitors within the marketplace.

- Helps the company to select the right marketing mix elements to support the product and/or service in relation to the position. For instance, promoting to the target audience through the most appropriate media channels.

- By selecting the right marketing mix elements the company seeks to maximise the effectiveness of the marketing budget.
- Supports both revenue and profit/surplus generation.

WHY DOES STP FAIL?

Whilst there are many examples of organisations using the STP concept successfully, there are equally cases where STP has been less successful.

- Some organisations do not utilise the technology available in terms of data warehousing and data mining to appropriately segment their potential audience.
- Markets are dynamic and organisations have to regularly review and update STP (when necessary) in order to remain competitive.
- A 'position' can change. For instance, a brand once considered 'luxury' may now be considered more mainstream if it fails to successfully under-pin its position within the marketplace. It could be argued that the Pierre Cardin brand lost some of its luxury appeal when the company offered various licensing agreements to a range of manufacturers from luggage to wallets (Reddy and Terblanche, 2005). The exclusivity invested in the clothing brand was reduced through the mass-market appeal driven by the various brand-bearing products, not all of which bore the quality hallmark of the original. Over the years various fashion houses, for instance, have sought to reduce the number of licences in order to have a much more focused control over their brands (Menkes, 2000).

KEY POINTS

In this chapter we have considered the following:

1. The interrelationship between segmentation, targeting and positioning.

2. Why it is important for organisations to undertake STP in order to reach the most appropriate customer groups and therefore maximise the value of their marketing budget.
3. How markets can be segmented using different frameworks such a geodemographics, behavioural and lifestyle analysis.
4. The possible reasons why the application of STP fails and therefore how organisations can mitigate against such a risk.

QUESTIONS

Here are a series of questions and activities for you to undertake to aid your knowledge and understanding of the points made in this chapter.

1. In Chapter 3 we asked you to create a questionnaire to gain information on various people's preferences for chocolate. Having reviewed that questionnaire as part of the previous activity, consider what demographic and lifestyle questions you might add to your revised questionnaire. Undertake the questionnaire again with the same family and friends as before. What does this exercise now reveal?

2. Visit two large supermarkets and look at the shelves displaying laundry washing powders, tablets, gels and liquids. Either write down or mentally note the position of the major brands, own-label brands, specialist products (for example, eco-friendly) and the cheapest products. Once you have visited the two supermarkets compare and contrast your findings. What have you discovered? Why is this important to your understanding of positioning? Equally, how can the supermarkets use the data collected at the point of purchase to better understand their customers?

3. Assume that you are buying a new car. What types of benefits (see Behavioural Segmentation) would you seek? Once you have noted your choice ask your friends and family to do the same – but do not reveal your choice. Once you have collected everyone's different views on 'benefits', compare and contrast them. What are the conclusions?

FURTHER READING

Epetimehin, F.M. (2011) Market segmentation: A tool for improving customer satisfaction and retention in insurance service delivery. *Journal of Emerging Trends in Economics and Management Sciences*. Vol 2 No 1. pp. 62–67.

Gbadamosi, A. (2012) Acculturation: An exploratory study of clothing consumption among Black African women in London (UK). *Journal of Fashion Marketing and Management: An International Journal*. Vol 16 No 1. pp. 5–20.

Hassan, S.S. and Craft, S. (2012) Examining world market segmentation and brand positioning strategies. *Journal of Consumer Marketing*. Vol 29 No 5. pp. 344–356.

Haverila, M.J. (2013) Market segmentation in the cell phone market among adolescents and young adults. *Asia Pacific Journal of Marketing and Logistics*. Vol 25 No 3. pp. 346–368.

McDonald, M. and Dunbar, I. (2012) *Marketing Segmentation: How to Do it and Profit from it* (4th Edition). Chichester: John Wiley & Sons.

Nella, A. and Christou, E. (2014) Segmenting wine tourists on the basis of involvement with wine. *Journal of Travel & Tourism Marketing*. Vol 31 No 7. pp. 783–798.

Rossberger, T. and Fiedler, M. (2014) Customer segmentation analysis in major sporting goods companies and its influence on strategic marketing decisions. *Review of European Studies*. Vol 6 No 4. pp. 268–276.

5

Branding

OBJECTIVES

By the end of this chapter you should be able to:

- Explain why products and services are branded.
- Explain the different types of branding.
- Discuss why some brands have longevity within the marketplace and others do not.
- Discuss how companies can build customer-based brand equity.
- Understand why it is important to protect brand trademarks.

INTRODUCTION

In this chapter we examine the importance of branding as an integral part of business and our everyday lives. Basically a brand is a form of identification, and in business terms this is a 'name' and/or 'symbol' that is trademarked or registered. By registering or trade marking, the organisation is stating that it has legal ownership and thus preventing use by anyone else, without express permission.

Organisations brand both themselves and the products or services that they create and market. Brands can be focused as Business to Business (B2B) or Business to Consumer (B2C). An example of B2B would be Rolls-Royce Aircraft Engines supplying major aircraft manufacturers/airlines with jet engines. A B2C example would be Heinz foods supplying products to ordinary customers via a supermarket.

We use the term 'organisations' rather than company as not-for-profit, non-governmental organisations (NGOs) and charities are also engaged in branding in a variety of different ways. Some of these points are explored further within this chapter.

Examples of Brand Names

Here are a few brand names that score high on recognition. Some we may encounter on a regular basis, for example, Microsoft; others, such as luxury car manufacturer Aston Martin are perhaps more akin to a wish list!

Apple

Aston Martin

British Airways

Cadburys

Carrefour

Coca-Cola

Heinz

Intel

Kraft

Microsoft

Nestlé

Renault

Tata

Tesco

Unilever

WORLD'S LEADING BRANDS

Each year the company Interbrand undertakes a detailed analysis of all major brands to determine the world's most powerful brands. In Table 5.1 we have compared the ten leading brands from 2014 with those of 2003 using Interbrand data.

The 2014 listing is dominated by technology brands. In addition to those in the top ten, Cisco (14th), Oracle (16th), HP (17th), SAP (25th), Facebook (29th), Canon (37th), Phillips (42nd) and Siemens (49th) are in the top 50 (Interbrand, 2014a).

WHY DO ORGANISATIONS BRAND?

Organisations seek to apply the concept of branding for several, often integrated, reasons:

Differentiation: To clearly define that the product/service is 'different' from the competition. If all chocolate bars, for example, had exactly that same wrapper, there would be no way of instantly recognising the difference between one chocolate bar and another. Branding provides a visual means of differentiating one product/service from another.

Table 5.1 Ten leading brands, 2003 and 2014

Ranking	2014	2003	Notes
1	Apple	Coca-Cola	
2	Google	Microsoft	
3	Coca-Cola	IBM	
4	IBM	GE	
5	Microsoft	Intel	12th in 2014
6	GE	Nokia	Nokia 98th in 2014, 57th in 2013
7	Samsung	Disney	13th in 2014
8	Toyota	McDonald's	
9	McDonald's	Marlboro	Marlboro not in 2012–14 lists. In 2011 it was ranked 18th
10	Mercedes-Benz	Mercedes-Benz	

Source: Interbrand

We can look at this as creating an 'identity' for the product or service and this, in turn, links to developing attributes for the brand.

Attributes: These are generally the 'features and benefits' that constitute the product or service. For example, we may know that a certain chocolate brand contains more cocoa, thus making it richer in taste than perhaps many other chocolate bars on the market. This becomes an attribute of the brand, which may well be reflected in both the marketing of the product and the subsequent price charged. Equally, when we consider opening a bank account we will probably compare and contrast the various features and benefits of different accounts on offer from a selection of local banks.

Recall: The creation and building of brand awareness (through various communication devices and tactics) can aid memory recall. The logos, colours and images used to identify a brand can be powerful symbols in brand recall. Thus if we consider petrol or filling stations we can easily recall the visual differences between BP stations from those of Texaco, due to logos, signage and particularly colours.

Recognition: We often associate our actions to purchase either a product or service through recognising the brand name. For us the brand carries, as stated above, certain attributes which helps us make our purchasing decisions. Moreover once we have purchased the brand we will draw our own conclusions in terms of, for instance, value for money. If we are satisfied with the brand then we will (1) seek repeat purchases and/or (2) recommend it to other people who trust our judgement.

Extensions: Building a brand provides some organisations with the opportunity to develop extensions. This is where other products are introduced into the brand range, thus building upon the recognition of the original product or service. An example is the Dove range of personal care products developed and marketed by Unilever. This brand originally started as Dove cleansing bar (soap) in 1957 in the US (Unilever, 2014a). Since its introduction into the UK in the 1980s it has been extended into a range of products under the broad headings of Washing & Bathing, Hand & Body Lotions, Deodorant, Hair Care and a Men's Range (labelled as Dove Men+Care). The products are branded as, for instance, Dove Body Wash, Dove Cream Bar, Dove Liquid Hand Wash and so on. This not only demonstrates the potential range of the extensions but also makes the direct link to the overall brand name – Dove. Unless you examine the packaging you would not necessarily know that it was a Unilever brand. Dove products are sold in over 80 countries (Unilever, 2014a). However, not all the extensions are necessarily available in all countries.

Building extensions provides various potential benefits:

- A reduced marketing spend is required as the brand name is already known within the market and target audience.

- Introducing a new product into the market can be risky. Using the extension approach reduces the risk as customers are already familiar with the brand. The key, of course, is that the extensions meet the expectations (quality, value, affect) of the current loyal customers.

Positioning: This links us back to Chapter 4 on Segmentation, Targeting and Positioning (STP). A brand needs to be positioned so that it can be marketed to the audience most likely to buy the product/ service. Whilst many of us know about Aston Martin sports cars (perhaps through the James Bond movies) and, probably, would like to own one, the marketers will position the marketing communications towards those who can afford one. Therefore upmarket brands will be advertised, for instance, in specific types of lifestyle magazines aimed at specific target audiences.

Valuation: Brands have a financial value to a company. When a company sells a brand or a company that owns several brands, the buyer is interested in, amongst other considerations, the value of the brands. When the world's second largest food company, the US-based Kraft considered acquiring the UK confectionery company Cadbury, the strategic and financial analysts advising Kraft examined the value of the individual brands within the Cadbury portfolio. In 2010 Kraft acquired Cadbury for £11.9 billion (Ruddick, 2010). For Kraft there were several potential advantages in this acquisition:

1. Provides access to increased growth potential in emerging/developing markets where Cadbury already has a presence with strong

distribution and supply-chain networks (Ruddick, 2010). Kraft aimed to use these networks to leverage brand recognition of their own brands.

2. Cadbury's world-famous brands – an international presence.

3. Combined brand strength – at acquisition the combined group had over 40 confectionery brands (Ruddick, 2010).

In 2012 Kraft Foods Inc divided into two separately traded companies. One brought various confectionery, beverage, cheese, grocery and snack food brands (including Cadbury) under the Mondelēz International name, creating one of the world's largest snack food companies. In 2014 the company held the number 1 market position globally in chocolate, biscuits, candy and powdered beverages, and the number 2 position in gum and coffee (Mondelēz, 2014).

Protection: Through registration, copyrights and trademarks, organisations seek to protect their brand and associated logos, attributes, typefaces, colours and names from being copied. Countries have signed up to various legal conventions to protect individual brands from counterfeiting and piracy. Unfortunately, such illegal activities remain a significant problem for many leading brands ranging from the luxury clothing and perfumier Chanel through to computer software multinational Microsoft.

Loyalty: The ultimate aim is that customers become loyal to a particular brand, for example, coffee, tea, chocolate, banking services or charitable giving. This brand loyalty leads not only to repeat purchasing of products and services but also recommendations to others who, in turn, may well become brand loyal and advocates (see Chapters 2 and 4).

Where there is extensive brand loyalty an organisation can tailor their marketing effort to:

• Further enhance loyalty: A charity may communicate, at a time of a specific crisis, with those who donate on a regular basis with the belief that they will make a further donation. A charity can use a variety of communication tactics linked to the donor's preferences – email, telephone and social media. This is a more cost-effective approach than targeting people who may have no previous links with the charity.

- Maximise marketing spend: This also links to Chapter 4 on Segmentation, Targeting and Positioning (STP). By judicious targeting of loyal customers with special offers, the organisation seeks to enhance revenue generation. Moreover, the organisation can focus attention on developing new segments/markets and thus target audiences. What is important to remember is that markets are not static and this fluidity needs to be monitored so as to support current customers whilst also seeking out potential future customers.

BRAND EQUITY

As indicated above, the aim of an organisation is to develop and maintain a strong viable brand. Brand equity can relate to two areas: (1) the added value given to products and services through the way customers feel, think and act towards them; (2) the brand's market share and the level of profitability it delivers to the organisation.

Keller (2001) suggests viable brand equity provides an organisation with a series of benefits including enhanced customer loyalty, increased marketing communication effectiveness, opportunities to develop brand extensions and potential for increased margins. However, whilst brand equity is important it may not be the only contributor to these particular benefits, as other factors may come into play.

Keller (2001) developed the four-stage customer based brand equity (CBBE) model, which explores how brand equity can be developed and measured. Keller's model focuses its attention on the customer, specifically in relation to their knowledge of and experiences with a brand. Keller (2001) suggests that each stage must be successfully completed before moving to the next.

Stage 1: Brand Identity

The organisation seeks to create salience or awareness in the mind of the potential and current customers. Keller (2001) suggests that there are two factors that distinguish brand awareness – depth and breadth.

- Depth refers to how easily a customer can recall, remember or recognise a brand, in addition to where and when they do so.
- Breadth refers to the range of purchasing situations where the brand can be recalled. The greater the convergence of depth and breadth the greater the salience or awareness.

Stage 2: Brand Meaning

This explores how both performance and imagery give meaning to the brand in the mind of the customer. These are about the associations that the customer makes with the brand, and Keller (2001) suggests that these need to be strong, favourable and unique.

Performance is where the product or service meets the functional needs of the customer. In terms of products these will include:

- Reliability: How reliable will the product be over the medium and longer term?
- Durability: How durable will the product be over the medium and longer term? Will it deliver value for money?
- Serviceability: How easy is it to service the product should it need repairs?

In terms of service, functional needs will include:

- Effectiveness: How effective is the service in meeting the customer's needs?
- Efficiency: What is the speed of responsiveness in delivering the service?
- Empathy: Does the organisation create a level of trust and caring in the mind of the customer?

Imagery focuses on the extrinsic properties of a product or service, specifically in terms of a customer's psychological associations with the brand. These associations include:

- History, Heritage and Experiences: These can be viewed from several different dimensions. As we explore elsewhere in this chapter, some brands have demonstrated longevity; they have been available and in people's subconscious for many years. The brand displays a history, a heritage that is often reinforced through the imagery of marketing communications. Even within a contemporary setting some brands will clearly identify their beginnings, their date of origin. Moreover some brands will closely identify with symbols or traits of their home country, even if they are marketing trans-nationally. For example, German efficiency in terms of engineering.

- Equally, we have experiences and a history with brands. These associations may have developed when we were children in the products we encountered, whether food or different makes of toys. As we age we still find a favourable association with a particular type of cereal or sandwich spread. These resonate in our subconscious.

- Personality: Aaker (1997) developed a framework which suggests that there are five types of brand personality which, in turn, display various facets or describers. The point that should be made is that this was US-focused research and that the brands, like us, may display different personality types within different cultural settings. However, this framework is a good starting point in helping us to relate to different types of brands:

  a. Sincerity: This personality can be described as down-to-earth, honest, wholesome and cheerful.

  b. Excitement: This personality can be described as daring, spirited, imaginative and up-to-date.

  c. Competence: This personality can be described as reliable, intelligent and successful.

  d. Sophistication: This personality can be described as upper class and charming.

  e. Ruggedness: This personality can be described as outdoorsy and tough.

- Purchase and Usage Situations: This is our association with the channel through which we make the purchase, whether it is normally in a particular store or online. For instance, we may only buy our clothes from one or two particular stores because we feel a strong association with those stores and the brands. Equally, we can associate the brand with when and where we use it. For instance, a man may buy formal suits of a particular brand that are only used for work. He may buy the same or another brand of clothes that he feels strongly associated with for more informal occasions.

- User Profiles: This is how we associate ourselves with other users of the brand. For instance, we may purchase particular clothing because we want to be associated with the style that is promoted by the brand. This may fit a particular age group, income level and attitude towards life. Equally, we may associate with a brand because of the values that it delivers in terms of a social consciousness. We could argue that the majority of people that started buying cosmetics and beauty products from the Body Shop had similar views against testing such products on animals. [Note: You may want to refer back to Chapter 4 and consider how organisations create profiles through segmentation in order to position their products and/or services to particular target audiences.]

Stage 3: Brand Responses

This is how customers respond to the particular brand. This response can be affected by marketing communications, other sources of information and customers' emotions. Keller (2001) suggests that these responses can be categorised as Brand Judgements and Brand Feelings.

Brand Judgements: These are the customer's personal opinions, which are linked to performance and the imagery associations that we experience.

- Quality: What is our view of the quality of the product or service? Is the quality of the product reflected in the price we have paid for it? Are we satisfied with the quality of the product or service?

- Credibility: Is credibility demonstrated in terms of Expertise (innovative, reliable), Trustworthiness (dependable) and Likeability (interesting, engaging)?
- Consideration: What is the relevance of the brand to us as customers? Is the brand appropriate for us? Does it have a meaning for us?
- Superiority: Do we as customers perceive the brand as superior or unique to other brands available within the marketplace?

Brand Feelings: These are the emotional reactions that the brand creates within customers. Keller (2001) cites the work of Kahle, Poulos and Sukhdial (1988) in terms of the types of feelings that can be related to brands. Although these authors' work was focused on social values within the USA we believe that generally these types of 'feelings' have a universality. You will also note that the final three in this list can also be linked to Maslow's Hierarchy of Needs discussed in Chapter 2.

- Warmth: The brand helps the customer feel peaceful, sentimental or affectionate.
- Fun: The brand creates a sense of amusement, playfulness and a sense of enjoyment. Many people may feel that the Disney brand, through its theme parks, conjures up this sense of fun within them. These feelings may remain with them through childhood and well into adulthood. Indeed, it may be an experience that they share with their own children. Hence these feelings can be shared across generations.
- Excitement: The customer feels energised by the brand; there is a sense of elation that the brand is 'cool'. This could relate to an association with a particular brand of theme park that delivers the thrills that we seek. We are elated every time we visit. Equally, the brand of clothes that we wear symbolises 'coolness', it makes us feel good when we wear the brand.
- Security: The customer feels comfortable, safe, self-assured. Certain car brands, for instance, seek to create this sense of security, of safety. Volvo is an example of a car brand that has been long associated with providing a safe and comfortable driving experience.

- Social Approval: These are where positive feelings or reactions are conveyed by others to the brand. Again we can refer to clothing brands that we feel are not only 'cool' but that are also considered 'cool' by others within our social circle.

- Self-respect: This is where the brand helps to create a sense of worth, of fulfilment within the individual. Earlier we used the example of purchasing a formal brand of suit for work. The style, design and the formality of the brand may convey within us a sense of self-respect that we have 'made it' within our career.

Stage 4: Brand Relationships

This is the final stage within Keller's framework and focuses on the level of resonance or bonding the customer has with the brand. Keller (2001) suggests that Brand Resonance can be subdivided into four categories:

- Behavioural Loyalty: This focuses on how much and how often the customer makes repeat purchases of the brand. [You may want to reflect back to Chapter 2 where we discuss different levels of loyalty.]

- Attitudinal Attachment: This is where a customer is passionate about a particular brand that they look forward to consuming/using and making the next purchase. Here we can think of the consumption of certain brands of chocolate, that there can be no replacement for this particular brand. The same can be said in terms of our attachment to certain types of perfumes and beauty products.

- Sense of Community: This is where we identify with a community that purchases the same brand; there is a sense of kinship. This reiterates some of the examples that we used in brand responses above in terms of wearing a clothing brand that we and others consider 'cool'. Equally, many brands have created social media forums on their websites where customers can share their thoughts and feelings about the brand. This helps to reinforce that sense of brand community.

- Active Engagement: This develops out of the sense of brand community discussed above, where the customer with a strong vibrant attitudinal attachment becomes a 'brand evangelist' or advocate. They become involved beyond the purchasing of the brand to actively promote the brand and engage (as stated above) in social media forums not just on the brand's own website but elsewhere. As discussed in Chapter 9, customer 'word of mouth' can significantly help to promote a brand both within the current brand community and beyond.

THE ROLE OF PACKAGING IN BRANDING

Although some authors (for instance, Groucutt, 2005 suggest that packaging should be a separate entirety, it is often positioned either under products or promotion (marketing communications). A consumer can often derive an understanding of a brand, along with its status, features and benefits, from the packaging. The packaging conveys the image that the brand owner wants to promote to the potential buyer.

We can look at packaging in several different ways, and this is perhaps exemplified by examining a luxury brand of perfume. In this case there are three sets of packaging:

- There is the bottle itself: This will consist of the bottle shape and accompanying labelling. Visit any perfume counter in a department store and you will see a variety of different shapes – some conservative and others perhaps more provocative and eye-catching. An example of the latter is Jean Paul Gaultier's classic women's fragrance, which has a bottle that follows the feminine form. The labelling can be simple, yet informative, restating the brand and any sub-brand.

- Outer Packaging: This has two main functions, firstly to communicate the brand name and image, and secondly, to protect the actual product. Whilst some perfume bottles are contained within cardboard packaging others, such as Jean Paul Gaultier's classic female perfume, is in a metal container. Again, this is another way of differentiating the brand from other brands.

- Branded Carrier Bag: This is the third and final packaging element. This can come in various physical forms, from plastic through to a ridged board construction. Moreover, it can be branded in one of two ways: (1) It can be the same as the perfume brand. This would be the case if the perfume was purchased within their own store, for instance, a Chanel store in Paris. (2) A department or specialist store's carrier bag, such as the luxury retail outlet Harrods in London.

What value does packaging add to a product or brand?
There are several 'value added' factors:

- As stated earlier, it conveys the image of the brand to the customer. It helps to create a perception of the brand and positions it in the mind of the customer. This positioning is also reinforced through marketing communications, such as advertising.
- Both inner and outer packaging helps to protect the product from potential damage.
- Packaging can help to keep the product fresh. For instance, chilled food products, such as pizza, may be sealed in a cellophane wrapping within a cardboard box. The cardboard box provides outer protection and the information about the pizza (ingredients and how to cook it).
- It can also protect from spillage – consider the cap/top on a tube of toothpaste or the cap on a bottle of expensive perfume.
- Conveys the various features and benefits of the brand. These can be communicated through images, colours and instructions on how to use it (for instance, application of paint onto the walls of a house or the cooking of a pre-prepared meal).

TYPES OF BRANDING

There are different types of branding structures that organisations can use to best suit their particular business and market requirements.

Family Branding

These are often called umbrella brands and usually carry the company's name, for example, the UK-headquartered private conglomerate Virgin Group. Figure 5.1 illustrates the span of companies under the Virgin Group umbrella. Apart from those clearly identifying themselves as country-specific,

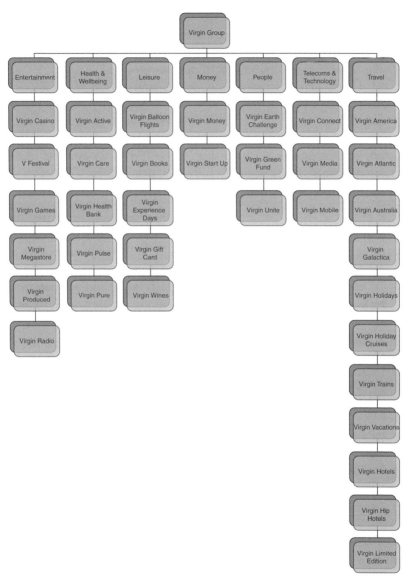

Figure 5.1 A diagrammatic representation of the span of the Virgin Group

[Correct as of September 2014]

for instance, the airline Virgin Australia, not all brands operate in all countries. Virgin Megastore, for instance, operates in parts of the Middle East but no longer in the UK (where it was originally created) and Virgin Trains only in the UK. However, the company has a significant international footprint.

H.J. Heinz, which is one of the world's largest food manufacturers, has a span of companies that include both family and individual brands (Heinz, 2014). Their products range from soups through to mayonnaise. (It should also be noted that the H.J. Heinz Company also own various brands such as Classico – pasta sauce; Lea & Perrins – Worcester sauce; Plasmon – infant nutrition products as well as many others.)

There are several advantages to using the family branding approach:

If the brand name has a heritage and there are loyal customers, the company can expand the range of products under the 'umbrella' of the name. The H.J. Heinz Company has significantly expanded its range of products under the 'label' since its foundation in 1869 (Heinz, 2014). Of course, where a company has used a family brand approach and seeks to continue to do so, there must be the ongoing quality standards and value that customers expect.

A further advantage is that the brand name is often easily recalled by customers. It can be argued that even if a supermarket shopper doesn't often purchase the brand, they will most likely know the Heinz name.

A solid, well-known family brand name will be easily recognised (see earlier points), and that will greatly aid marketing of the products/ services. Even if there is significant marketing spend to maintain profile within a highly competitive environment, name recognition will make an important contribution to product/service promotion.

However there can be disadvantages:

If there is a problem with a particular product/service within the family of brands, this can impact the remaining products/services. For example, if a food company has a product recall (which can happen to the most efficient of companies), customers may think that the remainder of the products (within the family brand) are equally 'problematic' and avoid purchasing until they deem it 'safe' to do so.

The company may launch a new product/service within the family brand. Regular customers will normally associate the quality of the new product/service with that of the existing products/services. However, if the new product/service does not meet customer expectations, then they may well believe that the overall quality of the company's products/services are in decline, whether they are or not. As indicated in Chapters 2 and 4, people's perception can make an important contribution to the success or otherwise of a product/service and, indeed, a company.

Individual Brands

Whilst some companies may opt for the creation of a family brand approach, others seek to develop individual brands.

This may be for several reasons:

- The company may be a diverse business operating over several market sectors and countries. It may have grown through the acquisition of various business operations, and such diversity may prove difficult (if not impossible) to collect under one family brand.

- The company seeks to create a range of similar products that can compete with each other, as well as competitors within the marketplace. Multinationals such as Procter & Gamble (P&G) and Unilever have developed a range of individual detergent brands.

- Through the development of individual brands a company can seek to gain greater shelf space within a retail outlet relative to its competitors. So you might see several individually branded products on a supermarket shelf, all apparently competing with each other, yet they are ultimately owned by the same company.

- Customers, even normally loyal ones, will switch brands that are close in features and benefits to another brand rather than their regular purchase. This may be for a variety of reasons, for example, they have been told it is a better brand by someone they trust, they are not satisfied with the performance of the current brand or it is on special offer. If a company has several individual brands present, even if the customer switches brand, there is the possibility that they will choose one of the company's brands.

- In one sense, developing a number of individual brands within a particular market sector, such as detergents, creates competition. However, the building, by several companies within a market sector, of a number of individual brands can reduce the threat of new entrants into the market as there may be no 'gaps' within the market for a new entrant to penetrate. Moreover, to enter the market may require significant investment in order to successfully compete.

- This strategy can create a level of healthy competition between the Brand Managers within the various divisions of the company. Brands, even well-established ones, require marketing investment (resources and ideas) to maintain/develop their position within the marketplace. Each brand will be expected to make a financial return to the particular division (for example, Detergents). In turn, that division will be expected to make a financial contribution to the parent company.

- If there is a problem associated with one particular brand, for example, a product recall, then the other brands are unlikely to be affected. Moreover, it might drive brand switchers to another one of the company's brands.

- It may provide greater opportunity for the development of brand extensions. As stated earlier, the Unilever brand Dove has been extended beyond the original moisturising soap to encompass a range of beauty products for both men and women.

Own-Label Brands

These are also known as supermarket brands, private labels, retailer brands and store brands.

Supermarkets, for example, normally do not develop and manufacture their own-label products. Various companies will be contracted to produce products on their behalf. One of Europe's largest manufacturers of own-label brands household and personal care products is the UK-based company McBride (McBride, 2015).

A supermarket's own-label brands can also cater for different segments of a particular market. For example, the UK-based supermarket Tesco, across its own-label chocolate biscuit range, has 'Finest' at one end and

'Value' at the other end. The pricing differentials will reflect product quality and packaging.

In many countries (such as the UK) supermarkets operate in a highly competitive marketplace. The level of competitiveness is often more apparent at times of recession, economic recovery and slow economic growth. At such times consumers may be particularly price sensitive, concerned about the amount of disposable income available to them. The supermarket's own-label brands, in many cases, will be cheaper than the 'mainstream' brands and thus particularly appealing to those customers who are price aware.

Co-Branding

This is also known as dual branding. Companies that have a strong reputation within different markets may seek to co-brand a specific product or service. This can assist in building brand loyalty across the two brands. A good example of this is two powerful brands, British Airways and American Express, where they have created a co-branded credit card for British Airways Club Members.

Case Study: Mountain Bikes & Raft Holidays

[Note: Although this is a fictitious case study it is based upon several real examples. In addition to an example of co-branding, it also demonstrates how companies with complementary products can collaborate to mutual benefit.]

JG Bikes Limited hires and sells mountain bikes and cycles to visitors in the Highlands of Scotland. With its beautiful and dramatic landscape, rivers and lakes the Highlands are a very popular tourist destination during the spring and summer months. JG Bikes Limited, which has been in existence for over 20 years, enjoys good business but seeks to add value for their customers, especially as they are facing growing competition. The company decides to discuss options with CJH Rafting Limited, who have been in business for approximately 10 years. CJH Rafting offer pack rafting holidays, which entails visitors walking across the countryside and when they reach water, unpack their inflatable raft and paddle for the rest of the way.

The two companies believe that there is potential for synergy. The visitors can have a choice of walking to the rivers/lochs (lakes) or using trail bikes. The inflatable rafts are lightweight and carried as a back pack.

The two companies decide to co-brand sharing logos, joint marketing communications (exhibition stands and website information) to market to individuals, hotels and travel companies. They remain as separate legal companies; however the action of co-branding and targeting a particular segment of the tourist market, will help both their businesses prosper within a competitive marketplace.

Re-Branding

Companies may seek, for various reasons, to re-brand a product/service. These reasons may include:

Seeking to harmonise marketing across several countries (see the case study on Cif). The original brand name may have another meaning in other languages, whether that is mainstream or in slang. What may be an innocent name in one language can be offensive in another. As companies market more of their brands internationally they have to be aware of the potential different meanings. This may lead to the necessity of re-branding in order to enter that marketplace.

There is an association with an ingredient, a location, a time in history that may be detrimental to the brand (see the case study on Sugar Puffs).

There may be a merger between two companies and, in some cases, this may result in the re-branding of the company name. A case in point was the merger of the US automotive manufacturer Chrysler with the German manufacturer Daimler to form the parent brand Daimler-Chrysler. However, this was a short-lived re-branding as the companies later de-merged.

Case Study: Cif

Cif is a range of cleaning products produced by Unilever and marketed in approximately 50 countries (Unilever, 2014b). Originally developed in France in 1969, Cif was launched in the UK as Jif in 1974 (Unilever,

2014b.) In 2001 the name in most countries was changed to Cif to har-monise marketing and distribution across borders (RF). In a few countries it is marketed at Vim, Jif and Viss (Unilever, 2014b). Over the years there have been various developments of the brand including extensions (addi-tional sprays and wipes).

Case Study: Sugar Puffs

Sugar Puffs had been a UK breakfast cereal brand since the 1950s when first launched by the previous brand owners, the Quaker Oats company (Montgomery, 2014). Since the late 1970s, the marketing of this prod-uct has been accompanied by a large, bumbling yellow furry 'monster' (Bamford, 2014). There were several slogans used in the print and televi-sion campaigns, with perhaps the most popular being 'Tell them about the honey Mummy', a reference to the cereal's honey ingredient.

Growing concern by parents, health experts and the government regarding childhood obesity and food ingredients in a variety of products from snack foods to cola drinks has resulted in companies reviewing ingre-dients. In November 2014 Sugar Puffs was re-branded as Honey Monster Puffs with a new recipe (less refined sugar, 20% more honey, no artificial colours, flavours and preservatives, virtually no salt) in a bid to distance itself from the overt 'advertising' of sugar (Halo Foods, 2014; Spary, 2014).

According to Bamford (2014), Halo Foods aims to grow their share of the breakfast cereal market through this re-branding and new marketing communications campaigns. Equally, Halo Foods parent company, the Finnish-based Raisio Group, blamed the UK cereal business for a UK£2 mil-lion reduction in operating profit in 2014 (Bamford, 2014).

BRAND LONGEVITY

This really poses the question – are brands here today and gone tomorrow or do they last?

The companies that own brands may merge with other companies or be acquired. The parent company's name may disappear – but the brands may continue to live on. Some brands go from strength to strength, some falter and disappear, some re-emerge after an 'apparent' absence whilst others are re-energised and become powerful once again.

Table 5.2 is a brief list of brands that demonstrate longevity and also includes a few relatively recent brand introductions.

Table 5.2 A selection of brands with date of origin

Year of origin	Brand name	Product/service type
1366	Stella Artois	Brewing
1706	Twinings	Tea manufacturer
1765	Lloyds Bank	Banking and finance
1824	Cadbury	Confectionery
1833	Shell Oil	Energy – Petroleum
1843	Macmillan	Publishing
1856	Burberry	Luxury fashion
1863	International Red Cross/Red Crescent	Medical charities
1864	Société Génerale	Banking and finance
1866	Nestlé	Food
1884	L'Amande	Soap
1886	Coca-Cola	Soft drink
1894	Lifebuoy	Soap
1899	Fiat	Automobiles
1902	Kraft	Food
1906	Rolls-Royce	Automobiles
1913	Aston Martin	Automobiles
1922	British Broadcasting Corporation (BBC)	Film, television and radio production and broadcasting
1923	Disney	Entertainment
1923	Warner Bros.	Entertainment
1924	International Business Machines (IBM)	Computing and IT consulting
1940	McDonald's	Fast food restaurants
1943	IKEA	Retail – furniture
1958	Sony Corporation	Electronics and entertainment
1968	Intel	Semiconductor chips
1971	Médecins Sans Frontières (MSF)	Medical humanitarian organisation
1991	Middle East Broadcasting (mbc)	Satellite broadcasting company
1998	Google	Internet services and products
2004	Facebook	Social networking service
2006	Twitter	Social networking service

[Details obtained from the individual organisation's websites. It should be understood that many of these organisations will have undergone structural changes (including changes in ownership) since their original formation.]

How Do Brands Maintain Longevity?

There are no exact rules as each brand needs to be considered on an individual basis. However, there are broad issues or factors that each brand may have to take into consideration. These issues or factors could include:

The Brand Owner Responding to Change: The company behind the brand responds to changes in trends. Whilst the brand may not change significantly (for instance, a food product), the packaging and the marketing communications tactics will do. In Chapter 1 we discussed the macro factors, and there are two that are particularly relevant to this point – societal and technological. What are the societal trends and how can new technologies influence/impact upon the brand?

Fulfilling a Need: The underlying product or service has to be able to fulfil current (and potentially future) customer wants and needs.

Investment: The level of investment required to support the product, for instance, in marketing communications and/or packaging updating will depend upon the financial returns already being received. The product may be in a position where there are reasonably high returns but it is unlikely that its market position will develop further. On the other hand, there may be growth potential and thus further investment can assist in gaining more market share. It is also important to consider that a brand may be in decline within its national home market but have significant growth potential in overseas markets.

Reinvention: Clearly there are products/brands that reach the end of their life as they are superseded by new technological developments. We can look at the typewriter and the various brands that adorned those machines that no longer exist, as an example. However, there are products/brands that can undergo a 'makeover' and in essence be reinvented. This 'makeover' can take various forms: (1) A new ingredient, a new formula that changes the essence of the product. (2) New packaging that perhaps provides a more contemporary look or style that appeals to a younger audience, potentially a new segment. (3) A radical change in the marketing communications, which may also be linked to the new packaging, segments and/or ingredients.

BRAND PIRACY AND COUNTERFEITING

It is worth noting that many brands, especially luxury brands, due to both their intrinsic and extrinsic values are pirated/counterfeited. This illegal action can take many forms and can be extremely damaging:

Creating a brand name (and accompanying packaging) or a design that is very similar to well-known brands. This is to give the impression that it is the brand that the customer normally relates to and uses. This is also known as 'passing off' and is deliberately created to confuse the consumer. The product is most unlikely to have been manufactured to the standards and quality of the real brand, indeed, it may even be damaging to the consumer's health.

Counterfeit Goods: Where products are sold as genuine but are fake, in other words, the counterfeiters are 'hijacking' the brand. This is an international problem across many sectors ranging from alcohol and medicines through to software and tobacco products. As stated above, these types of products are often not made to the exacting standards required by both the original brand manufacturer and regulatory authorities. The counterfeit goods can also cause harm, as in the case of 43 people who died in the Czech Republic from drinking alcohol made with the toxic ingredient methanol. Such ingredients can cause blindness as well as death (IPO, 2014).

Illegal Copies: This particularly relates to the illegal production of CDs/DVDs and the downloading of music and films from unauthorised sites. Such actions affect the revenues for artists and production companies, which in turn potentially reduces new investment in films and music.

Impact of Brand Piracy

Such illegal and unethical action, as highlighted above, can have a range of consequences for the brand itself and those who purchased the illegal products.

1. In the worse cases it can affect the health and wellbeing of the consumer. They may or may not be aware that they are buying an illegal product. They may be price sensitive and thus the price is the key determinant.

However, as evidenced above, fake alcohol along with other items, such as fake medicines, can have serious health consequences.

2. Impacts upon the real brand's image. The real products are often made to exacting manufacturing and regulatory standards, and this can be reflected in the price. Think of designer luxury handbags that retail for £800 to £1,500 in London's fashionable Bond Street. A 'copy' being sold for £30 will not possess the quality of an original, for instance in terms of the material used and the stitching along the seams. It is not just the buyer who has been deceived it is also the people who see the 'copy' and believe it to be genuine. Thus their impression of the brand may be a negative one.

Where there is the case of 'passing off' with similar brand names, the customer may feel that there has been a lack of trust in producing an inferior product. However, it is not the fault of the genuine brand, yet that lack of trust may remain.

3. Impacts upon the real brand's revenues and financial resources. This has an impact in three ways: (a) There is a potential loss of revenue to the genuine copyright/trademark owners if fake copies are circulating within the marketplace. This can impact upon the future development of the business, including employment and contracting suppliers, who in turn can be affected financially. (b) Major companies are investing, along with regulatory and law enforcement agencies, significant financial and other resources to prevent such illegal actions. Tracking fake goods is a painstaking operation, and it could be argued that if companies did not have to undertake such work, the resources could be used to create new products and enhance existing ones. (c) Companies invest in technologies to prevent/reduce illegal copying of products, for example, the use of seals, holograms and blocking websites. This approach requires investment that is again not focused on developing and enhancing the brand itself.

OUR FUTURE RELATIONSHIP WITH BRANDS

Interbrand (2014b) consider that we are entering a new phase in our relationship with brands. They have called this 'The Four Ages of Branding'.

With changes in technology and the way we live, brand owners will seek to create fully personalised experiences delivering to our own wants, needs and desires (Interbrand, 2014b). This will mean understanding and tailoring 'Big' data in such a way as to meet various demands. We could argue that mass customisation set out to tailor, within parameters, certain products to meet our needs. Indeed, the computer manufacturer Dell has long been a leading proponent of mass customisation. However, what is being proposed is a greater connectivity between the customer and the brand.

KEY POINTS

In this chapter we have considered the following:

1. The various reasons why organisations brand themselves as well as their products and/or services. These include STP (see Chapter 4), differentiation, recall, recognition, enhancing loyalty, building financial value, creating opportunities for extensions, protection (patents, trademarks and copyrights) and maximising the value of the marketing budget.
2. How the implementation of a brand equity framework can help secure a strong brand over the longer term.
3. The different types of branding that organisations can undertake, including own-label, family, co-branding, individual and re-branding.
4. The reasons why organisations may change the name of the particular brand (re-branding) either in its home market and/or internationally. This may be due, for instance, to translations or changes in political/legal/societal attitudes (see also Chapter 1).
5. Some of the factors that help brands to survive longer within the marketplace in comparison, perhaps, to some of their competition. These factors include focusing on features and benefits that meet customer needs/wants, levels of marketing investment (including marketing communications), responding to external changes and reinvention.
6. The perceived and real impact of counterfeiting and piracy on brands, particularly in terms of reputation, costs, revenue and profit.

QUESTIONS

Here is a series of questions and activities for you to undertake to aid your knowledge and understanding of the points made in this chapter.

1. Explain why so many organisations place a high priority on branding a product or service.

2. Are there situations where a product is not branded? If so, why? Can you think of examples?

3. What do you think are the potential advantages and disadvantages of co-branding? Use examples to support your perspective.

4. Select two different types of brands that you use on a regular basis. Examine the various attributes of the brands and answer the following questions: (a) What are the attributes? Could you explain them to a friend? (b) Why do you think these attributes are important to these particular brands? (c) What attracts you to these particular brands? (d) Would you switch from these brands to others? Why?

5. Briefly outline the different types of branding, using different examples from those stated in this book.

6. There is a view that a brand can create emotional attachments and reactions in customers. Do you share that view?

7. There are times when a company decides to change/modify the brand name of a product or service. Under what circumstances would they seek to change/modify the brand name? What do you think are both the positives and negatives of making such a change? Use examples to support your answers.

8. Whilst companies may change ownership, be acquired or merge with others, their brands remain visible within the marketplace. Provide additional examples (different from those in this book) of brands that have been in the marketplace for over 40 years. Why do you think these particular brands have lasted in the marketplace for so long? What do you think their position will be in the next 20 years and why?

9. There has been extensive media coverage on the counterfeiting and piracy of brands. What is the business case for seeking legal redress against those who engage in counterfeiting and piracy?

FURTHER READING

Aaker, D. (2012) *Building Strong Brands*. London: Pocket Books.

Bastos, W. and Levy, S.J. (2012). A history of the concept of branding: Practice and theory. *Journal of Historical Research in Marketing*. Vol 4 No 3. pp. 347–368.

Jones, C. and Bonevac, D. (2013) An evolved definition of the term 'brand': Why branding has a branding problem. *Journal of Brand Strategy*. Vol 2 No 2. pp. 112–120.

Jones, R. (2012) Five ways branding is changing. *Journal of Brand Management*. Vol 20 No 2. pp. 77–79.

Kapferer, J.N. (2012) *Strategic Thinking (New Strategic Brand Management: Creating & Sustaining Brand Equity)* (5th Edition). London: Kogan Page.

Leek, S. and Christodoulides, G. (2011) A literature review and future agenda for B2B branding: Challenges of branding in a B2B context. *Industrial Marketing Management*. Vol 40 No 6. pp. 830–837.

Temporal, P. (2000) *Branding in Asia: The Creation, Development and Management of Asian Brands for the Global Market*. Singapore: John Wiley & Sons (Asia).

Temporal, P. (2011) *Islamic Branding and Marketing*. Chichester: John Wiley & Sons.

Van den Bergh, J. and Behrer, M. (2013) *How Cool Brands Stay Hot: Branding to Generation Y*. London: Kogan Page.

6

Value and Price

By the end of this chapter you should be able to:

- Understand the relationship between value and price.
- Explain the factors that influence the pricing of products and services.
- Explain the different types of pricing structures that organisations might use and why.

INTRODUCTION

In this chapter we examine the relationship between value and price, considering what constitutes both.

VALUE

From the Consumer Perspective

As indicated in Chapter 2, we place a perceived/real value on the products or services that we purchase. Whether we pay a relative small price, say a Dollar, a Pound Sterling or a Euro, or not we normally still seek a 'value' in the product that we exchange for cash.

However, how do we define 'value'? We could argue that this is subjective, the perception of the individual as to what 'displays' value and what does not. Do we mean 'quality' or 'performance'? Two exceptionally wealthy individuals may disagree over the 'value' of a product even though both, without any difficulty, could afford to buy the product.

As we discussed in the previous chapter individuals will determine, perhaps through product performance, what is value to them. For example, take two washing up liquids – Brands A and B. Brand B is marginally more expensive than the other. Several scenarios could be played out:

Brand A may perform as well as Brand B in the number of dishes cleaned.

Brand A may clean the dishes as well as Brand B.

In this scenario Brand A, the cheaper brand, delivers the best performance and thus the better value for the shopper. However, the alternative scenario may well be true, that the marginally more expensive brand delivers on value. For the consumer, it may be a case of trial and error before they know which of the washing liquids delivers the best value for them.

A further point that must be taken into consideration is the level of price sensitivity. Whilst it could be argued that Brand B is the better product – delivering value – the individual's amount of disposal income may prevent the purchase. Except for the exceptionally wealthy, most consumers have limited disposable incomes. However, for some, on very low incomes or government support, every cent/penny must contribute to delivering the necessary products/services. Nothing can be wasted. In such cases, price sensitivity to some extent will dictate the 'value'.

Adding Value

Many companies seek to add real and/or perceived value to their products and/or services. This may take the form of 'extras' to the standard offering. For instance, a toothpaste manufacturer might, for a limited time period, add a toothbrush to the toothpaste package at no additional cost to the consumer. Whilst this is adding value to the toothpaste product, it is also promoting the company's range of toothbrushes.

When movies are shown on TV or in the cinema, it is just the movie. However, production companies have realised the value of providing 'bonus' material on DVDs and Blue-ray Discs. For example, Paramount Home Entertainment released a two-disc DVD collector's edition of *Mission Impossible III* (2006) with 'over four hours of exclusive bonus material'. Initially this would retail at a higher price than the standard single disc containing just the movie, however for those interested in learning more about the making of the movie, this would be considered value for money.

From a Business Perspective

As stated in Chapter 5, companies seek to allocate a value to the brands that they own. This, in turn, contributes to the overall financial value of the company. There are situations where companies market either themselves or subsidiaries for sale. Potential buyers will consider the valuation of the brands (and their future potential) when considering the purchasing price.

Equally, companies market products and services to other companies. In these cases 'value' may be determined by the quality of the product/service on offer. In various industries (for instance, engineering, aircraft and car production) components, for both design and safety reasons have to be made to exacting high-quality standards.

In Figure 6.1 we have sought to depict diagrammatically the various operational stages from the extraction of raw materials to the final product where value can be added. We can deconstruct the framework as follows:

Extracting Raw Materials: Raw materials can be anything from copper ore to wheat, sugar and cocoa. The processes in extracting or harvesting these raw materials will be very different. Some will require careful handling to reduce the risk of damage so that quality is maintained.

Refining of Raw Materials: The raw materials will then be processed to form either an ingredient (for example, refined sugar) or an element that will form part of a component (for example, copper wire).

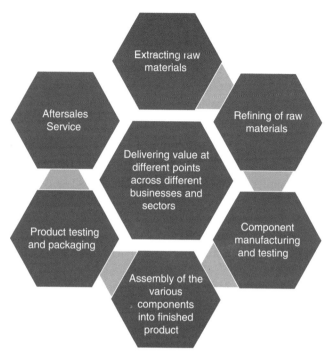

Figure 6.1 An illustration of where value can be added across different businesses and sectors

Component Manufacturing and Testing: A component can be described as a finished product (anything from a screw or a circuit board to a car door handle) that are used to make another product. The component will be tested to make sure that it meets the required quality control standards of both the supplying and purchasing companies.

Assembly into a Finished Product: This is where the various components are brought together and assembled into the finished product, for instance, a family car or a bar of chocolate.

Product Testing and Packaging: Whether it is a car or a bar of chocolate there will be sample testing to make sure that the product meets the required quality standards, as set not only by the company but also any regulators. Packaging, as stated in Chapter 5, can add value through product protection and reinforcing brand identity.

Aftersales Service: The service available after delivery of the product. It can include insurance, repairs and technical support (for instance, assistance for computer software problems). Some of these may be available free under a guarantee (this will depend upon the type of product and the legal regulations within a country), but for others it might be a chargeable item.

Value Delivered: This is the overall value delivered to the customer and how the customer feels about the product they have purchased. It can be linked to aspects of the Post Purchasing Behaviour or Brand Responses that we discussed in Chapters 2 and 5. Many companies will have exacting requirements for the materials used throughout the production of their products, often to meet the equally exacting requirements of regulators. Consider, for instance, the range and quality of components that must be used to build a safe and reliable jet engine for an Airbus A380.

KEY FACTORS THAT INFLUENCE PRICING

Figure 6.2 depicts the various factors that either influence or impact upon the pricing of a product and/or service. It is important to remember the following:

- They will not have equal levels of influence/impact.
- The level of influence/impact will vary over time depending upon variable circumstances.
- There can be interconnectivity between the factors so, for instance, changing regulations may impact upon the cost of production. For example, governments may impose new environmental regulations, which result in higher production costs as the company modifies its plant and equipment to meet the regulatory standards. The company may decide to absorb such costs, which would result in reduced margins

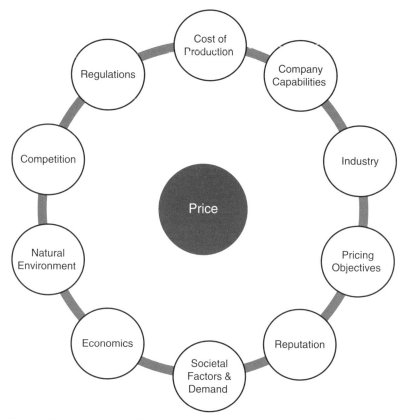

Figure 6.2 Factors that influence/impact pricing

and level of profitability. This action would thereby reduce the 'shock' of a price rise to their customers. However, the company may decide to raise prices over the medium and longer term to absorb some of the additional costs as a result of regulations.

Cost of Production

There is a production cost to every product that we purchase, whether it is a bar of chocolate, a tin of soup, a TV monitor or a car.

As we discussed in Chapter 4, there are many different kinds of chocolate bars. The extent and quality of their ingredients may determine the positioning of the chocolate bar within the marketplace. The higher the quality of the chocolate (and hence richness of the taste), the higher the costs of manufacture and thereby the price to the targeted audience.

A car manufacturer will source the various components from numerous suppliers. Whilst all car manufacturers will source reliable components (especially for safety reasons) some components will be of a higher quality than others. Examples could include seat covering in an expensive sports car compared to an everyday family car. Or the number of airbags in a more expensive model compared to an everyday standard vehicle.

With developments in technology and globalisation since the 1970s, components are now sourced internationally. This provides manufacturers the opportunity to source quality components at competitive prices.

In addition to ingredient/component sourcing, labour is often a major factor in the cost of production. Many companies seek production overseas in order to reduce labour costs yet produce goods of a high standard for the international market.

Another contributor to the cost of production is gaining economies of scale. A good example of this is the car industry. If we consider the mainstream car industry – the Fords, Volkswagens, Renaults and so on – automation of production, the purchasing of components in bulk and large-scale production reduces the unit costs. The automotive companies know that there is a market, albeit a competitive one, for their products. It is the mass production techniques, established at the turn of the 20th century by people like Henry Ford, that have enabled car manufacturers to promote their products at an 'affordable' price to the market.

However, not all cars are mass produced in the same way as an average family car. Some 'top of the range' sports cars are made by hand. Although contemporary as well as traditional manufacturing techniques may be used, the scale of production is not the same as that of the mainstream car manufacturers. Therefore a greater level of costs will be incurred, which will be reflected in the showroom price. This limited number of cars produced each year adds to the collectability or exclusivity of the car.

Company's Capabilities

Organisations seek to use their capabilities (resources and competences) to provide a product and/or service that either allows them to operate within the market or gives them an advantage over competitors. Both the quality of and how the capabilities are used can influence/impact upon pricing. If the use of the capabilities is highly efficient, thus enabling the company to reduce their costs, then they can reflect that efficiency in the prices charged.

A good example of this is the low-cost airlines, which tend to operate regionally, rather than internationally. Whilst they must operate within strict safety regulations, these airlines have sought to use, for instance, their resources more efficiently. Many of them have used the following approaches to reduce costs:

- Shorter turnaround times at airports reduces both airport costs and means that the aircraft can be better utilised for more journeys over the day. This allows the airline to move more passengers per day over its scheduled routes.

- No full-service on-board catering reduces both costs and turnaround times. Normally, on such flights tea/coffee/light refreshments and sandwiches are available for purchase. These are easier to load on-board the aircraft compared to full-service meals, require less space and are less costly to purchase from airline catering companies.

- Rather than take cleaning teams on-board the aircraft at each stop, the cabin crew undertake a general clean-up prior to the boarding of passengers. Once the aircraft has returned to base, then it can have a thorough clean. Again this approach can reduce costs, specifically airport and cleaning charges.

The result is that these airlines are able to reduce their airfares, and many have been able to build a relatively profitable business.

Industry

Here we can consider industry from several different perspectives:

Size: If the sector is small and relatively specialised (a niche) it will significantly influence the price that can be charged for the product or service on offer. This can occur in both the B2C and B2B environments. For instance, there may be relatively few companies that produce luxury hand-made chocolates, which are distributed through specialist outlets and/or online. These will be more expensive to purchase than mass-produced chocolates from the major brands available via the local supermarket. Equally, specialist firms supporting the major oil exploration companies will be able to charge a premium price due to the 'unique' capabilities that the company possess and the oil exploration firms need.

Cartels: These are illegal within many countries and regions, however they do exist. This is where companies collude to 'fix' prices across a particular sector. This can mean agreeing a minimum price that no competitor will sell below. It can also mean agreeing price increases and thus adjusting the minimum price. Governments consider these actions illegal as customers, whether businesses or individuals, do not benefit from the freedom of price competition.

Monopolies: This is where one single company, operating within that industry, supplies a specific product or service. Monopolies have been prevalent within the utility industries (power, telecommunications and water) and transportation. This one supplier has to some extent 'control' over the market. Therefore, because the service is needed, it can charge a premium price. Many countries, for instance the UK, have changed such state-owned enterprises into for-profit companies and have opened the markets to other companies to supply products and services. By opening up the markets, for instance in the provision of domestic energy supplies, government is providing consumers with the opportunity to switch to the provider that best meets their needs.

Reputation

This links to branding and positioning of the product or service in the customer's mind. As indicated in Chapter 5, gaining a positive reputation is important for brands in order to build a successful long-term position within the marketplace.

Due to their reputations (including image) many brands are marketed at premium prices. Consider, for instance, luxury sports cars (Aston Martin), upmarket watches (Patek Philippe), bespoke hand-made shoes (Gaziano & Girling), private jets (NetJets) and six-star plus hotels (Burj Al Arab Jumeirah). Due to their reputation and limited availability they command a higher value in the minds of those customers who can afford the ultra-luxury.

However, this is only one part of the marketplace. Companies such as Cadbury, Heinz, Citroën, Sony, Kellogg and the Financial Times, among many others, have all built brands on reputation. Whilst they may not charge a premium price for their products, they may have higher pricing points than some of their competitors.

Natural Environment

In Chapter 1 we referred to the macro or Pestel factors, one of which is the natural environment. As indicated in that chapter the natural environment can impact/influence organisations in many different ways. Here are a few examples that we can link to pricing.

Poor Harvests: A poor crop harvest in one part of the world can affect the price of either that food item (for example, oranges) or as part of the ingredient costs (for example, cocoa in chocolate). There are means by which producers and retailers can reduce price increases to customers. For instance, they can 'absorb' the additional costs within their profit margins with the aim of retaining sales revenue. In some cases ingredients, such as cocoa, can be bought on a futures market. This is where the chocolate manufacturer will buy cocoa, at a fixed rate per tonne, in advance of the harvests. If the company buys at a fixed price, for say, two years and the cost per tonne increases, then the manufacturer has made a good deal. However, if the cost per tonne falls below what the company has paid on the futures market, then the company has to accept any associated disadvantages. If direct rivals have been able to agree a better financial arrangement on the futures market, there is the potential for selling the chocolate product at a discounted price. Therefore these companies have the potential to gain an additional share of the market. However, there are a range of ingredients that comprise food products, especially in prepared meals (either tinned or within chilled/frozen cabinets) so where there may be a shortage of one ingredient (hence higher costs) there may be an abundance of another (possible lower costs).

Poor Summer: Here we can use the example of ice cream and a 'poor' or colder summer period. Ice cream companies and retailers will gear up for what is hoped to be a hot summer period where they can sell more ice cream generating strong revenues. However, if it is 'cold, overcast and miserable' then there is the likelihood of deflated sales. Retailers may choose to discount products or combine them in special offers (for example, 3 for the price of 2) in order to clear stock and generate some revenue.

Societal Factors and Demand

When examining societal factors they should be considered not only from a localised perspective but also from a trans-national point of view. To some extent this integrates with the economic environment.

As discussed in Chapter 2, there are various factors that influence us when considering purchasing a product or service, and these factors can include culture and our views of the world. How we view the value of a product in one nation may be very different to how we view it in another. For instance, in certain countries there are foods that may be considered high-priced delicacies yet in other countries either avoided or of low value.

We have also included 'demand'. Demand can be considered from two perspectives:

- Overall demand for the product and/or service: Some products and/or services may be in greater demand than others. If there is a shortage of supply this tends to increase prices (see Chapter 2 and the umbrella example).

- Demand changes over time: Earlier in this chapter we referred to the low-cost airline sector and how they seek to reduce costs and thus prices. However, with many airlines the price will change in relation to the demand and time. So if you book a seat three months in advance of the flight date then it will be cheaper than booking it one week before travelling, assuming that there are seats still available. The same principle can also be applied to other forms of transport, such as trains and coach services.

Economic Environment

Consider the case of taxation policies. There are two main types: direct taxation (tax that comes directly out of a wage or salary) and indirect (a tax that is added to a product or service). They are considered 'indirect' in that the customer can choose to buy or not to buy the product or service on offer, whereas with 'direct' taxes that individual has no choice other than to pay.

Governments impose indirect taxes on various products and services in order to raise revenue for the State. These taxes may be in the form of 'duty', 'value added' or 'sales taxes'. Some products and services may be exempt from additional taxes. For example, in the UK, there is no VAT on food items.

For the average consumer these taxes are included in the price at the time of purchase. However, this may vary from country to country.

When a government increases indirect taxes (for example, VAT) a company may, for a short period of time, absorb that additional cost. This can create a short-term advantage over close competitors.

Intensity of Competition

The intensity of competitive rivalry can influence the pricing of products and services, especially where they display similar features and benefits. The greater the number of competitors within a particular market selling similar products, the greater the opportunity for price competition.

Perhaps the key factors here are the perceived or real similarities in the features and benefits of the particular product or service. Companies that can provide features and benefits that differentiate a product or service from its nearest rivals may have greater scope to charge a higher price. However, as discussed earlier in this chapter, the customer must be able to determine 'value for money' before they will purchase the product or service.

Case Study: UK Supermarkets and Milk

In many countries products such as bread, milk and rice are staple foods. During early 2014 the UK's four largest supermarkets (Tesco, Sainsbury's, Asda and Morrisons) reduced the price of milk in a bid to outperform each other on the sales of this product (BBC, 2014c). This market competition reduced the average price of milk to approximately 31 pence per (UK) pint (0.56 litres); in some cases this was a reduction of 20% over the space of one week (BBC, 2014c).

According to Defra (2014), the average farm-gate price (the average price paid to farmers, net of delivery charges) in December 2014 was approximately 60 pence per UK pint (approximately 33.84 pence per litre). On this simple analysis, taking into consideration volume purchasing and sales, supermarkets will have significantly reduced their margins, some to below break even. However, there are two points to reflect upon:

1. Total milk production in the UK in 2013 was approximately 13.5 billion litres (Baker, 2015). Approximately 5.2 billion litres of liquid milk is purchased in the UK each year (DairyCo, 2014), so it is a significant market.

2. Retailers may adopt a loss-leader approach (break even or slight loss) on one item to drive footfall into the supermarket. This increases the opportunity for the customer to purchase other products as part of their daily/weekly supermarket purchases. The margins on the other products may well compensate for the loss-leader approach on milk.

Regulations

Governments through their legal systems may seek to impose specific pricing regulations on products and services. For instance, in the UK there are various regulations and guidelines associated with how products and services are priced. Specifically the regulations prohibit the seller from misleading the customer on the price of the product or service and how that price was calculated (BIS, 2010). These regulations are designed to prevent unfair commercial practices that 'harm the consumer's economic interests' (BIS, 2010).

Mini Case: Alcohol Pricing

In the UK there has been much debate regarding the introduction of minimum pricing for alcoholic products. In May 2014 the UK Government introduced a ban on supermarkets selling alcoholic drinks as a loss-leader, that is, selling below the cost that the supermarkets pay (including taxes) for the products (BBC, 2014d). Until then some supermarkets were selling lagers and beers at low prices, usually associating their sale with major sporting events on television. The purchasing of low-priced alcohol, it was assumed, would also increase the purchasing of other products that might go well with watching such events, for example, pizzas and other snack foods.

Market Conditions

Markets are not static but in a constant state of flux as they are affected/ influenced by several external factors. These factors will include the following:

Economics: This is a broad area of study and one that can have a profound effect upon market conditions. The state of a country's economy will determine the level of disposable income available to the overall population. Generally at times of economic growth there is a greater opportunity for employment, entrepreneurial development and manufacturing/service outputs. In turn there is normally a greater level of disposable income available.

However, the converse is true when there is recession or an economic slump. There is less stability, higher levels of unemployment and greater uncertainty. It is at such times that many families self-impose austerity measures to reduce expenditure and, where possible, increase savings.

These situations can be further impacted by inflationary pressures and a central bank's approach to reduce such pressures via increasing interest rates. The increase in interest rates will benefit savers; however, there will be a resultant increase in credit costs, which, in turn, may reduce expenditure on various goods and services.

The economic conditions will also be affected by the government's approach to taxation policy, as discussed earlier in this chapter.

Societal Conditions: This also links to the economic wealth of a nation. Here we need to consider the geodemographic structure of a country. As stated in Chapters 1 and 2, organisations need to understand how the structure and requirements of society may change over time. This may not only influence the price of the product/service but whether it actually has a future within those specific marketplaces. People's tastes and preferences may change, and a product/service that once was popular and achieved a high-price point may no longer do so.

Population structures are also changing. According to the UK Government, some ten million people in 2010 were over the age of 65 with the projection being almost 20 million by 2050; that will be one in four of the population (Cracknell, 2010). In 2008, there were some 3.2 people of working age for every person of pensionable age, however this is expected to fall to 2.8 by 2033 (Cracknell, 2010). Now it has to be taken into consideration that these are projections and various other factors could come into play over time, such as migration into the UK. There may be greater longevity, however there are costs in terms of healthcare provision and the concern expressed by various governments, especially in Europe, is how will these costs be met (Cracknell, 2010).

This is perhaps also compounded by the increase in obesity rates in younger people, and both the short-term and longer-term affects that these may have in both economic and societal costs. In England it is estimated that the direct health costs of treating overweight and obesity have escalated from £479.3 million in 1998 to £4.2 billion in 2007 (Morgan and Dent, 2010). Governments have implemented action via better labelling of food products, encouraging food companies to reduce sugar, fat and salt contents in food, and promoting healthier lifestyles in terms of food and exercise. They could also impose additional levies on food manufacturing and supply to reduce the intake of certain food items.

Researchers writing for the *British Medical Journal* have suggested that a 20% tax on sugary drinks would reduce the number of obese adults in the UK (Briggs et al., 2013). However, this has become an area of debate and as yet (2015) the Government has not sought to impose such a tax, seeking voluntary reduction in sugar content by the manufacturers. However, there have been discussions in other countries, namely the US, regarding such taxes as a means of modifying societal behaviour.

There may also be sharp economic contrasts within society itself. India, for example, demonstrates extremes of wealth and poverty. Pricing will often reflect the economic characteristics of a country. Even though the Indian economy is growing overall, a vast proportion of the population would not be able to pay the same price for a product as the average person living within the UK.

Pricing Objectives

Bearing in mind the various factors that contribute to costs, organisations will seek to develop a pricing strategy that best suits their products and services. The pricing strategy used may well change or develop over time due to market conditions and other external factors. Therefore the approach to pricing should not be considered as 'static'.

This section is broadly divided into Business to Consumer (B2C) and Business to Business (B2B) to highlight some of the key approaches that organisations may undertake to pricing.

Business to Consumer Pricing (B2C)

Pioneer Pricing

When an organisation develops a new product or service, they will have to take into consideration various factors (some have been mentioned earlier in this and other chapters). They may have to enter the market with a 'base' price in order to 'test' what is acceptable to the market. Entering the market with a low base price may gain some market share – but this could be short-term as the organisation must consider cost, profitability and competitive pressures.

In the pharmaceutical industry, for instance, the base price may be significantly higher due to the research and development costs that have been invested into the product. Prices may remain high until a generic version is more widely available. An example of this might be mild pain suppressants or analgesics such as Paracetamol. This is now a widely available as an Over the Counter (OTC) medicine in many countries under various brand names such as Panadol and Tylenol.

Price Skimming

This is where a manufacturer/retailer may set a particularly high price for the introduction phase of a new product. This approach may be taken where there is a particularly high demand for a specific type of product, such as a branded tablet or mobile phone. Price skimming is often used with technology-related products as this is an area of constant development and newer versions coming to the market.

The appeal to acquire the latest version is known as Innovators (see Chapter 2). An example of this can be seen where customers queue on the day of product's release in order to be one of the first to purchase it.

This approach can also be used to seek early recovery of research and development, as well as production costs. It is also beneficial where there are no direct competitors who can deliver similar product features and benefits.

As new models are introduced the price of current models are normally reduced with the models eventually being phased out.

Penetration Pricing

This is where the price of a product or service is set deliberately low, although it should not be below 'break even', with the aim of gaining as much market share as possible within a short time frame. This can be undertaken if the manufacturer can achieve efficient economies of scale. This is a way of creating a new low-price segment within the market.

Psychological Pricing

There are several different approaches that can be taken with this pricing method.

Prestige: Products and services may have a high price to reflect an associated psychological value and attract wealthy customers; the food product caviar is an example.

Single Price: This is where a retailer offers a single price for the products on sale in the store. In the UK there has been a rise in the number of retail outlets that advertise all products at either 99 pence or £1.00. In such cases the customer 'believes' that because the product is either only 99 pence or £1.00 it will be cheaper than elsewhere. This may or may not be the case. Whilst some products are cheaper than say a supermarket or DIY store, others (even at £1.00) will be more expensive. The attuned customer, who is aware of local supermarket prices, will be able review what is a 'bargain' and what may not be.

Variable Pricing

This is sometimes called flexible pricing. The price may be contingent on the time of day or months in the year, the level of demand and the services required. This is the reason why vacations at the time of school holidays are generally more expensive than at other times. There is greater demand over a certain number of weeks with limited resources available (for instance, flights and hotel rooms). During the peak season, family vacations whether in their country of residence or overseas will normally be more expensive.

Low-cost airlines use variable pricing in several ways:

1. If you book several weeks in advance it is normally cheaper than booking a few days in advance of the flight.
2. If you are taking luggage with you there are different prices depending upon whether they are bags that can go in the cabin or need to go in the aircraft's hold.
3. Other requirements such as priority boarding and choice of seat can incur additional charges.

Promotional Discount Pricing

Often retailers will offer discounts on a particular range of products. The approach has been used for everything from books (usually novels) through to cosmetics and food. Buy One Get One Free (BOGOF) is one method. Another can be buy one and get another at half price.

This is a means of getting people to purchase a product that they haven't used before. If the incentive is successful they will likely purchase more in the future. It also allows the retailer to move stock faster, especially if they are items that are not 'moving as fast' as originally hoped.

Business to Business Pricing (B2B)

Organisations will need to take into consideration costs when determining the pricing of products and services within a B2B environment. Some of these costs will be similar to those within a B2C environment; equally there may be specialist costs that differentiate one business activity from another.

Professional Services

These can include advertising, accounting, legal, marketing, public relations consultancy and the provision of security. The pricing of professional services can vary depending upon the nature of the service and the reputation of the service provider. The fees charged can be based upon an hourly rate or fixed, perhaps, for a particular project.

Competitive Tendering

We also referred to competitive tendering in Chapter 2. This is where companies are invited to bid for specific projects. These can range from advertising accounts through to building design and even stationery supplies. Governments are normally the largest users of the competitive tending method in order to demonstrate transparency and fairness in the allocation of contracts. In many countries, for example the UK, it is a legal requirement for government departments to use the tendering process for purchases over certain financial amounts.

The approach to competitive tendering may vary from organisation to organisation. However, there are two basic approaches:

> Potential suppliers are required to state what they could do for a fixed amount of money. Here the tendering company needs to be realistic in terms of costings so that they do not promise what cannot be achieved for the fee, otherwise it will incur losses.

> The potential client sets out a brief of what they want to see achieved within the time frame of a contract. The tendering company then develops the brief into an action plan with associated costings, which are then presented to the potential client for consideration. The client company may ask several companies to respond to the brief. The decision to award the contract may not be based purely on price but on how the brief is met and the overall value delivered.

As indicated above, advertising agencies, marketing and public relations consultants are often required to tender for projects and longer-term accounts.

Leasing

This is where a supplier (the lessor) 'rents' the product to a customer (lessee) for 'normally' a set payment over a specific period of time. In a B2B environment the product can range from photocopier machines to company cars and passenger aircraft. In some contracts between the two parties there may be clauses relating to additional payments for the early termination of the contract within a specific time frame. For instance, a university may have a lease agreement with a photocopier company for a ten-year period. If they seek to terminate that contract within, for instance, within the first three years, there may be additional charges incurred. This is because the photocopier company will make its return on investment that period of time. After three years there may be the need to upscale the machine due to increasing obsolescence and the potential needs of the university.

Pricing and Ethics

This issue is discussed in more detail in Chapter 11 where we examine specific pricing tactics that are unethical and in some countries also illegal. However, it is worth noting here that consideration should be given to the following points:

1. A pricing policy may be deemed legal, but is it always an ethical approach? Should it be left to consumer choice? How do pricing policies influence relationships between the customer and supplier?

2. What may be deemed legal in one country may not be so in another. Once again are there ethical issues that need to be considered?

KEY POINTS

In this chapter we have considered the following:

1. Price is one of the most effective marketing tactics available to an organisation. Various authors have suggested that it is the premier factor within the marketing mix.
2. How customers view 'value' in relation to price. [This can also be linked back to brand equity in Chapter 5.]
3. How organisations seek to add value to their product and/or service.
4. The key factors that influence/affect the pricing of products and services. These include cost of production, an organisation's capabilities (resources and competences), societal and economic demand, reputation and levels of competition.
5. Different types of pricing tactics within a B2C context. These include pioneer, skimming, penetration, psychological, variable and promotional.
6. Different types of pricing tactics within a B2B context. These include professional services, competitive tendering and leasing.
7. A brief overview of the ethical issues associated with pricing tactics. This is examined in greater detail in Chapter 11.

QUESTIONS

Here is a series of questions and activities for you to undertake to aid your knowledge and understanding of the points made in this chapter.

1. Citing examples, explain some of the factors that may influence the pricing of a product or service.

2. Using your own personal examples discuss your perception of 'value' in relation to the 'price' that you have paid for a product or service over the past six months.

3. Find examples local to you of psychological and promotional pricing. What were the products being sold using these tactics? How do they compare to comparable products being marketed by competitors?

4. Imagine that you are employed in the Estates and Facilities department of a local hospital. The hospital requires five new photocopiers for administrative purposes. They must be able to handle a reasonable volume of work, be reliable and provide value for money. You have several possible options: buy outright five new photocopiers, lease five copiers, buy five previously used copiers or ask photocopier companies to tender. Using the Internet to help your research, what approach would you take and why?

5. What do you think are the potential ethical issues associated with the pricing of a product or service? [You may also want to read the relevant sections in Chapter 11.]

FURTHER READING

Drozdenko, R., Jensen, M. and Coelho, D. (2011) Pricing of green products: Premiums paid, consumer characteristics and incentives. *International Journal of Business, Marketing, and Decision Sciences*. Vol 4 No 1. pp. 106–116.

Hazledine, T. (2011) Legacy carriers fight back: Pricing and product differentiation in modern airline marketing. *Journal of Air Transport Management*. Vol 17 No 2. pp. 130–135.

Hinterhuber, A. and Liozu, S. (2012) Is it time to rethink your pricing strategy? *MIT Sloan Management Review*. Vol 53 No 4. pp. 69–77.

Hinterhuber, A. and Liozu, S.M. (2014) Is innovation in pricing your next source of competitive advantage? *Business Horizons*. Vol 57 No 3. pp. 413–423.

Johansson, M., Hallberg, N., Hinterhuber, A., Zbaracki, M. and Liozu, S. (2012) Pricing strategies and pricing capabilities. *Journal of Revenue & Pricing Management*. Vol 11 No 1. pp. 4–11.

Leventhal, B. and Breur, T. (2012) Intelligent markdown pricing. *Journal of Direct and Digital Marketing*. Vol 13 No 3. January–March. pp. 207–220.

Mattimoe, R. and Seal, W. (2011) Pricing in a service sector context: Accounting and marketing logics in the hotel industry. *European Accounting Review*. Vol 20 No 2. pp. 355–388.

Özer, Ö. and Phillips, R. (Eds). (2012). *The Oxford Handbook of Pricing Management*. Oxford: Oxford University Press.

7

Delivering Service

OBJECTIVES

By the end of this chapter you should be able to:

- Explain what is meant by delivering a service.
- Consider the differences between how services are marketed compared to products.
- Explore value in relation to service delivery.
- Explain why efficient and effective service delivery can help a company develop a competitive advantage.

INTRODUCTION

In the previous chapters we have referred, in our discussions, to both products and services. In this chapter we focus on the importance of delivering service within a marketing context. Some organisations, indeed some countries, are better at delivering a higher standard of service than others. Through various concepts and examples we will explore why efficient service delivery is important in creating an effective relationship between an organisation and its customers.

In Chapter 6 we explored the idea of 'value' and what that might mean to the average customer. This idea of 'value' can equally apply to the delivery of a service in terms of the customer's level of satisfaction. The more satisfied the customer the more likely that they will: (1) make further purchases of the services, for example, book more flights on a particular airline, and/or (2) recommend a service provider, for example, an accountant. In this case the satisfied customer is becoming an advocate of the services provided by the accountant.

DEFINING AND DELIVERING SERVICE

There are many definitions of service delivery. However, we can look upon service delivery broadly as the various processes and performance levels that a consumer of the service believes are beneficial to them. This will include interactions with employees of the organisation, for example, the aircrew on a flight or the staff in a hospital. Of course, what one person considers is 'beneficial' to them may not be to another person. It may depend upon a range of factors including upbringing, education, personal values, lifestyles and our own experiences over time. What we might consider a good level of service delivery when we are young we might not when we are older, having possibly encountered a wider range of service performance levels.

In our highly competitive Internet-connected world the quality of service delivery has played an increasingly important role in organisational success. Competition means that companies need to match or surpass the quality of service delivery in order to maintain or gain market share. Whilst we may focus on larger companies, it is also the small and medium-sized enterprises (SMEs) that must consider the effectiveness of their service delivery.

Moreover the development of the Internet (including social media) means that there are a greater number of 'public' channels through which to share information. For instance, booking a flight, hotel or vacation through a third-party site (for example, hotels.com) means that not only will the hotel request feedback on your stay but also the third party provider, in this case hotels.com.

CHARACTERISTICS OF SERVICE DELIVERY

There are five generally accepted key characteristics of service delivery, which can operate individually and/or collectively. In many cases, some highlighted below, they operate together and therefore should be considered in an integrated context in order to maximise value for the customer.

Inherent Intangibility

A product, such as a tin of soup, can be held, the contents clearly identified, cooked and consumed. We can see it, touch it and feel it. The difficulty for marketers is to 'demonstrate' how an intangible service will benefit the customer. Groucutt, Leadley and Forsyth (2004) use the example of a person visiting a psychotherapist to help them reduce their stress levels. Such emotional support services are widely promoted in many parts of the world. However, the client (patient) will not know if the counselling has worked until the end of the designated sessions. Neither can the psychotherapist guarantee that the sessions will actually create a positive outcome for the patient. Clearly this is different to the various features, benefits and the accompanying guarantees that we have come to expect from a product.

Perishability

This is where a service has to be consumed at a particular time. Good examples of perishability are train and airline services, which have set departure and arrival times. The role of the train and airline providers is to make sure, working in conjunction with other companies and organisations (rail networks, airports, air traffic control and so on) that the service can be delivered at the designated time. As the train or plane departs the customer is beginning to 'consume' the service and experience being offered.

Heterogeneity or Variability

The quality assurance processes in manufacturing generally means that mass-produced products, for example, tins of tomato soup produced by a company such as Heinz or Baxter's, will all be of the same standard. However, as services are delivered by people it is not always possible for everyone to maintain the same standard of delivery throughout. True, some organisations, such as the fast-food restaurant chain McDonald's produce detailed operational manuals on the service deliverables required. An airline's cabin crew will all be trained to the same standards. However, some of the crew will display the basic minimum standards to serve the passengers, whilst others will seek to 'add value' to their interaction with passengers. For instance, in making sure that all passengers, no matter what class they are flying on the aircraft, have a pleasant difficulty-free experience.

However, each person is different and thus the level of service, although good, may not be equal.

Inseparability

This is where the actual service cannot be separated from the organisation providing the service. An example of this is that the service provided on an aircraft is inseparable from the flight itself. The service does not exist until it is 'consumed' by the person on the flight. The 'experience' of the flight and the service provided on that specific flight may determine whether or not the passenger uses that airline again. Of course, if the passenger is new to this airline and they are disappointed with the service, then they may consider either an alternative airline or different form of travel in the future.

Ownership

This is a point of significant difference between the provisions of a service when compared to that of a product. The purchasing of a service provides the buyer with an 'access' to or right to 'use' that service – not ownership of the actual service. However, the outright purchase of a product normally gives the buyer ownership of that specific product, for example, the purchase of a watch or a household appliance.

However, it is important to note here that there may be limits placed upon the buyer of the product as to what they can do with that product. For example, the purchasing of a computer software program gives the buyer the right to install and use it for as long as they want. However, they would not be allowed to copy it and give those copies to friends and relatives. The ownership of the product resides in the CD, not the intellectual property rights associated with the software code and the company that owns it.

Case Study: Classical Music Concert

Although we have chosen a classical music concert it could be any form of music event. Such a concert demonstrates the key characteristics of service delivery: Intangibility, Perishability, Variability, Inseparability and Ownership.

The musicians of a symphony orchestra take their seats in a grand concert hall. Shortly afterwards the conductor arrives and begins conducting the orchestra in the first work in that evening's programme. After two hours, including an interval, the orchestra stands to take their applause from the audience. Conductor and orchestra leave the stage tired but thrilled with their performance that evening. Various members of the audience leave the auditorium in animated discussion about that evening's concert, with many stating that it was the best of the season, so far.

Unless this orchestral performance was recorded for CD release, television or radio (to be broadcast at another time) it cannot be consumed again. Whilst it may linger in people's memories the 'performance' has gone – it has been 'consumed'.

KEY FACTORS IN DELIVERING SERVICE

The following is based on the work of Booms and Bitner (1981), who argued that what we could call the building blocks of marketing – the 4Ps – were too limiting in explaining service delivery. They contended three additional 'Ps' needed consideration – People, Physicality and Processes. These combined with the tradition 4Ps now comprise the generally recognised generic 7Ps of the marketing mix.

We will explore each of these factors. However, it is important to view these factors both collectively and individually.

People

People are at the 'front line' of service delivery in several ways:

The interface between the organisation and the customer. This delivery can be online (email, social media), via the telephone and/or face to face (such as the cabin crew mentioned earlier in this chapter).

'Behind the scenes'. These are often referred as the 'backroom' people, however they provide an invaluable contribution to the operations of a business. These are the people who are engaged in various activities from updating the computer systems (ironing out the bugs) through to packing and delivering the products that you have ordered online. In some cases more than one company may be involved in providing this service to you. Consider the sorting and packing of products at an Amazon warehouse. Depending upon location it may be delivered by the national postal services, as in the UK.

We inhabit a globalised 24/7 world where increasingly customers expect reliable service delivery and appropriate interface. Some people have a good instinct when it comes to delivering service, be they a bank teller or working on a supermarket check-out. Skills and abilities can be enhanced through appropriate ongoing training. However, as indicated above, we cannot assume that there will be homogeneity in delivery of the service.

Physicality

This is also sometimes referred to as 'physical evidence', and it's how the interaction between the customer and the environment influences their buying behaviour.

We suggest that this covers several different areas:

What we see: We can consider this from two different overarching environments. Firstly, the actual physical environment that we associate with a supermarket or other retail outlets. This can include colour schemes, signage, the shape and height of the internal structure of a building, the ambient lighting and layout of the space (consider, for instance, the seating arrangements in a restaurant).

Secondly, the 'physicality' that we see within a virtual environment. Whilst we may not be able to 'touch' it we are affected by the layout, signage and colour schemes. There is also a direct link to 'Process', which is examined later in this chapter.

What we hear: The level of 'noise' can either be inviting or distracting. In a nightclub, disco or rave we would expect to hear loud music, appropriate to the venue. However, the choice (and volume levels) of background music in a restaurant or clothing store can significantly contribute to the level and duration of footfall. The difficulty for retailers and restaurateurs is that what is music to one person can be an irritating noise to another. A clothing retailer, for instance, may want to appear 'current' in their choice of music but it may be inappropriate, even for its target audience, within that specific retail environment. It may be appropriate in the mind of the target customer for dancing but not for shopping.

Companies such as the coffee and sandwich outlets Starbucks and Pret A Manger use jazz and classical music to create a 'chilled no rush and relaxing environment'. Indeed Starbucks sell jazz compilation of the CDs used in their US outlets.

What we sense: As indicated in Chapters 2 and 5, psychology is a significant contributor to how and why we purchase a product or service. What we sense (within physicality) is a combination of the above factors and our own psychological makeup. What we sense is how we feel when entering a store, a hotel or a restaurant. Do we feel comfortable? Do we feel welcomed? Do the staff 'appear' interested in us as customers? Some of these feelings may be due to our backgrounds, our experiences and how confident we may feel as individuals.

A smile and a hello, whilst simple activities, can provide the customer with a sense of welcome, of inviting them into the store, hotel or restaurant. Of course, that is only the start, as the customer needs to feel or sense that they are welcomed throughout their stay. They need to sense that they are as 'valued' as any other customer.

Processes

We can consider processes from two broad perspectives, Technological and Non-technological.

Technological: This we can subdivide into physical location and virtual.

Physical location: As customers we continually encounter technological processes that have been introduced to make purchasing either of a product or service more convenient. Moreover, the technological processes can also assist with future service delivery (see the point on RFID tags below).

Virtual: In addition to major organisations the vast majority of SMEs will have some form of online presence, providing customers with the opportunity, 24/7, to view, select and purchase anything from an e-book through to a fully-inclusive vacation.

As indicated earlier, colour and layout within a physical environment are important emotional clues for the customer. This is equally important within a virtual environment; however, what is fundamental is the ease of navigation, selection and payment. Many sites, for example, Amazon, provide secure facilities, which store credit/debit card data, thus allowing the minimum number of clicks between selection and verification of purchase.

The development of online banking provides customers with the opportunity to make payments and transfer funds (both nationally and internationally) at a time that best suits them. Banks, even with the necessary security checks, have sought to minimise the number of clicks to expedite the transactions.

In addition to banks there are other online payment systems, such as PayPal, which provides real-time payments for both individuals and small businesses within e-commerce sites. These online payment systems store a customer's credit/bank card details, allowing for a one-click process for the payment transaction. This reduces the customer's time in re-inputting data on every occasion that they want to make a purchase.

Such processes also provide opportunities for data capture. This will include what products are selling well (and which are not) as well as the individual's preferences. Loyalty cards, for instance, can provide supermarkets with an array of information on their customers' purchasing habits. The company will already hold basic information on the cardholder – gender, age and address. However, the company will be interested in additional customer information. They will be able to use this data to understand the broader purchasing habits of their customers (within particular geographical areas) and to target customers with appropriate and specific offers.

So, many supermarket chains will be interested in a customer's purchasing habits, such as:

- When do they buy? This can be times and dates.
- How often do they purchase online and/or in-store?
- If purchasing in-store – which ones do they use? Is there a pattern, for instance, shopping in-store every Friday afternoon?
- What do they buy? This is both in terms of produce and manufacturer, for instance, own-label or major brand.
- What is the quantity of specific purchases?
- Do they take advantage of special offers both in-store and online? If so, which ones?
- Do they use special offer coupons? If so, what frequency are redeemed online and/or in-store?
- Have their spending and purchasing habits changed? If so, what could be the indicators? For instance, the purchasing of nappies and other items signifying a baby in the family.

Technology allows companies to store vast amounts of data and to interrogate that data. This can allow companies to be more efficient and effective in terms of their relationship with the customer and the operation of the business.

Case Study: Supermarkets

We can consider this from the perspective of a supermarket chain (based upon UK examples) where various processes have been developed to provide service to customers.

Barcodes: These are attached to either price tags or packaging and can be scanned at the check-out. Additionally, with some supermarket chains, customers can verify the price at scanners placed around the store before making the final purchase.

Radio Frequency Identification Devices (RFID tags): These are small tags that can store a larger amount of information in comparison to the standard barcode. In terms of food items, such information as the required ambient temperature for storage, use by date and prices can be included. At check-out pricing information is relayed to the service till (self-service or staff operated) through wireless technologies.

As nanotechnologies develop more home appliances will include the facilities to read the RFID tags, store and display the information. Already various industries use RFID tags in logistics and warehouse management. The transport networks in London and Hong Kong use cashless pay-as-you-go cards (Oyster and Octopus respectively).

Types of Check-out: Increasingly in different parts of the world self-check-outs have been installed alongside the more traditional assisted check-out. Self-check-outs allow the customer to control the scanning, bagging and payment activity, which can be as fast or as slow as they want it to be. However, it should be noted that technology does not always work effectively and some people prefer the interaction with staff rather than machines. This point links back to the importance of people in delivering value.

Payment Systems: Cash and the use of credit/debit cards (with pins) are standard in most parts of the world. Additionally, contact-less payment systems have been introduced to pay for low-cost items. In Hong Kong, an Octopus Card is not only used for payments on the Rapid Transit system but also for the purchase of newspapers and other small items.

Loyalty Schemes: In addition to many supermarket chains, various companies have created loyalty cards. As the name suggests, the aim is to increase the customer's loyalty to a particular company or group of companies. In the UK, for instance, the use of loyalty cards is particularly well developed, and major supermarket chains support them with points that can be converted into products and services from chosen companies. For example, points accumulated on the loyalty card provided by UK-based supermarket Tesco can be converted to British Airways' air miles scheme.

Online Ordering and Delivery: In various countries, such as the UK and France, supermarkets provide 24/7 online ordering for a range of products from groceries through to fashion and home-ware. The customer can book a delivery slot to best suit their needs across the day, often until late into the evening.

Click and Collect: Several supermarkets provide the ability to order and purchase a non-food item online, then go into a designated store to collect. In the UK several retailers offer such services. This allows customers to use the online store (24/7) to view, make a purchase, then collect it, as opposed to waiting for a delivery that they might miss and have to reorganise. Therefore for some people it may be a more effective and efficient way to acquire the product.

KEY POINTS

In this chapter we have considered the following:

1. The definitions of service and service delivery.
2. Why service and service delivery are important in providing value to the customer and creating a competitive advantage within the marketplace.
3. The key characteristics of service delivery, inherent intangibility, perishability, heterogeneity or variability, inseparability and ownership.
4. The key factors in delivering service are people, physicality (also known as physical evidence) and processes.

QUESTIONS

Here is a series of questions and activities for you to undertake to aid your knowledge and understanding of the points made in this chapter.

1. Research two different examples (other than those stated within this chapter) that clearly demonstrate two of the characteristics of service delivery. In your opinion, do you consider that the two examples are delivering a quality service to their customers? If not, what do you think needs to change in order for them to do so?

2. To what extent does the 'people' element of the generic marketing mix drive the success or failure of a business?

3. Compare and contrast four different examples of physical evidence and how they contributed to service delivery. What are your findings, and what conclusions have you drawn?

4. What are both the positive and negative aspects of the 'process' element of the marketing mix?

FURTHER READING

Bowie, D. and Buttle, F. (2004) *Hospitality Marketing*. Oxford: Elsevier Butterworth-Heinemann.

Drury, P. (2015) When marketing is everyone's business. *Strategic Direction*. Vol 31 No 1. pp. 24–26.

Gilmore, A. (2003) *Services Marketing and Management*. London: Sage Publications.

Lovelock, C.H. and Wirtz, J. (2010) *Services Marketing*. Harlow: Pearson.

8

Marketing Operations and Distribution

OBJECTIVES

By the end of this chapter you should be able to:

- Explain the concept of marketing channels.
- Evaluate non-retail methods of distribution.
- Discuss how the use of different technologies can contribute to supply chain effectiveness.
- Explain how the effectiveness of marketing operations and distribution influences customer satisfaction levels and contributes to competitiveness.

INTRODUCTION

In this chapter we examine marketing operations and distribution. In Chapter 1 we referred to the generic marketing mix of the 7Ps. A component of the 7Ps is 'placement', and this is generally accepted in marketing as encompassing distribution and logistics.

Marketing is perhaps often considered as the front-end of a business transaction, creating the image, developing the brand, providing the 'show room' for the product or service on display. However, as indicated in Chapter 7, there is significant activity, behind the scenes, that enables the product or service to be delivered to the end user.

We, for example, place an order with an online retailer and then wait for delivery. However, we may be one of hundreds if not thousands placing an order that day that needs to be fulfilled, tracked and despatched.

This chapter considers the variety of ways a product or service can be delivered to the end user; sometimes this is direct, at other times it is via a series of intermediaries. In each case the 'intermediary' is also engaged in a marketing operation. A problem at any point can mean that the end user doesn't receive their order at a designated time and date. This can create inconvenience, loss of trust and a lost customer. In highly competitive markets, where brand switching is relatively easy, this is not only a lost customer but also lost revenue. Moreover, in the world of social media, one customer's experience (good or bad) can be shared with many others not just locally but internationally. Again, there is risk of loss of custom and revenue.

CHANNEL MANAGEMENT

Although there are overlaps it is worth separating out B2B and B2C in order to better understand the complexity of channel management. Equally, as stated in Chapter 1, we consider the role of C2C as a channel along with P2P.

Developing channels is about building partnerships between suppliers (raw materials and components), service providers (transport companies, web hosting companies), manufacturers and retailers. Such activities need to be considered both in a competitive and global context.

B2B Channel Management

In this context B2B can be the first part of a channel process that subsequently links to a consumer – so B2B2C. Equally, it can remain purely within the business domain.

There may be several channel stages prior to the manufacture of a product. A chocolate bar, for instance, manufactured in the UK comprises ingredients that are sourced from other parts of the world, for example, cocoa and sugar (see Figure 8.1). The farmers may sell either directly to the chocolate manufacturer or to another company that supplies several chocolate companies. The cocoa, along with other ingredients, has to be transported (logistics) to the manufacturer, who combines the ingredients to produce the chocolate bar.

The chocolate bars are then transported (logistics) to wholesalers and distribution centres for the major supermarkets. The wholesalers will stock a range of products supplying smaller retail outlets (the local convenience store). Normally the convenience store owner will visit the wholesaler on a regular basis to purchase new stock (logistics). In the case of the supermarket, the managers of the individual stores will inform the central distribution centre of their stock requirements, which are then delivered (logistics) to the store. Increasingly the reordering becomes an automated process once stock levels within the supermarket reach a specified level.

In this case there are numerous companies involved in the operation of producing, gathering and transporting the raw ingredients both to the point of manufacture and the final product to the retailer. So from the producer to the customer there are a number of intermediaries who are crucial in delivering the product to market.

B2C Channel Management

Davidson (1997) suggested that consumers seek eight broad requirements from marketing channels. We have also added to this framework.

Clarity: This relates to how the customer will receive the product being offered and when it will be received. Many companies provide information and links to allow the customer to track their parcel from warehouse

Figure 8.1 Broad, simplified outline of the channel from grower through to consumer

despatch to delivery, informing them at each stage of the operation. As we discuss in this chapter, items provided within a 'digital domain' such as music and ebooks can be downloaded directly from an online store to an electronic device, such as smartphone or an eReader.

Convenience: The customer finds the product easy to obtain. We can view this from several different perspectives:

Retail Outlet: This will include store opening hours, parking facilities and ease of access to the store. Store opening hours will depend upon local and national regulations. In the UK, for instance, many stores are open 7 days per week, although there may be restricted hours on a Sunday. Some supermarkets operate on a 24-hour basis 6 days per week with, again, some limited hours on a Sunday. In other countries stores may be closed or partially open on their religious day of the week.

As stated in Chapter 7 (Delivering Service), 'click and collect' customers can place an order online and collect from their local store. Depending upon location and availability of the product this can be either the same day (if ordered before a certain time in the morning) or the next day.

Deliveries from Retail Outlets: Here the customer places the order in-store for a large item (for instance, a household appliance such as a washing machine) so a delivery date and time needs to be fixed. Increasingly retailers, working through third-party logistic companies, seek delivery slots that are convenient to the customer. Again, due to competition, companies have sought to expand the number of slots available from early morning to late evening across a 7-day schedule. Moreover, many retailers will not only connect the household appliance, for example a washing machine, but also remove the old machine for recycling. Some companies may charge extra, others not. However, we can make a link to value added as part of service deliverables.

Online: Online retailing has grown significantly since the 1990s, providing customers with the convenience of shopping within a 24/7 environment. Retailers who have a 'bricks and mortar' presence are most likely to have an online one too. Equally, some companies only interface with their customers online.

As discussed in Chapter 7, an Internet presence needs to be supported by effective design and ease of navigation across the website. Enhanced and secure payment processes have reduced the number of 'clicks' between choosing the product and purchasing. A developing trend has been the purchasing of music online to download, so within a matter of minutes a whole CD can be available on an individual's various devices – netbook, smartphone, ipad, laptop and/or tablet.

Deliveries from Online Retailers: As with deliveries from retail outlets, Internet providers seek to provide, where possible, a range of delivery options for customers. In the UK, for instance, supermarkets provide online customers with delivery slots across 7 days from early morning to late evening. Charges usually apply, however, where customers have placed a large order, the convenience of the home delivery outweighs the additional delivery charge.

Product Returns: Customers may receive goods that do not meet their expectations, are missing a component or are faulty. In these circumstances the customer should be able to return the goods in a manner that reduces any further disruption and disappointment. The efficient and effective handling of product returns can result in the customer remaining loyal to the company and reordering in the future. In addition to providing customer convenience it also can build a positive image and trust (reflect back to the comments in Chapter 5 on brand equity).

Environment: This relates to the environment in which the product or service is consumed. An example would be ordering a takeaway meal, either via phone or the Internet. The customer will expect their meal to be as advertised (in leaflets/online), be delivered at the approximate time stated, in containers to retain heat and to be properly cooked.

Image: We suggest that this goes beyond the image of the product or service being delivered to include that of the retailer and delivery company. The customer will consider the product in relation to price and value. However, they will also consider the place of purchase, how and when it was delivered. Where there are multiple companies offering similar products at equally similar prices, the image associated with distribution may provide the competitive edge. This may be one of the reasons why the UK supermarket chain Tesco was able to gain significant market share in the online/home delivery market.

Price: Companies that operate within highly competitive marketplaces may compete on the basis of price. Where the customer is having the product delivered to their home they will also have to consider any additional delivery charges. Some retailers may provide free delivery on orders above a certain financial value, which may, in turn, add to the customer's overall perception of value.

Quality: Here the customer is seeking value for money. However, we suggest not just in terms of the purchased product or service but also in terms of the efficiency and effectiveness of delivery. Does the quality of delivery (including packaging) meet the customer's expectations?

Range: This relates to the selection of products or services on offer to the customer. Even a large department store is limited to the range of products it can display and store. However, the move to online retailing has provided many companies with the opportunity to 'display' a much wider selection of product across categories. Businesses, such as the UK supermarket company Tesco, have increased their online presence beyond groceries to include home-ware, musical instruments, furniture, clothing and financial services. Some companies, however, may take a niche approach, focusing on a limited and specialist range of products. This niche allows them the opportunity to determine a particular (sometimes unchallenged) position within the marketplace.

Service: This is the level of customer support provided during and in the post-purchase phase (see Chapter 2). The support potentially covers general/specific queries via telephone and email, and the opportunity to easily return goods if they do not meet the customer's expectations.

We would also add a further category to Davidson's list of qualities.

Experience: This can be considered as the customer's overarching response to the transaction, from initial browsing (be it in-store or online) to the receipt (use/consumption) of the product or service. The quality of the experience (this can be linked to real/perceived value) will also determine whether or not the buyer becomes a repeat customer (see Chapters 2 and 5).

In order for companies to meet and, where possible, exceed customer expectations they have to be agile in their supply-chain operations. The ability to be agile is increasingly one of the measures that provides companies with a competitive advantage over rivals.

B2C Channels

There are several different channel formats that can be used to distribute the product to the customer.

Manufacturer/Producer to Customer

Arguably there are few producers/manufacturers that actually sell their products or service 'directly' to their targeted customer group. There are also situations where it is perceived by the customer that there is a direct channel; however, there is a third-party or intermediary link.

Here are a couple of examples to illustrate this direct channel format:

Pret A Manger: This UK-based fast food retailer makes all their sandwiches fresh each day in their respective outlets. They are sold directly in store to their customers.

Traditional and Farmers' Markets: In many parts of the world there are weekly markets where farmers bring their produce to sell directly to consumers. These may be either street markets or within designated halls.

Manufacturer/Producer to Customer via Intermediaries

As stated earlier, this is where several companies engage in the delivery of the product from the producer to the end user, the customer. In terms of the average consumer perhaps the most common is manufacturer – transportation – retailer – customer. A local supermarket would be a prime example.

There are cases where we think that the channel is direct between the supplier and ourselves as customer. This may be only partially correct. We perceive that there is a direct channel between us and the manufacturer/

service provider where, in fact, there may be one or more intermediaries even if the purchase is purely electronic. The intermediary may be the company providing the electronic interface between the producer and ourselves.

The following are two examples where the point of contact is with the producer but via a company providing the electronic interface. It may appear seamless to us, as the customer, but there is an intermediary nonetheless.

Airlines: Traditionally airline tickets were purchased only through independent travel agents who could often provide a selection of airlines for specific routes. In many countries travel agents still provide such services, however, increasingly flights can be booked directly with an airline. This provides the customer with various choices: outbound and return flights (dates and times), seat allocation (within the designated class), listing the number of bags for the flight and any special dietary requirements. The chosen flight can be purchased with the customer receiving an email conformation and an eTicket.

Newspapers: Generally newspapers are available both in a print format (via intermediaries such as street vendors and newsagents) and online. It is the online version that provides a direct link between the newspaper and the consumer. Moreover, where the print version is 'static' the online version can be updated throughout the day. Whilst some online newspapers remain free, others charge for access to different levels of content.

C2C Channels

As stated in Chapter 1, this is often viewed as a relatively new channel of activity and very much born out of the development of the Internet and social media. To some extent this is true, especially in volume terms. However, in itself it is not a totally new concept. In suburban America it is traditional that neighbourhoods hold yard or garage sales where local people sell their unwanted goods to other people in their area. Equally, as we stated in Chapter 1, there has been a long tradition of selling our unwanted goods via the classified 'for sale' section of newspapers and magazines.

Although we state that, in terms of the Internet, it is customer to customer there are various intermediaries involved. Let's subdivide the channel into the constituent parts using an example.

Customer 1: This customer, based in the UK, wants to sell their collection of watches. He decides to sell them over the Internet and seeks an appropriate platform.

Platform: The most well-known is perhaps eBay, although there are several others. Customer 1 uploads the details of the watches and either states a fixed price or opens it for bidding. In order for Customer 1 to sell effectively they will need to provide as much information as possible for those individuals looking to make a purchase. Let's say in this instance that Customer 1 has a fixed price.

Customer 2: Having viewed the watches online and read the various descriptions and seen the photographs, Customer 2 states that she wants to buy, and Customer 1 acknowledges the purchase. Customer 2 completes the purchase through the payment process – this may be via PayPal.

Postal Service: Customer 1 takes the package, containing the watches, to the Postal Service and arranges delivery to Customer 2, who receives it the following day.

Customer 1 may have more watches to sell and informs Customer 2 that if they are interested in making additional purchases they can discuss via telephone, email and/or Skype. This could lead to real direct selling/ buying, which removes the platform interface – thus creating truer C2C activity.

Peer to Peer (P2P)

As stated in Chapter 2, an example of P2P is crowdfunding, where a group of individuals may invest in an entrepreneurial business for a fair return on their investment. Whilst there are platforms through which this form of regulated funding exists it is seen as a direct peer-to-peer venture, thus reducing the number of intermediaries in the channel.

Supply Chain Management and Logistics

The Council for Supply Chain Professionals define supply chain management as:

> … encompassing the planning and management of all activities involved in sourcing and procurement, conversion, and all logistics management activities. Importantly, it also includes coordination and collaboration with channel partners, which can be suppliers, intermediaries, third party service providers, and customers. In essence, supply chain management integrates supply and demand within and across companies.
>
> (CSCMP, 2014)

The Council for Supply Chain Professionals define logistics as:

> … that part of supply chain management that plans, implements and controls the efficient, effective forward and reverse flow and storage of goods, services and related information between the point of origin and the point of consumption in order to meet the customer's requirements.
>
> (CSCMP, 2014)

This is a broad area and encapsulates several key factors:

Customer Services: This can be viewed from both a B2B and B2C perspective. Firstly, in terms of its business client, for instance, an online retailer and secondly, from the perspective of the customer who has ordered goods from the online retailer. Both need to be informed of the progress of any order and any difficulties encountered. Ineffective customer service from the logistics/distribution company can have a negative impact upon the retailer's image, with potential loss of customers.

As stated in Chapter 7, the quality and efficiency of the service provided can be a game changer within a highly competitive marketplace. In choosing a logistics/distribution company, the manufacturer/retailer will consider their customer service reputation as well as overall efficiency.

Demand Forecasting: Various techniques can be employed to estimate demand for a product or service at different intervals (perhaps times of the year). Companies aim to forecast customer demands so that sufficient product is available and ready to be shipped. Traditionally, even using mathematical equations, this was based on previous experiences to trend forward. With dynamic markets, historical data may not be able to always provide reasonable forecasts.

Various companies such as Oracle and SAS have developed integrated software packages that can monitor real-time customer interactions and reactions to price, promotional activity and product changes. Such information, along with monitoring changing external factors (for instance, economic and social factors), can assist companies in predicting possible trends, not just for their products but for the market as a whole.

Inventory Control: This links to demand forecasting and the ability to understand trends. Holding a large amount of stock (be it components and/or finished goods) is relatively expensive. Not only are there warehousing costs (space, heating, labour and so on), there are the costs associated with purchasing components and finished goods. Which do not generate revenue. Whilst they may, from an accounting perspective, be assets to the business they are not generating revenue and profit.

In order to reduce warehousing of components, for instance, companies operate on a Just in Time (JIT) system of supplier delivery. This is made possible by the use of technologies that alert the company's suppliers to stock levels (a point that we referred to earlier in this chapter). When an agreed minimum stock level is reached a new order is automatically triggered and delivery made. The objective is to deliver at the right time to the right location.

Groucutt, Leadley and Forsyth (2004) outlined five requirements for successful JIT operations:

High Quality: That high-quality standards must be sought throughout the production and supplier process.

Speed: The operation must be designed to be fast and efficient.

Reliability: Systems and procedures must be robust and reliable in order to reduce disruptions.

Flexible: There must be flexibility built into the processes and systems to respond to customer requirements.

Seeking lower costs: With fast, reliable and robust procedures there should be either a reduction or elimination of various costs.

Materials Handling: Materials, whether they are raw materials, components or finished products, display a range of different characteristics. These can include size, shape, fragility and volatility (think of petroleum, gases and radioactive materials). These various characteristics will determine how the materials are transported, whether by road, and/or sea or air.

Technological developments, across the decades, have had profound effects on the ability to transport goods across borders and globally. These developments have witnessed the more cost-effective and efficient handling of goods and completed products. An example that revolutionised cargo handling was the introduction of shipping containers. As of 2015 the world's largest container ship, the China Shipping Line's *Globe*, was capable of carrying over 19,000 containers (Telegraph, 2015). When fully laden the ship could carry 156 million pairs of shoes, 300 million tablet computers or 900 million tins of beans (Telegraph, 2015).

Packaging: As ordinary consumers our experience of packaging is twofold. Firstly, as the material (paper, plastic, cardboard or combinations thereof) that contains and protects the product, for example, washing-up liquid. This also acts in a promotional and informational context identifying the brand, the ingredients, how to use the product and, usually, how to contact the manufacturer. Secondly, additional packaging that may be added to aid shipment of the product to our home. Think of the packaging that surrounds a product that you have ordered online. As well as displaying address (and courier/postage details) the packaging protects the product in transit. (Refer also to Chapter 5 on the link between packaging and branding.)

In a B2B context products may be shipped on pallets or in specialist containers, for both ease of movement and protection.

Over recent years there has been increasing discussion, across societies, regarding the amount and type of packaging used. These discussions have generally centred on the impact upon the environment from raw material consumption (trees for paper/cardboard and fuels for energy) and the ability to effectively recycle after use to reduce the impact of landfill (dump) sites.

Governments in some countries, such as France and those that comprise the UK, actively encourage recycling of packaging as part of the weekly general household rubbish collections. Product and packaging companies have sought, where possible, to create packaging materials that can be either recycled or are biodegradable, thus reducing impact on landfill sites.

Return Goods/Products Processing: As stated earlier and in Chapter 7, there must be mechanisms in place for customers to return products that do not meet their expectations (for instance, wrong colour/size, material/ texture). These can be a combination of Return Postage labels, collections or specific 'drop points' (which are likely to be stores). Many companies offer 'no quibble' returns policies if the product is returned within a certain time frame. This is often considered an important aspect of customer service.

Tracking: This is used in both a B2B and B2C context and allows both the company and the customer to identify the location of the product within the delivery cycle.

Transportation: This is the function of the physical movement of raw materials, components and finished items from one location to another. In addition to transportation by road, rail, air and sea we should also include, rivers, canals and pipelines.

Transportation tends to be multi-modal, that is more than one form of transport is used to move the goods. For example, oil may be pumped via a pipeline from a drilling site in the desert to a port location where it is loaded onto oil tankers for shipment to a refinery in the UK. Once it has been refined the petroleum may be transported by road tankers to petrol stations within the UK.

Warehousing: This is the storage of raw materials (for instance, copper ore), components or parts and finished goods. We may traditionally think of warehousing as a covered or semi-covered building. However, it can also include large open spaces – new cars, for instance, are often stored on large car parks prior to shipment to distributors.

As stated previously in this chapter, companies seek to minimise, where possible, warehousing to reduce inventory costs to the business. As we see in the Zara case study, here is one company that seeks to avoid warehousing through developing hyper-efficient supply chain and logistics processes.

Case Study: Zara

The clothing and home-ware brand Zara is owned by parent company Inditex S.A., which is the largest listed company on the Spanish stock market with a market capitalisation of some €65 billion (Bloomberg, 2014). Inditex has also become the world's largest clothing retailer (2014), with Zara delivering approximately 80% of the group's revenues (Inditex, 2014).

Zara is an interesting example of a company that has deployed many aspects of supply chain management and logistics discussed elsewhere in this chapter. In the 1980s Zara, along with other retailers such as H&M, began to develop a concept that is widely known as fast fashion (Mihm, 2010; Berfield and Baigorri, 2013). The concept of fast fashion is threefold:

- Firstly, to stay ahead of the trend curve. This means being able to spot trends developing, perhaps styles emanating from the catwalks of Paris, Milan, London and New York.

- Secondly, to be able to design, manufacture and distribute clothing ranges within very short time frames. Traditionally, clothing companies would work in 6–12 month cycles from design to delivery, focusing more on 'seasonal' collections, for instance winter and spring. By reducing lead times Zara has been able to react to market changes more effectively. This is what Sull (2009) describes as Organisational Agility, the 'capacity to identify and capture opportunities more quickly than rivals'.

- Finally, for store managers to be able to reorder stock efficiently with equally efficient delivery times.

The company developed a highly centralised design, manufacturing and distribution system, which means that Zara can deliver from pattern to store within two to three weeks (Inditex, 2014). Moreover, twice a week store managers place their orders and twice per week garments arrive (Berfield and Baigorri, 2013).

This has been achieved through several key actions:

Zara remains in control of its manufacturing as part of a tight vertical integration approach to business. Approximately 50% of its production comes from Spain and relatively near neighbours Portugal, Turkey and Morocco (Berfield and Baigorri, 2013). This allows Zara, through its 5 million square foot distribution centre in Arteixo in Spain, to control its inventory. Approximately 150 million garments pass through the distribution centre each year (Berfield and Baigorri, 2013). More basic garments, such as T-shirts, which can operate on longer, more traditional scheduling flows, are ordered from factories in the Far East. These garments are shipped to the distribution centre for checking and processing.

The clothing made at the 11 Zara-owned factories within the area is sent to the distribution centre via an automated 124 miles of underground monorail (Berfield and Baigorri, 2013).

Near the distribution centre is an open-planned structure known as The Cube. Here real-time information from store managers is gathered and discussed by cross-functional designers, planners, buyers and the marketing teams (Sull, 2009). The store managers provide an important link to the distribution centre on fashion trends in their particular location (Butler, 2012). Moreover, the company uses 'trend spotters' who seek out fashion trends and ideas for new designs (Lo, Rabenasolo and Jolly-Desodt, 2004).

From this and trend information the teams are able to make reasonably fast decisions on style changes and production quotas (Sull, 2009; Berfield and Baigorri, 2013).

From the distribution centre goods are shipped twice weekly to the Zara stores using scheduled cargo flights (Inditex, 2014). Within Europe shipping will take 24 hours and for the US and Asian markets, 48 hours (Mihm, 2010).

The company has invested in technologies and extra capacity that can accommodate fluctuations in demand, reacting to trends as they emerge. According to Berfield and Baigorri (2013), this is an approach that few Asian garment manufacturers would be able to achieve. However, we should note that many Far Eastern and Asian companies have sought to emulate, indeed surpass, Western approaches to manufacturing in the past.

The company believes that speed and responsiveness are more important than cost (Berfield and Baigorri, 2013).

Challenges

Whilst the above has provided Zara with the leverage to gain a competitive advantage within the marketplace the company faces several potential challenges:

Companies learn from the approaches taken by competitors. Other companies, such as H&M, have adopted the fast fashion approach to retailing.

As clothing manufacturers in Asia develop new approaches and technologies, they too will be able to increase speed of design, production and delivery.

As Zara expands globally there will be greater pressure placed upon its supply chain, especially as it seeks to develop markets in the Far East. The question remains can they operate a centralised model out of Spain or will they have to develop another 'distribution hub' in the Far East?

KEY POINTS

In this chapter we have considered the following:

1. The different types of channels from the traditional B2C and B2B to the emerging C2C and P2P.
2. The nine broad channel customer requirements: clarity, convenience, environment, image, price, quality, range, service and experience.
3. The role of supply chain management and logistics in contemporary marketing: customer service, demand forecasting, inventory control, materials handling, packaging, returns, tracking, transport and warehousing.
4. The different elements that comprise the storage and distribution of items, from raw materials through to finished goods. There is a clear overlap between the channels used in B2B and B2C operations.

5. The development of information technologies has greatly enhanced the speed and efficiency of delivery. Moreover, this technology has heightened customers' expectations of high-quality service delivery (this links back to our discussions in Chapter 7).

6. Demonstrated that when companies harness new technologies and approaches to supply chain management a competitive advantage can be gained.

QUESTIONS

Here is a series of questions and activities for you to undertake to aid your knowledge and understanding of the points made in this chapter.

1. Following your next visit to a supermarket, take a selection of items, for example, bagged fruit and a frozen food product. Reflect upon the source or location of the ingredients and consider the various and number of channels possibly used to bring that food to your table.

2. With the potential development of 'click and collect', what are the possible challenges for both suppliers and retailers?

3. Companies such as Amazon and Apple market music downloads whereby tracks from CDs or complete CDs can be purchased online and immediately downloaded to your computer or a cloud. This has changed the way many people shop for their music as now they can undertake an instantaneous purchase 24/7. This is convenient for the buyer in various ways as the B2C channel is greatly shortened. However, the more traditional 'bricks and mortar' retailer remains. Consider previous chapters as well as this one. What actions can the more traditional retailers take to remain viable businesses?

4. There has been much discussion of the positive value that JIT contributes to supply chain management and logistics. Reflect upon the potential problems/difficulties that can also be attached to JIT.

5. Re-read the Zara case study and consider the following: (a) What could be the potential supply chain and logistical challenges as the company expands its 'bricks and mortar' and online retailing operations? (b) What lessons, if any, can other fashion retailers learn from the approaches taken by Zara?

6. What can companies in one business sector or industry learn from companies in different sectors or industries regarding supply chain management?

FURTHER READING

Ellinger, A., Shin, H., Magnus Northington, W., Adams, F.G., Hofman, D. and O'Marah, K. (2012) The influence of supply chain management competency on customer satisfaction and shareholder value. *Supply Chain Management: An International Journal*. Vol 17 No 3. pp. 249–262.

Inditex (2014) Annual Report and Accounts. Inditex.

Mangan, J., Lalwani, C., Butcher, T. and Javadpour, R. (2011) *Global Logistics and Supply Chain Management* (2nd Edition). Chichester: John Wiley & Sons.

Soosay, C., Fearne, A. and Dent, B. (2012) Sustainable value chain analysis: A case study of Oxford Landing from 'vine to dine'. *Supply Chain Management: An International Journal*. Vol 17 No 1. pp. 68–77.

9

Integrated Marketing Communications

OBJECTIVES

By the end of this chapter you should be able to:
- Explain the purpose of a marketing communications strategy.
- Identify the key tactics used in marketing communications.
- Debate the potential value to an organisation of integrating marketing communication tactics.
- Develop an outline marketing communications campaign.

INTRODUCTION

There is no absolute definition of marketing communications. Texts will vary. One defines them as:

> *The instruments (tactics) by means of which the company communicates with its target groups and stakeholders to promote its products or the company as a whole.*
> (De Pelsmacker, Geuens and Van den Bergh, 2010)

Equally we could encapsulate marketing communications as:

> *A variety of integrated methods or tactics through which an organisation communicates and promotes the values of the organisation*

and its brands to a range of selected and relevant stakeholders with the aim of gaining greater understanding and, where appropriate, a competitive advantage.

Whilst this 'definition' may be 'wordier' we feel that it seeks to also explain possible outcomes, these being a greater understanding of the organisation (company, NGO, charity or government unit) and supporting the moves towards gaining a competitive advantage. Additionally, we have focused on the integration of tactics, a point that we will return to later.

In this chapter we explore the various methods or tactics that encompass integrated marketing communications (IMC); also sometimes known as Omni Communications. Many texts and degree courses include IMC under the heading of 'promotion', one of the 7Ps of the generic marketing mix. Often promotion and integrated marketing communications are seen as interchangeable. The use of the term integrated marketing communications may be the result of a greater emphasis on the integration of the tactics or instruments of communication together to seek a greater synergy. Therefore providing a greater impact than a series of standalone tactics.

Virtually every waking moment of our lives we are exposed to marketing messages, whether they are online, in magazines, on billboards or via television. Organisations use a variety of methods or tactics to communicate key messages to their target audiences. Moreover, the challenge, within highly competitive markets, is to create marketing communication campaigns that clearly resonate with customers.

Marketing communications can be used to achieve several, often broad, key objectives:

- Build brand awareness within new developing markets.
- Reinforce brand awareness, especially within highly competitive markets.
- Influence members of a target audience to take action, be that to purchase a product/service or campaign against a perceived injustice.
- Provide aftersales advice and customer service support.

Marketing communications operates within both B2B and B2C environments. In this chapter we will not delineate the two but will include various examples to illustrate the context.

Value of Integration

- Reinforcement of brand message – increases brand recognition.
- Potential to create interest and action (purchases).
- Potential increased effectiveness of resources (especially financial).
- Opportunity to create 'value added'.

Understanding Communications

There are various communication theories and models, some basic, others more advanced. What is important to understand, within the confines of marketing communications, is that there are eight key features to how an organisation communicates. These are Sender, Encoding, the Message, Decoding, the Receiver, Feedback, Noise and Clutter. This concept is based upon the work of Schramm (1955) and his adaptation of Shannon's model (1948). Although the original work was produced some time ago, the basic premise of the ideas remains true, even within the fast-paced Internet age – perhaps even more so (see Figure 9.2).

Figure 9.1 The key components of the communications mix

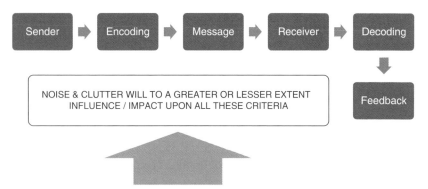

Figure 9.2 A general communications model based upon the work of Shannon (1948) and Schramm (1955)

Sender: The organisation, whether a government department, charity, non-governmental organisation (NGO) or a for-profit company, that sends the communication.

Encoding: The combination of the channel of communication (for example, television) and the 'elements' of the advertisement – imagery, words, music, sound effects and so on.

Message: This is the key idea or point of view that the organisation is seeking to communicate to its target audience. This can range from the importance of health screenings for men to reduce the risk of prostate cancer through to the value-added features and benefits of a particular new car model.

The Receiver and Decoding: This will be a member of the target audience who will *decode* the message. Decoding is identifying, interpreting and understanding the key elements of the message that has been sent.

Feedback: The receiver may consider possible actions that they could take as a result of decoding the message. This can be either seeking further information or/and making a purchase. If we look at the two examples provided, on seeing the message regarding health checks for detecting prostate cancer, a man might make an appointment (by phone or email) at their local health clinic. They are reacting to information being provided by either a cancer charity or a government department (for example, the Department of Health in the UK). Equally, a person thinking about buying a new car might seek further information (by phone or online) prior to discussing the idea with other members of their family and visiting a car dealership.

Noise: This can be described as something that 'interferes' with the communication of the message. We suggest that this can happen at any point within the communication process. Here are a few possible instances:

- Clutter: This is where there are too many marketing messages all vying for the customer's attention. The sheer volume of daily messages creates its own form of 'turbulence', leading to the consumers 'switching off' from advertising in whatever form it takes.

- The encoding itself: We probably all have favourite and, perhaps not so favourite, advertisements. Our likes and dislikes may be personal preferences; however, if an advertisement, for instance, is not communicating a message effectively then it is not achieving its true objective. It could be argued that what is in the mind of the advertising agency's creative team doesn't always translate well into an effective and positively memorable advertisement. Thus the style and design of the advertisement creates, in effect, its own noise.

- Semantic noise: This can be partially linked to the above point. The message is received exactly as transmitted but is not understood. This may be due to various factors, including social, economic and educational background. Whilst it can be argued that this is applicable to all nations, it is particularly important when considering the use of marketing communications in poorer developing nations. What may be reasonably understood in one country or region may not be in another. Whilst we may live in a highly globalised world, it doesn't always mean that one standard marketing message is easily translated and understood trans-nationally from one language and culture to another.

Marketing Communications Strategy

The aim of a marketing communications strategy is to fulfil the objectives set out within the overall marketing strategy. This, in turn, needs to support the objectives as presented within the organisation's corporate strategy. It is a cascading approach.

Consider this brief example:

A company seeks to increase overall revenue with the intention of also increasing profits. The marketing team respond by examining which markets have growth potential and for which brands. To meet the corporate objectives, the marketing team may propose to increase its market share within a particular market by, say, 5% over two years, for a specific brand. From this the marketing team need to create a plan. The marketing communications strategy sets out, stating various tactics, how the marketing objective will be supported.

So a marketing communications strategy (and related tactics) can be crucial to the future success of an organisation.

Why Integrate?

As we work through this chapter we will examine individual tactics or methods that comprise marketing communications. Yes, these tactics can operate independently and in many cases do. However, an integrated approach provides opportunities for synergies across the tactics, thus providing a stronger and consistent message to the target audience.

In the longer term it may also be more cost effective for the organisation. By creating synergies there is also the opportunity to reduce duplication of effort and waste. However, this means bringing together different groups (advertising agencies, PR consultants, sales people and so on) to share ideas and approaches to build the consistent message. Such an activity must be driven and controlled by the marketing team within the organisation.

However, an organisation needs to carefully select which tactics or methods are best suited to (1) meet the objectives of the marketing communications strategy and (2) create an effective synergy.

Communication Objectives

There are many reasons why an organisation communicates with its current and potential target audience. These can include:

- Launching of a new product or service.
- Prolonging the life of a product within a declining market.
- Rejuvenating a brand within a changing market.
- Promoting new versions of a product – think of brand extensions.
- Informing customers of changes in the way the organisation will operate. An example of this might be a bank that is changing/enhancing the way customers' accounts operate.
- Stock clearance: A retailer will seek to promote a sale, thus clearing space for the introduction of new stock.
- Overcoming resistance to new approaches, new concepts and new ideas. A government might undertake such promotion to support the introduction of new legislation or major new infrastructure investments.
- Promoting the corporate brand identity.
- Announce major structural changes to the organisation and how this will benefit customers. For example, the acquisition of a company.
- To attract and support individuals and/or companies that will operate as product sellers/distributors.
- To increase footfall in retail outlets.

Communications Mix

The communications mix comprises the following tactics or methods:

Advertising

Direct marketing

Exhibitions

Merchandising

Product placement

Public relations

Sales promotion

Sales force

Sponsorship

Word of mouth – Social media

Guerrilla marketing

We will examine each of these within this chapter.

ADVERTISING

There are several important factors that we need to consider when examining advertising:

Paid Communication: Fees are paid for the placement of an advertisement whether it is in a magazine or on television. This is in addition to the costs of creating the advertisement. The amount paid for the advertising space often varies depending on, for example, the position (location) in the magazine or when it is shown on television. Some of the most expensive advertising slots are for the US Super Bowl American football match where a 30-second slot can cost in the region of £3 million, although it needs to be stated that the audience is normally in excess of 100 million people (Siltanen, 2014).

Gain Attention: As indicated earlier, one of the challenges for marketers is the level of clutter or overexposure to marketing messages faced by consumers. Marketers will seek to cut through the clutter with advertising that gains attention and is memorable, thus creating interest (inform and/or influence) and possible action (seeking further information and/or purchase).

Inform – Influence: Advertising can be used to purely inform the public. For example, a government might use advertising to inform us of changing legislation. During 2013 and 2014 the UK Government used television advertising to inform the population of a new workplace pension scheme that was being introduced. For the majority of viewers this was just informing them of changes taking place and that they need to take no action as it would be the responsibility of their employers to organise.

Advertising can also influence or attempt to persuade people to take action. In the case of the workplace pensions cited above, those viewers running a business that employed staff would need to explore how this would affect their particular operations. Equally, we might be influenced to purchase certain food items that are on special offer or consider whether it is time or not to buy a new car.

Creating Cognitive Dissonance: Companies may, through advertising, seek to create a level of uncertainty in the mind of the consumer that their current purchases may not satisfy their particular needs (see also Chapter 2). The UK supermarket sector is particularly competitive, especially between the big three – Tesco, Sainsbury's and Asda. During 2013 and 2014 Asda's television campaign focused on comparing their prices on specific products with those of both Tesco and Sainsbury's, the aim being to show that they were significantly cheaper. Here advertising is used to persuade people to switch from one supermarket brand to another.

Reinforcement: Advertising can be used to reinforce the benefits of using a particular product or service. This assists in influencing repeat purchasing.

Level of Targeting: As stated above, advertising incurs costs. Therefore marketing teams and advertising agencies need to target the advertisement to the most appropriate segment of the population. This may be choosing a particular magazine as the readership is more likely to be interested in the specific product/service being promoted. Equally, the same applies to slotting advertisements before, during and after specific television programmes.

Advertising Media

In this section we examine the range of advertising media, however not all organisations will use the full range of media available. This may be for several reasons:

Budget: Major organisations such as Unilever, Procter & Gamble, BP, Nestlé, the US Government, Tata and Johnson & Johnson can dedicate significant budgets to advertising. Even then they will seek to use the most appropriate media and gain strong return for their investment.

However, the vast majority of organisations do not have the financial resources to use a broad range of advertising media. They will need to be particularly selective in their choice of media with the aim of maximising return on investment. So a company might opt for a series of advertisements in a magazine over a 12-month period rather than the weekend supplements in a national newspaper. Both publications may be aimed at the similar target audiences, even though the newspaper's weekend supplement may have a greater circulation.

Media Availability: Some countries have a greater spread of advertising media than others. This may be due to the historic development of the media providers, the sheer size of the country, level of communications development, culture, economic development and educational levels. In some countries terrestrial television stations may be state-controlled and carry no advertising. However, the influx of satellite providers can provide an advertising alternative. Equally, video advertising may be available via the Internet.

Media Regulations: Each country will have its own set of media regulations governing what can be advertised in what media and when. Certain products, for example, tobacco-related although available for sale, may have significant restrictions, as in the UK, placed upon them in terms of how these products can be advertised and promoted (CAP, 2014).

Print Media

This is can be described as traditional media in the form of newspapers and magazines. There are two broad, yet important characteristics, in print media – level of readership and their buying power. These will depend on the type of print media, its circulation and audience segmentation. In some countries, for instance the UK, the circulation of traditional printed newspapers is steadily declining (Media Week, 2014) in favour of more online delivered material. Yet in other countries newspapers may still have a mass appeal.

Newspapers

These can be subdivided into the following groups:

Daily: These tend to be national or local newspapers that are published five to seven days per week. They are generally published in tabloid (also known as Compact), broadsheet or Berliner formats. Many of the national newspapers also are available overseas and carry an international reputation for their high-quality journalism. Examples include, *The Financial Times*, *The Washington Post*, *The Times* (of London) and *The Wall Street Journal*.

Weekly: These are newspapers published once per week, and the day of publication may be for historic reasons (original owner wanted to launch on a particular day), religious reasons, by design (a weekend publication) or by circumstance. They may be local, regional or national newspapers.

Trade or Industry-focused: These usually take the format of a newspaper (for example, tabloid or Berliner) and may be published either weekly or monthly. They focus on a business-related field and may be only available by subscription. Organisations advertising in these publications are able to focus on specific target audiences. For example, *The Times Education Supplement* (TES) published weekly in the UK provides advertisers the opportunity to communicate with teachers in secondary education. This can be valuable when promoting new textbooks and other resources.

Newspapers may be Either Charged for or Free: The Evening Standard Limited newspaper group publish two newspapers in the London region – *The Metro* (Monday to Friday mornings) and *The London Evening Standard* (Monday to Friday evenings). Both are free newspapers (often known as Freesheets) and are available at London Underground stations and major supermarket chains; they are aimed at commuters.

The newspapers carry news and feature stories, from a local, national and international perspective. The newspapers are supported by advertising and both also have an online presence.

Magazines

These can be broadly subdivided into the following groups:

Business-oriented: These are magazines that are targeted at specific business audiences and can range from aviation, through catering to travel and tourism. These are usually published on a monthly basis although some are published weekly.

These publications may be available on both subscription (sent direct to the subscriber's home or office) or via a news vendor/newsagent.

Examples of weekly magazines are the UK publications *Campaign*, which covers advertising and the commercial media industries, and *PR Week*, which focuses on the public relations industry.

Specific consumer interests: These are usually monthly publications that focus on specific topics ranging from art and crafts through to fashion and style. These publications may be available on both subscription (sent direct to the subscriber's home) or via a news vendor or newsagent.

Customer Magazines – In-store – Inflight: These are publications developed specifically for a company. Perhaps the most common are airline or inflight magazines. The airline may have a general publication (focusing on vacation destinations and lifestyles) and one for business-class passengers that centres on general business issues, such as leadership skills. Examples include British Airways' *High Life* and *Business Life* magazines.

Various retailers have created their own magazines as a means of highlighting what is available both in-store and online. One such retailer is the UK-based supermarket Tesco. Their free glossy magazine includes recipes (often focused on certain events and seasons of the year), all made from ingredients available at Tesco. There are also sections on health and fitness, home life (including makeovers). Major brands, such as Colgate, advertise their products, which are also available at Tesco.

Television

Since the 1990s, with the development of digital technologies, there has been a burgeoning of terrestrial, cable and satellite television stations. This, in turn, has provided greater opportunities for companies to advertise on television. However, it should be noted that not all publicly owned television stations have advertising, for example, the BBC in the UK.

However, several factors need to be taken into consideration:

Cost of Production: Generally the production of television commercials is relatively expensive – just consider the costs associated with writing the script, assembling a production team, location shooting, the actors (especially if they are well known), the visual effects and postproduction (voiceovers, editing, sound effects and music). Many of the car commercials have employed elaborate visual effects and location shooting, the aim being to differentiate themselves from other cars and to 'hold' our attention.

Transmission – Choosing transmission times is governed by a number of factors:

1. Cost: The peak time slots, normally 17.00–22.30 (although this may vary country to country), command a higher cost than other times. This is when the most popular programmes are normally shown – 'soaps', major drama series, sporting events (see earlier comment on Super Bowl) and game shows. This is the usual time when the major retails, banks and Fast Moving Consumer Goods (FMCG) manufacturers advertise their brands.

2. Regulations: There may be regulations that stipulate that certain products and how they are portrayed can only be advertised after a certain time. This is often known as 'the watershed' by which time younger children are normally in bed and the programming is more adult-focused. This is particularly the case with terrestrial channels. In the UK, for instance, the 'watershed time' is normally considered 21.00. In many countries the advertising of products, such as tobacco and alcohol, may be banned or highly restricted. Equally, there are generally specific regulations regarding advertising to children.

3. Target audience: Due to the costs of both production and transmission, the advertising agency must seek the slots that best reach the client

company's target audience. This may be the main 'commercial break' in the middle of a 'soap'.

Return on Investment: This is applicable to any form of marketing communications. The company needs to see that its objectives have been achieved by investing in the right form of media.

Radio

Radio stations often operate on a local, regional and national basis. They can be accessed via standard household radio, digital TVs (free to air programming), in-car radios, smartphones and tablets. Thus technology has widened the opportunities for current and new target audiences to be reached by advertisers.

Radio stations are often segmented into contemporary, jazz, classical, sport, talk, comedy, easy listening, religious and so on. Stations will have profiles of what constitutes their typical audience. This can assist advertising agencies in knowing where and when to place their client's advertising.

As with television some radio stations, for example, those operated by the BBC, do not carry either advertising or sponsorship.

A criticism often stated of radio advertising is that 'there are no pictures'. However, the use of an imaginative script, the right tone/style of voice and accompanying sound effects and music can create an effective piece of communication. The inventive use of words and sounds can 'paint' an image or series of images in the mind of the listener.

Cinema

The enthusiasm for visiting the cinema does vary from country to country. Movie makers, through the use of new technologies such as CGI and enhanced 3D, have sought to create an entertainment experience. However, cinemas are competing, in many countries, with home cinema systems that seek to re-create, albeit on a smaller scale, that experience. Moreover, in many countries, the cost of a large-screened HD television is relatively low. This is due to the development of new technologies and increasing price competition.

Within these settings advertising agencies will need to consider the effectiveness of cinema-related advertising. Equally, box-office successes not only draw audiences but also advertisers as well.

Online

Increasingly advertising agencies and their clients have invested in advertising their products and services online. Additionally, advertising via the Internet is becoming interactive. For instance, the Napolina brand range of Italian food (pasta, tomatoes, sauces) have used interactive advertising online in the UK to market various recipes using their products. These advertisements have appeared during the commercial breaks on ITV Player (a UK terrestrial station catch-up TV service online).

Sophisticated analytics allow companies to track consumer online behaviours, thus channelling advertisements that would appeal to particular segments of the online audience.

Equally, when you undertake an online search via a search engine, for example, Google, advertisements will normally appear related to the search.

Outdoor Advertising

This is also known as posters, billboards, hoardings and out of home. This type of advertising is normally positioned at roadsides, on the sides/backs of buses, sides of taxis, phone boxes, at shopping malls, train/metro stations and airports – basically any location where there is a heavy throughput of people (walking and driving). Such locations provide the advertiser with a greater 'opportunity to be seen'.

(Although it is generally known as 'outdoor advertising or media' this does include within buildings such as airports and metro stations.)

Research can determine the profile of people who are likely to pass the site. For example, a provider of an internationally recognised accounting qualification could choose metro stations in and close to the business district of a major city. They will be targeting junior employees who are seeking qualifications to enhance their chances of promotion.

Equally there will be posters advertising local restaurants, both fast-food chains and individual ones.

Poster Sizes:
There are many different types and sizes of posters available to advertisers. Here is a brief selection (Tfl, 2014):

Adshel (6 sheet): 1200 mm × 1800 mm
48 Sheet: 6000 mm × 3000 mm
96 Sheet: 12000 mm × 3000 mm.

Outdoor advertising usually takes three forms:

Static: These are fixed posters of varying sizes. In some countries, India is an example, the posters are hand-painted *in situ*.

Mechanical: These are posters that are fitted on a mechanical system that revolves, thus allowing more than one poster to be viewed at that particular site.

Digital: In essence these are TV screens of varying sizes that allow numerous different posters to be displayed over the course of the day.

Ambient Media

This is advertising that can be described as 'in the background' as opposed to being at the forefront, which we would associate with, for instance, TV advertising.

An example is 'giveaway' postcards that you might find in cinemas or restaurants. They are the same shape as a tourist postcard and can be posted like any other card – but they are really advertising a product or service.

DIRECT MARKETING

This varies from providing a 'basic' directness (a leaflet/flyer for a local takeaway pushed through the letterbox) to personalised letters and emails which indicate knowledge of the customer and their buying habits.

Whilst both seek to 'build' a relationship, it is the more contemporary approach that often enhances that relationship. For instance, a bank writing directly to an individual customer offering them a new loan rate. Of course, banks do not just write to one customer, they will select an appropriate segment of their customers to communicate this offer. However, the intention is to personalise the marketing offer.

Technological development, especially in terms of computing power and software, provides organisations with the opportunity to store and analyse vast amounts of customer data. This data can include credit ratings, lifestyle information, purchasing history (think of online shopping or stores where there are loyalty cards), income level and educational qualifications. This data helps to build profiles and segment target groups (see Chapter 4).

Direct Marketing Methods

Door Drops: These are simply items that are placed through an individual's letterbox. They can be:

1. Sealed envelope: These might be addressed to 'the occupier' above the actual address and contain information regarding special offers within the local area. These offers could include installation of broadband and/or satellite receivers.
2. Free samples: These will usually be in special packaging and may include special discounts for the full-sized product from a local store.
3. Flyers: These are usually advertising services from home repairs through to local takeaway/home delivery fast-food services.

A major problem associated with door drops, especially in high-density areas such as London, is the volume. The inundation of flyers advertising yet another pizza outlet with home delivery services leads to door drops often being categorised as 'junk mail'. This inundation can result in the door drops cancelling each other out as households ignore them and place them in recycling. Therefore the use of door drops needs to be carefully considered in relation to the location and other available means of advertising the product and/or service.

Direct Mail: In many countries this has become an increasingly sophisticated means of communicating with current and potential customers. As indicated above, technology has assisted in revolutionising this approach. Today, companies can use a range of measures to target specific customers with 'individual' offers. These can range from banks offering loans at low interest rates to creditworthy customers through to supermarkets with special offers based upon the customer's buying preferences.

Traditionally, direct mail was delivered through mail services, however increasingly such targeting can be achieved via email and smartphone texts.

EXHIBITIONS

These can be classed as major events that expand over two or more days where a range of exhibitors display their products and services. The aim is for the companies to choose the events that most likely target both current customers and potentially new ones. Some exhibitions operate on an annual basis within one location, whilst others, such as the postgraduate education MBA Fair, operate across several countries.

These can be divided into three main categories of B2B, B2C and a combination.

1. B2B: This is where companies market to other companies. These can range from catering equipment for restaurants and hotels to new movies. The Cannes Film Festival in the south of France, for example, includes an exhibition space where companies seek buyers for their movies and countries can market their locations for filming.

2. B2C: This is where companies market to ordinary consumers. Exhibitions can range from education (where agents and universities market to potential students, an example being study abroad fairs) to home improvement shows.

3. Combination: Some exhibitions are generally aimed at a B2B audience, although they may have limited opening times for the general public. One such event is the Farnborough Airshow in the UK. The principal

activity of this show is for aircraft manufacturers to exhibit their range of aircraft and accessories to potential international buyers. On public open days there are also air displays, usually of vintage as well as the latest aircraft technologies. Several countries operate similar types of exhibitions.

MERCHANDISING

There is occasionally confusion around the use of the word 'merchandise'. In the fashion industry, for instance, 'merchandise' refers to the actual fashion item being sold. Merchandising (within the context of the marketing mix category, Promotion) often refers to branded items that are used to support the marketing of another product and/or service.

Merchandising is used by a wide range of organisations to promote their brand. For example, universities with sweat shirts, T-shirts, jumpers, cases and umbrellas. Movies, from James Bond through to the Star Wars series and Disney, have greatly benefited from the sale of models, posters and books. Equally, companies such as Disney have promoted some of their movies with merchandise in joint arrangements with companies, such as the fast-food outlet, McDonald's.

PRODUCT PLACEMENT

This is extensively used in the movie and television industries. This is where a company pays to have their product used/on show within the actual movie or TV programme. Virtually every type of product has been marketed through product placement from drinks, cars, fast food, designer clothing and hotels to watches. The movies do not have to have a contemporary setting either – futuristic sci-fi thrillers have also incorporated logos of contemporary global brands.

Some countries, such as the UK, regulate the use of product placement on terrestrial TV stations (OfCom, 2014). Certain products, such as tobacco, alcoholic drinks and gambling products (as of 2014), cannot be product placed on UK-originated programmes (OfCom, 2014).

PUBLIC RELATIONS

There are many definitions in the literature covering Public Relations, whether they are developed by organisations, authors or, indeed, PR companies themselves.

The Public Relations Society of America (PRSA) defines PR as:

> ... *a strategic communication process that builds mutually beneficial relationships between organisations and their publics.* (PRSA, 2012)

The definition refers to 'publics'.

As we discussed in Chapter 4, there are significant benefits in focusing on those customers (current and potential) who are most likely 'interested' in the product or service being marketed. In public relations, the targeted group is known as 'publics'.

The types of activities undertaken by PR teams include:

- Media Relations: Building and maintaining appropriate relationships with journalists in the relevant business areas.

- Community Relations: Organisations often need to work closely with local communities. For example, a local supermarket engaged in charity fund raising.

- Consumer Relations: PR teams can often be the interface between the organisation and the customer. This can be through written and verbal communication. Complaints, for example, regarding a product or service has PR implications for the organisation, especially in a world of social media. Therefore the organisation needs to have mechanisms in place to respond to such complaints.

- Planning and Implementing Events: These can range from product launches (perhaps at an exhibition), a major sporting event (World Cup Football or Formula 1 racing) through to a company's Annual General Meeting (see the section on Investor Relations below).

- Employee Relations: PR practitioners can also be engaged to advise on enhancing the relationship between the organisation and their employees. This is particularly important, from a marketing perspective, if the employees are a direct interface with the customer. As discussed in Chapter 7, people are a key factor in delivering quality service.

- Government Relations: As discussed in Chapter 1, governments and politics can have a significant impact upon organisations and how they operate. Individual organisations and trade bodies representing companies seek, through PR, to discuss issues that may have an impact upon operations. These issues can include regulations relating to the marketing of products and service.

- Investor Relations: This is where a company listed on a stock market (for example, the London Stock Exchange) seeks to keep investors informed of the company's activities and plans. This would be particularly important, for instance, in the case of a potential acquisition or merger with another company. Listed companies hold an Annual General Meeting to which shareholders are invited and may be requested to cast votes on, for instance, re-electing members of the Board of Directors.

- Crisis Management: This is a specialist area within Public Relations. A crisis can range from a product recall through to a major incident/accident at the other end of the spectrum. In all cases of crisis management, there is a risk to the viability of the brand. For example, the sinking of the cruise liner *Costa Concordia* off the Italian coast in 2012 was global news (BBC, 2014f). The sinking, the loss of life, the resultant court cases, the salvaging of the ship and its eventual dismantling had been a recurring news story for over two years. This was a major crisis for both Costa Cruises (based in Italy) and its parent company Carnival (based in the US), and specialist PR firms were engaged to provide information, transparency and to protect the brand (Luker, 2012).

SALES PROMOTION

This is something that we see virtually every day in retail outlets, with companies providing customers with incentives to purchase. Sales promotions may coincide with certain festival periods, a particular month or be for a longer duration.

Sales promotions can include:

1. **Buy One Get One Free**: This is known as a Bogof and is a means of increasing sales of a product that has perhaps been slow-moving or is nearing its expiry date.

2. **Buy Three items and Get the Cheapest One Free**: This is often used for a specific selection of products, for instance, a branded skin care beauty range. In addition to selling product it is a means by which new customers have the opportunity to try several products within the brand range.

3. **Buy Two and Get the Second Half Price**: This has been a type of promotion used in various airport and high-street bookshops in the UK. Used on a selected range of books, it is a means of not only increasing the readership (thus promoting) several authors but also revenue generation.

4. **General Sales**: This is where product is reduced for a specific period of time. Such sales are not only prevalent in shopping malls but also through companies operating online, for example, travel companies and hotel comparison sites.

SALES FORCE

This also links to Chapter 7 and the relationship between people and delivering service.

Even with the exponential rise of the Internet and online shopping, companies still employ a range of sales people, whose role it is to interface with the customer/potential customer. This approach can come in many forms and includes:

1. **Door to Door Salesperson**: In many countries, such as the UK, this was the traditional view of the salesperson. However, this practice is now much less popular; that said, some charities in the UK still employ people to market the charity on a local door-to-door basis. Whilst of

declining popularity in places such as the UK, in other regions of the world it remains one of the most effective ways of marketing and selling products to a local community.

2. B2B Sales Visits: Whilst the Internet has also aided B2B marketing, there remains a significant role for the specialist salesperson. As discussed in Chapter 2, buying decisions within a B2B context are often complex, requiring expert knowledge from both the buyer and seller.

3. Call Centres: Various organisations either operate directly or contract out call centre operations. Often these provide both customer service and the opportunity to market a product or service over the telephone. Even the paying of a bill can prompt a discussion regarding additional services that are available.

4. Online Assistance: Various Internet sites provide the opportunity to undertake an online discussion with a salesperson. Software tracks each entrant and their movements whilst on that site, for example, looking for a potential vacation on a travel company website. Where the potential customer is browsing – not sure of a particular destination/hotel/package – an icon can appear asking whether the person needs assistance. The icon can be disengaged or indeed be the link to starting a conversation.

Whilst organisations retain sales forces, how they interact and the methods used, will often vary trans-nationally.

SPONSORSHIP

This is where an organisation either financially or in-kind supports a particular event, activity or charitable cause. Sponsorship is a means of marketing and reinforcing the brand to a wider audience. Organisations may be sole sponsors or acting within a consortium. Within such a consortium there would be non-competing brands, although they may display complementary linkages, for example, a cola drink and a fast-food outlet.

Regulatory organisations provide advice to companies on sponsorship, including the brand benefits. Examples can include:

The Arts:
Sponsorship can range from artists, art installations, art centres, television programmes and classical music concerts.

Sport:
Sports sponsorship ranges from football teams, football and tennis tournaments (including the World Cup and Wimbledon) to stadiums and international athletic meetings.

WORD OF MOUTH – SOCIAL MEDIA

This is also known as Viral Marketing. As we stated in Chapter 2, individual consumers can be influenced by the views of others. As we discussed, these may include friends and family. From a traditional marketing perspective these 'word of mouth' influences operated within a relatively narrow circle of influence. This circle of influence began to widen with the development of the Internet, the use of email and social media.

The subsequent development of social media has meant that:

1. The potential circle of influence is much larger. Consider the number of followers a celebrity might have on Twitter. Celebrities can influence lifestyles through, for instance, their actions, music, films and clothing.
2. The speed of contact (and thus potential influence) can be rapid. With the Internet operating 24/7 and access via smartphones, individuals have instant access to an array of information and ideas.

Organisations have realised the power of 'word of mouth' and have engaged in the use of social media to both promote brands and also to counter negative comments (Refer to Public Relations).

GUERRILLA MARKETING

This can be defined as deploying atypical, unconventional or unusual methods or tactics, often beyond the mainstream approaches, to communicate a message. This approach is often used when the company has a small budget available to promote their product and/or service. However, there are cases where major companies have equally used unusual approaches to promote a product or service. Examples have included advertisements that have covered all the steps of an escalator, sculptures of people that look as if they are coming out of the ground along a sidewalk to flooring of a metro train that looks like half water and half beach with footprints in the sand.

There has to be care given to the tactics used in guerrilla marketing. Among the numerous examples cited on the Internet, for instance, is the use of graffiti. The use of graffiti to deface either public or private property to promote someone else's products and/or service is both illegal and unethical. Additionally, it is self-defeating as it will impact upon how people perceive the values of that brand – most likely in a negative light.

Mini Case: Parking a Car on the Side of a Building

In 2011 an agency working for a BMW dealership mounted a fiberglass replica of a BMW Mini Cooper on the side of a building in Houston, Texas. However, the city authorities issued a ticket, not for parking, but for not seeking permission to erect it on the side of the building. Thus its presence was breaking building regulations rather than any other laws. The issuing of the 'ticket' led to more interest and making the front cover of the local *Houston Chronicle* newspaper (Boerlu, 2013).

MARKETING COMMUNICATIONS PLAN

As indicated above and elsewhere in this text, it is important to develop workable and realistic plans.

A communication plan normally includes the following components:

Objectives: These are usually developed out of the marketing strategy – in essence what the marketing department seeks to undertake to meet the overall objectives of the organisation. So, for instance, if a company seeks to increase their market share by 'X' percent, then how does the marketing department seek to achieve that goal? One method may be to raise the profile of the brand by emphasising its various features and benefits. This may be achieved through a combination of communication tactics – targeted advertising, direct marketing, public relations and so on.

Background Research: As stated in Chapter 3, marketers must be researchers seeking to better understand what customers require and how best to meet those needs and wants. Research is also required for marketing communications. Here the task is examining the objectives of the communication plan and seeking the most effective and efficient tactics (advertising, direct marketing, public relations and so on) to meet those objectives.

Budget: The overall marketing strategy will have a designated budget that will also include finance for an integrated communications plan. Even global businesses, such as Unilever and Nestlé, who allocate multi-million dollar budgets to marketing, seek to be effective and efficient in their use.

Timing: Timing can be everything in terms of a successful product launch or gaining additional market share. Consideration is given to what media is used over a specific period of time, for instance, 12–18 months.

Tactics: Out of the research, an understanding of the overriding objectives and budgetary and resource constraints will come the choice of appropriate tactics to operationalise the plan. Choice of tactics can be critical to the success or failure of a campaign. Often students immediately pinpoint display advertising as the tactic that should be paramount. However, this is not always the case. Choice will depend upon many factors, and sometimes the least likely is the most effective, as it captures the public's imagination. Consider our brief examples of guerrilla marketing above.

Implementation: How and when will the communications plan be implemented? This will include allocating appropriate resources (finance, equipment and people) to operationalise the plan.

Monitoring: In addition to implementation, there must be a mechanism to monitor the ongoing effectiveness of the plan. As we saw in Chapter 1, the operations of companies can be affected by changes within the macro or external environment. Equally, the plan may not be as effective as originally conceived. In both cases, the marketing department may have to intervene and revise the plan according to the changing situation. This may mean diverting resources to other tactics to concentrate on a particular segment of the target audience.

Measurement: As we have stated above and elsewhere in this text, marketing should be driven by 'objectives'. These objectives or outcomes need to be measurable so that the organisation knows whether or not they have achieved them. For a charity, for instance, it may be a significant positive response to a disaster appeal. For a company it might be an increase in sales of a particular product over the length of the campaign.

Review: Every plan should be reviewed at the end of its cycle. Measurement allows the organisation to gauge how successful a campaign has been, what has worked, what has not worked, what can be modified and what could be used again in future campaigns.

KEY POINTS

In this chapter we have considered the following:

1. Organisations need to develop an overarching communications strategy that meets the goals of the marketing strategy, the aim being to fulfil the marketing strategy in order to fulfil the overall goals of the organisation (see Chapter 1).

2. The objectives of marketing communications can be many and varied, including maintaining brand awareness in existing markets and building awareness in new markets.

3. The most appropriate tactics need to be combined or integrated to fulfil the marketing communications strategy. This will also depend upon the available budget.

4. Marketing communications plans generally consist of: objectives, background research, budget, timings, tactics, implementation, monitoring, measurement and review.

5. In highly competitive markets the challenge is to develop a marketing communications campaign that can 'break through' the noise and clutter that can disrupt the message.

QUESTIONS

Here is a series of questions and activities for you to undertake to aid your knowledge and understanding of the points made in this chapter.

1. Select one newspaper and one magazine. The newspaper can be local, regional or national. We suggest that you choose a lifestyle/fashion-related magazine to provide more advertising options. Examine both publications, looking specifically at the advertisements. Are there any advertisements that particularly impress you? If so, why? Equally, are there any advertisements to which you have a negative reaction? If so, why? Once you have completed this exercise, ask a friend to review the same advertisements and answer the same questions. Do they have the same reaction as you? Compare and contrast the reactions. What is similar/different about your reactions? Why might they be so?

2. Select two to three newspapers, they can be local, regional and/or national. Read through them and mark off those articles (news and features) that you believe have been created through public relations activity as opposed to investigative journalism. Once you have completed this exercise, add up the number of PR-generated articles and

consider it as a percentage of the total number of articles within the newspaper. Reflect upon the outcome and consider the importance of PR as a means of communication.

3. The local outlet of a nationally branded fast-food retailer, located near a major financial centre, plans to offer Internet ordering and fast delivery service for business lunches. They have worked out the logistics of the service. Now they need to market it to both current and potential local customers. What marketing communications approaches would you advise them to use to 'pull' customers to use their new service? Provide a rationale for your suggestions.

4. Organisations increasingly seek value for money in terms of their advertising spend. This is especially the case during times of economic recession and within highly competitive markets. Explain how segmentation, targeting and positioning can help advertisers to maximise the value of their budget. [You may want to refer to Chapters 1 and 4.]

5. The following can be undertaken as either an individual or group exercise. Adopting the role of a marketing communications consultant(s), create a marketing communications plan for the launch of a new organic chocolate bar. [Note: You can launch the chocolate bar in a country of your choice. However, the plan must reflect the key points below.]

The key points are:

a. The target group are 18–25 year olds.

b. The plan is to cover an 18-month period.

c. Create a brand name – remember that brands have values and those values should link to your marketing communications. In other words, what intrinsic values are you seeking to communicate? [Note: You may want to refer to Chapters 5 and 11.]

d. Your overall budget is UK £3 million (or equivalent if you have decided to undertake this launch in another country).

e. You need to outline the media that you would use and a rationale for your choice of each type of media.

f. Outline any potential marketing communication risks or issues.

g. How would you measure the performance of the campaign?

Finally, when you have completed your plan reflect upon it. What have you learnt from this exercise? What would you do differently if you had to undertake it again?

FURTHER READING

Amoako, G.K., Dartey-Baah, K., Dzogbenuku, R.K. and Kwesie Jr, S. (2012) The effect of sponsorship on marketing communication performance: A case study of Airtel Ghana. *African Journal of Marketing Management*. Vol 4 No 2. pp. 65–79.

Carrillat, F.A. and d'Astous, A. (2012) The sponsorship–advertising interface: Is less better for sponsors? *European Journal of Marketing*. Vol 46 No 3/4. pp. 562–574.

Egan, J. (2014) *Marketing Communications* (2nd Edition). London: Sage.

Groeger, L. and Buttle, F. (2014) Word-of-mouth marketing influence on offline and online communications: Evidence from case study research. *Journal of Marketing Communications*. Vol 20 No 1–2. pp. 21–41.

Papasolomou, I., Kitchen, P.J. and Panopoulos, A. (2013) The accelerative and integrative use of marketing public relations in Cyprus. *Public Relations Review*. Vol 39 No 5. pp. 578–580.

10
Relationship Marketing

OBJECTIVES

By the end of this chapter you should be able to:

- Explain the concept of relationship marketing.
- Explain how relationship marketing could enhance revenue generation and, potentially, profitability.
- Explore the links between relationship marketing and other aspects of marketing such as the marketing mix.
- Consider to what extent relationship marketing may differ between B2B and B2C environments.

INTRODUCTION

We are all involved in relationships, whether family, friends, neighbours, work colleagues or our fellow students. In many cases these relationships will be long-term sometimes for our entire lifetime.

What Do We Mean by Relationship Marketing?

Gronröos (2000) defined Relationship Marketing as:

> *The process of identifying and establishing, enhancing, and, when necessary terminating relationships with customers and other stake-holders, at a profit, so that the objectives of all parties involved are met, where this is done by mutual giving and fulfilment of promises.*

Groonröos (2004) then goes onto explore the link between exchange and 'value added' when he states:

> *The relationship marketing perspective is based on the notion that on top of the value of products and/or services that are exchanged, the existence of a relationship between two parties creates additional value for the customer and also for the supplier or service provider.*

Why Is Building a Relationship Important?

In Chapter 1 we began to highlight the importance and value of customers who engage in repeated purchases of the same product and/or service. In that chapter we depicted the levels of loyalty and engagement (which we have reproduced in Figure 10.1). This diagram is a good starting point in order to understand the value of repeat purchasing compared to continually seeking to acquire new customers.

There are various reasons why building a 'relationship' with a customer has longer-term benefits for an organisation:

Acquisition Costs: Organisations incur both direct and indirect costs every time they seek new customers. The direct costs include

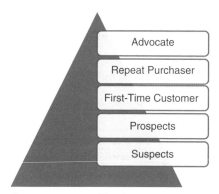

Figure 10.1 Levels of engagement and loyalty

marketing communications' campaigns and resources (people's time, product samples, credit-checking costs, administrative costs, salaries (including possible commissions), costs associated with data warehousing and data mining).

Whilst there is no definitive answer, the CIM (2010) suggest that it costs between four and ten times more to acquire a new customer than retain an existing one. Ozimek (2010) writes that it takes approximately 'three times as much money to attract new customers via traditional forms of advertising as to re-attract a repeat customer'. Reichheld (1993) proposed that it can be up to five times as much money to gain a new customer whilst Jobber (2004) suggested as much as six times.

Ozimek (2010) adds that it takes approximately '30 times as much marketing spend to attract a new customer via traditional forms of advertising as to have a satisfied customer find new customers'. This is playing the role of advocate.

The majority of business owners spend less than 5% of their marketing budget on their current (repeat) customers but 95% of this spend on attracting new customers.

In addition to the direct costs there are the indirect costs associated with non-acquisition of a new customer. Could someone else have been acquired instead? Could the resources have been devoted to enhancing already established relationships?

Sectors/industries will have variable conversion rates. Where there is a low level of conversion from a prospect to a customer, the organisation will have to find the means of recovering costs due to the failure to convert.

In addition, we need to consider the contribution that existing customers make towards repeat purchases and may even become advocates (see Chapter 2). Repeat customers may actually purchase in larger volumes than new customers (Ginn, Stone and Ekinci, 2010). Again there are no absolute statistics; however, depending upon markets we can assume that this could be significant.

From this perspective retention becomes an important aspect of relationship marketing. Ginn, Stone and Ekinci (2010) define retention and
retention management as the

> *customer's declared continuation of a business relationship with
> the firm. Customer retention management is defined as develop-
> ment and implementation of a customer information-based
> customer-centric marketing strategy for managing and nurturing
> a company's interaction with specific customers or groups.*

Whilst we generally agree with these definitions we would replace
'firm' and 'company' with 'organisations' as this provides a much
broader scope, encapsulating charities, NGOs and even, where relevant, government departments.

Life-time Value (LTV): As indicated above, retained customers add
value (revenue and profits) to the organisation through a combination
of repeat purchasing and advocacy. The more satisfied the customer is,
the more likely that they will purchase more of the product or service.
Equally, the more likely that they are to recommend and champion the
product or service to friends and family. The life-time values of customers can be calculated, and various studies have been undertaken in the
financial sector to determine such values (Reichheld and Sasser, 1990
among others).

Profitability: Although figures do vary, Reichheld (1993), Buttle (1990)
and Bowie and Buttle (2004) suggest that an increase in customer
retention of 5% would increase profits in the range of 25–95% within
some service-oriented companies. Levels of profitability will vary due
to the characteristics of a particular sector/industry, along with the
efficiency levels of that company.

Competition: A recurring theme of this text has been 'competition'.
Organisations operate within generally competitive environments with
varying degrees of rivalry. Companies will seek to build relationships
in order to retain, if not grow market share. Losing customers means

loss of revenue from departing customers and the cost associated with acquiring new ones. Moreover, if the lost customers were particularly profitable for the organisation there is no guarantee that the newly acquired customers will be as profitable.

WHY DO CUSTOMERS DEFECT?

In order to enhance relationship marketing we need to understand why customers defect. DeSouza (1999) provides a foundation for customer's reasons and we have added a few of our own. It should be noted that whilst these factors can operate in isolation they could also be combined – for instance, the combined impact of pricing policy and poor service provision.

Price: Where switching costs are low/non-existent, a customer may switch to another cheaper alternative. For example, this could be changing supermarkets due to their close proximity. This may occur when customers are particularly price sensitive, perhaps at times when the local/regional/national economies are close to or are in recession. In such cases, customers will be seeking to maximise the value of their disposable income.

Product/Service: This is where the customer seeks a superior product and/or service. For instance, the introduction of a new smartphone with a more flexible tariff arrangement by a rival provider. Here the customer, by switching, is provided with two major benefits – a new phone (with extras) and perhaps a more financially beneficial tariff. The defection may be enhanced by the rival provider offering to cover any contract severance costs. However, the new provider will seek a 'lock-in', that is a particular time period before the customer can leave the contract, for instance, 18 months.

Quality of Service Provision (see also Chapter 7): Whilst it is impossible to maintain 100% service perfection, many organisations have gained international reputations in terms of the quality of their service delivery. However, service provision can be problematic, as what is good service to one person is poor service to another. This is partly due to our experiences as customers. However, many organisations seek to deliver a 'service standard'. When a customer feels that they have not received either the acceptable service standard (as promoted by the organisation) or an acceptable response to their complaint/concerns, then they might switch to a rival company. Where switching costs are low, the customer can move relatively easily to a competitor provider.

Lifestyle Changes: A customer may seek to exit a market as it no longer fulfils their needs and wants. For instance, a customer who has bought a particular car brand and has used their after-sales service for several years may move from a semi-rural location to the centre of a major city. They could still retain their car but they would incur parking charges. However, they may decide to relinquish the car and use the local public transportation system instead. Equally, an individual may become more affluent, perhaps through their career development. As a result they 'trade up' in terms of the products and services that they seek to fulfil their needs and wants.

Lack of Engagement: There may be a lack of engagement, a lack of communication on the part of the supplier whereas competitor organisations stay in contact with their customers through a steadily balanced stream of information and updates. This information can be via email, physical mail, text messaging and/or telephone calls. If switching costs are relatively low this may provide an incentive for the customer to defect.

How a Company Corresponds with a Customer: There may be various methods by which an organisation can communicate with a customer, however it is also the tone and style of communication that affects customer retention. As we state in Chapter 11, the customer is not always right, especially in terms of ethical and legal behaviours. However, if we set aside these caveats then a genuine customer may become irritated if an organisation uses a tone, language or style of writing that is disproportional to an issue (for instance, late payment reminders) or their name is spelt incorrectly, even though they are a regular customer. The technology available used to mass-customise correspondence should prevent (or at least greatly reduce) errors such as miss-spelling of customer's names.

Where there is competition within the marketplace and switching costs are low, again the customer may decide to change suppliers on the basis of how they feel treated. In some cases the customer may not care that much and just look at it as incompetence on the part of the supplier. However, another person will seek to change their supplier and may not even notify the organisation of the reasons for switching. A company could be losing a larger than acceptable proportion of their customers to competitors, not because of the quality of the product or even for the prices being levied – but through how they interact with the customer.

All organisations will state that they are engaged in customer service. It is one thing making such statements – however actively engaging and practising it to retain customers is another.

Organisational Requirements: Within the B2B context, an organisation may decide to end the relationship with a particular supplier. This may be due to costs; however it may be as a result of other factors. These factors can include:

1. **Internal political reasons:** The senior management team no longer wants to purchase supplies from a particular company, on ethical grounds, due to its reputation. For instance, a fashion company that discovers that a supplier has employed child workers, against the specific contractual agreement. Although there will be switching costs for the fashion company, its reputation may be intack, whereas the garment manufacturer may find it difficult to gain replacement customers.

2. **External political reasons:** As stated in Chapter 1, the actions of governments can give rise to both opportunities and threats. Governments can impose multi- and unilateral embargoes and sanctions against another country. This may result in a company having to end their business relationship with a supplier, as not to breach the embargoes/sanctions and incur legal penalties.

3. **Changes in requirements:** A company may change their requirements for a particular product and/or service. It is therefore whether or not the supplier can accommodate these changes. If not, the company may have to seek an alternative supplier.

Technological Changes: Rapid changes in technology could result in a customer seeking alternatives. This may occur when the current supplier cannot meet the customer's requirements. For instance, the introduction of netbooks, notebooks, tablets and smartphones provide greater flexibility than the traditional desktop computer. In such a situation an individual or organisational customer may seek to replace their desktop computers with devices that deliver greater portability. If the current supplier is not manufacturing/retailing such devices, then the customer may switch supplier in order to meet their specific requirements.

Ethical Reasons: A customer may switch to another provider because they believe that they are a more ethical business than the original supplier. For example, a customer shops at a particular clothing retailer where they like the style and believe that they obtain overall value for money. However, they later learn that the clothes are made by low-paid employees working long hours in difficult conditions. On these grounds the customer seeks out an alternative retailer who clearly states that they only use suppliers who meet their specific and exacting regulatory standards.

Promiscuity: Gilligan and Wilson (2003) among others have suggested that some customers are 'promiscuous' in their actions, that is they have a tendency to switch brands frequently in response to the various promotional offers available. The customer may not necessarily be 'dissatisfied' with the product and/or service but has been offered a 'better deal' elsewhere. Whilst this is a valid perspective, we suggest that there are additional issues that need to be considered:

Rather than the use of the term 'promiscuous' we suggest that customers are exercising choice.

Customers may be actively encouraged to seek out the 'best deal' and make a switch not by competitor companies but by government. In the UK, for instance, the Government, through various regulators, encourages customers to 'explore offers' especially within the energy supply market. As regulations have made it easier to switch electricity and gas providers, the Government believes that this will enhance competition among the providers, thus providing enhanced services to the customer.

With the multitude of loyalty cards available it is most likely that customers will hold more than one card, especially for a supermarket chain. Consider this scenario: an individual holds loyalty cards for both supermarket X and supermarket Y. There may be a branch of supermarket X relatively near their home which is used during the weekend, perhaps for buying a large quality of groceries. However, there is a branch of supermarket Y near their place of work. They use this supermarket to buy *ad hoc* items for dinner in the evening as well as items for their lunch. In both cases the individual is collecting points and perhaps money-off coupons and is exercising their choices.

Other Factors: It is worth noting that there are other factors, though not strictly 'defecting' that mean that the customer no longer engages with the brand. These include:

1. The customer no longer has a requirement for the product or service. This could be for numerous reasons including outliving the use of the product, the person is ill or infirmed and can no longer use the product, or there has been a lifestyle change and there are different requirements.
2. The customer has died.
3. The customer has moved away to a place, perhaps another country, where the product or service is not available. This may be particularly the case with certain localised retailers, banking services and restaurants.

In some of the above cases it is not possible to prevent defection. However, in others organisations can stem the tide of defections by instigating a more customer-focused approach.

CHARACTERISTICS OF RELATIONSHIP MARKETING

So, as we have explored elsewhere in this text (for instance, Chapter 6), there is an exchange (usually a financial transaction for goods/services provided). However, the goods and/or services that we acquire have a value attached to them, hence the price we are prepared to pay for them. Yet there is the opportunity for further value through the mutual development of a relationship (see Chapter 5).

Blomqvist, Dahl and Haeger (1993) outlined key characteristics of relationship marketing as follows:

1. **The Individual**: This is where every customer is considered from the perspective of 'an individual'. This links back to Chapter 4 where we discussed STP. Marketers seek to subdivide the wider population into target groups. Through the use of sophisticated database management, organisations can seek to build enhanced relationships with groups and individuals within those groups.

2. **Customer-focused**: The activities of the organisation are predominately directed towards existing customers. As depicted in Chapter 2, organisations seek repeat purchasers and advocates who will champion their products and/or services. This is equally applicable to charities and NGOs, such as the Red Cross/Red Crescent and Unicef as it is for Apple or KFC. However, the point that should be made is that there needs to be customer replenishment as customers (a) no longer require the product and/or service, (b) can no longer afford the product and/or service, (c) move away from the particular location where the product and/or service is available or (d) pass away.

3. **Interactions**: Relationship marketing is based upon interactions and dialogues. The key is being able to develop communications that enhance the interactions rather than become a disincentive to the customer. The act of 'over communicating' with customers can actually turn customers away from the company, especially where switching costs for the customer are low.

4. **Being Profitable**: The organisation is seeking to achieve profitability (or surplus for a not-for-profit organisation) through the decrease of customer turnover and the strengthening of customer relationships. Recruiting new customers through various forms of marketing communications, as we have seen, can be expensive compared to maintaining customers through a relationship-building approach.

These factors can be supplemented by additional characteristics suggested by Bowie and Buttle (2004), which include:

1. Service Culture: As stated above, a customer may defect because of the quality of service that they receive. In order to implement and importantly maintain an efficient and effective service culture, organisations have to invest in the appropriate systems, procedures and training. People are core to the successful implementation of a service culture, and not just those who are customer-facing. The staff who work behind the scenes, for instance, in packing goods for delivery, building the websites and developing procedures all have a responsibility for service delivery (see Chapter 7).

2. Trust and Commitment: Bowie and Buttle (2004) suggest that it 'is helpful for the customer and the company to have shared values'. This links back to our comments, above, in Organisational Requirements, where we state that a customer may defect for ethical reasons. Where customers and companies hold shared values then there is a greater opportunity to build a relationship.

   In 1976 when Anita and Gordon Roddick founded the cosmetics and beauty company, The Body Shop, in the UK it was born out of the idea of using natural ingredients that were not tested on animals. This was not the overall general approach of the time, although there were a variety of smaller companies treading similar paths to that of The Body Shop. However, it could be argued that the success of The Body Shop was, in part, due to the values that customers shared with the Roddicks on animal testing and other social and environmental issues that they promoted.

   Of course, where trust can be gained it can equally be lost too. Companies that have publicly stated, through their marketing communications, that they uphold certain values only for it to be revealed otherwise, have lost that trust. This can result in boycotts with accompanying reduction in both revenue and profitability.

3. Rewards and Recognition: Bowie and Buttle (2004) suggest that there can be mutual rewards. For the company it is additional revenue, for the customer it is a tangible reward. Many companies offer loyalty

cards to their customers, and the greater the 'loyalty', the greater the number of rewards (usually points) that the customer receives. Of course, as we stated above, a customer's loyalty can be spread over several similar organisations. For instance, in the UK a shopper may have both a Tesco Club Card and a Nectar Card, thus gaining points whether they are shopping at either a Tesco or a Sainsbury's supermarket. Arguably the shopper is loyal to both supermarkets; it depends upon what benefits they are seeking from the two supermarkets at particular times (see our earlier point/example regarding customer choice).

National Cultural Dimensions

It is important to realise that whilst the concept of Relationship Marketing is very much a European and American area of research, the idea doesn't just pertain to those cultures or the late 20th century. Indeed, it could be argued that the concept of relationships in marketing long precedes the discussions in Western universities. Successful relationships are built and maintained on 'trust'. Trust is often at the forefront, for instance, of Middle Eastern business relationships. Some of that will be underpinned by tribal loyalty, yet those of other tribes, whether local or indeed international, can be welcomed into the relationship. An acceptance may take time – yet it can often lead to long-term respect and mutual business benefits.

Therefore it is valuable for organisations, especially those operating trans-nationally, to understand how relationships and trust operate within different nationalities and cultures. In one country, the organisation may be able to build and maintain a relationship within a relatively short period of time. However, that may not always be replicated in others in the same way.

Are Relationships Possible in All Situations?

This very much depends upon the product or service being offered. Car companies realised that there were opportunities in developing 'after-sales service' for those who had purchased one of their cars. Today this includes: financing, warranties and servicing after so many kilometres.

For high-ticket purchases, such as sports cars, there is usually an exclusive members' club where additional accessories, including branded clothing, can be purchased. Whilst the car may be a single purchase that will not be replaced for five or more years, the company can continue to maintain a relationship with the customer. When the time arrives for the individual to purchase a new car then the 'relationship' can carry them over into a new purchase. Most likely as an 'ongoing' customer there would be a price reduction for their continuing loyalty.

As with cars, many products can build in a relationship approach to their offer. Another example would be computer software. Once acquired and registered, the user will normally receive updates free of charge. Equally, there may be a mix of free and for-purchase 'add-ons' for the software.

However, it is unlikely that all transactions can be accompanied with a relationship-building approach. Whilst a small newsagent, within a business district, may have a few regular customers, it may be dependent more on transient trade, perhaps from tourists. In such cases it may be convenience and price that gains the business – purely a transactional relationship.

Different positions can be adopted in relation to a customer's level of significance in terms of value. Where the level of engagement (or spend) is low then the 'relationship' is purely a transactional one. Where there is an increased frequency of engagement and an increased opportunity for life-time value, then there is the opportunity to create a marketing relationship.

Relationship Marketing in B2B

This is where building long-term relationships can be mutually beneficial, especially where the customer purchases contribute significantly to revenue. The transactions can range from components through to fully manufactured products.

The question is how deep and integrated are these relationships? Moreover, how much are they dependent upon a relatively small number of people across the organisations? It is often key people within the supply and procurement departments that build the relationships. Both sides seek to negotiate – usually for more business on one side and specifications and value on the other. A rapport can develop between both individuals and teams, seeking the best for both organisations.

A difficulty may arise when one of the key individuals leaves the organisation. They may take with them the tacit knowledge of how the relationship developed and how the negotiations are handled, with an understanding of the personalities involved. A relationship will most likely continue, unless the parameters of the relationship change significantly. If they do, and both organisations can obtain other buyers/suppliers, then the relationship will come to an end. There will be immediate cost implications; however, one or both parties may recoup those costs through the next relationship.

RELATIONSHIP MARKETING AND THE MARKETING MIX

Figure 10.2 simply illustrates that we need to consider that relationship marketing integrates not only to customers but with the marketing mix

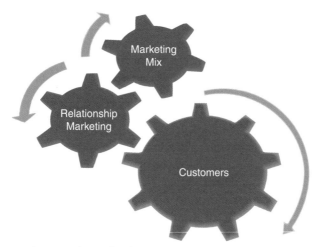

Figure 10.2 The interrelationship between customers and the marketing mix via relationship marketing

as well. We have used the concept of cogs to show that there is this inter-connectivity, this dependency between relationship marketing and the marketing mix to fulfil the needs and requirements of customers. Many of the fundamentals of the marketing mix – people, process, physical evidence, promotion (marketing communications) and placement (logistics and delivery) – strongly associate with building and maintaining relationships with customers.

APPROACHES TO CUSTOMER RETENTION

Both academic and practitioner literature suggest different approaches to customer retention. We have sought here to encapsulate some of the key approaches. What is important to consider is that such approaches do not work in isolation, and that marketing teams have to seek real and effective integration.

Loyalty Programmes: As the name implies, and indicated earlier in this chapter and elsewhere in this text, these are developed to encourage loyalty. The development of data warehousing and data mining techniques provides organisations with the ability to contact current customers on a regular basis with information, offers, incentives and rewards. Ginn, Stone and Ekinci (2010) suggest that data analysis focuses on seven factors:

- What are the expectations of the customers?
- What actions can be taken to meet them?
- What is the growth opportunity with existing customers?
- Who are the valued customers who should receive better treatment, and what treatments are they likely to respond to? [We suggest that there is a focus on enhancements to service levels.]
- How do customer interactions affect satisfaction and loyalty?
- How can interactions be improved?
- What strategies are required to take customers to higher loyalty levels?

Predictive modelling (neural networks, regression analysis, decision trees) can be combined with marketing metrics (profitability per customer, longevity of each customer) to develop and initiate personalised approaches to retention. In Chapter 5 we referred to Interbrand's research on the relationship we will have in the future with brands. Through various technologies we will have a closer, more personalised relationship with products, brands and organisations than perhaps ever before.

Application of 'Real-Time' Marketing Tactics: This is real-time personalisation operating within an online environment. Consider this scenario. You go online to a clothing retailer that you have previously visited and have purchased goods from, so they have your email address and data from your previous purchases. On this occasion you navigate through the site viewing various fashion items, and there are some that you are interested in buying. You place the details in your electronic shopping basket, however you do not go to checkout but decide to exit the site. Your exit from the site may be for many reasons, for instance, doubts about spending the money, you have to leave for a meeting or its time to join other family members for a meal. The items that you have placed in your electronic shopping basket remain. Now depending upon whether or not the online retailer has the e-commerce software with the functionality to monitor and respond to 'abandoned' shopping baskets/carts, the retailer could respond in several ways. These can include:

1. Doing nothing – leaving you to make the decision whether or not to return to the site and make the purchase.

2. Contact you via email after you have exited the site. This will be a computer-generated personalised email enquiring to see if 'everything is OK' and reminding you that there are items still in your electronic basket. Additional contact details may be provided in case you have any queries regarding your potential purchase. These details will normally include a free-phone number.

3. At a later stage (thus not in real time), if you have been a good repeat customer and you have a reasonably large order waiting in the electronic basket, the retailer may offer you an incentive to

complete the transaction. This incentive may be a discount on the purchase (for instance 5%), additional points on a loyalty card (if a scheme is in operation) or free delivery.

4. Additionally, many online sites display a pop-up icon that appears no matter what page you are visiting where you can enter real-time online discussions with a salesperson. Some sites offer the additional option of a telephone conversation, if preferred.

Employees Passionate about the Brand: This is particularly important with front-line employees (sales staff, cashiers, customer service and technical support). Their enthusiasm not only can create repeat customers but enhance the opportunity to create advocates. However, in order for employees to be enthusiastic about the brand, the organisation needs to be enthusiastic about the employees. This 'enthusiasm' can be through leadership styles, support, compensation and benefits, strong ethical policies, empowerment, respect and encouragement. Various companies have, over the years, exemplified this approach, and include the social media company Twitter, the specialist fabric manufacturer, W.L. Gore & Associates, the US retailer Nordstrom and the ice-cream manufacturer, Ben & Jerry's.

Reassurance: In order to build a relationship customers have to be reassured in relation to both privacy and security. The first affects both in-store and online where details are provided to the company, for instance, name, date of birth and address. Online the level of detail provided can be far greater and include passwords, security questions (for example: Mother's maiden name) and credit/debit card details. There has been significant media coverage over recent years regarding loss of data, weak online security and hacked sites. It is not only the risk of stolen credit data but also identity theft. Whilst it is incumbent upon customers to have their own anti-virus and firewall protection, it is equally incumbent upon organisations to have reliable protection for their customers. It is unlikely that such risks will ever be eliminated, but, that said, relationships will only ever be maintained if companies can genuinely reassure their customers.

Reacting to Complaints: There will be occasions when there is a 'service failure'. At whatever loyalty level the customer is placed, the organisation needs to have an effective means of response. Bell and Zemke (1987) suggest that there are five elements to 'effective service recovery': apology, urgent reinstatement, empathy, symbolic atonement and follow-up. However, there are other factors that also need to be considered:

1. The customer is not always right: This is a point we explore further in Chapter 11, however it is important to reflect upon it within this context. Whilst the customer, in an objective sense may not be right, the organisation still has to manage the complaint within a fair and transparent manner.

2. Ozimek (2010) suggests that dissatisfied customers can become 'hostile' towards the brand. His definition is that of an individual who 'is both dissatisfied with the organisation's products or services and prepared to spread dissatisfaction by word of mouth (WOM) among friends and colleagues' (Ozimek, 2010). This is no longer limited to just friends and colleagues, as the use of social media allows the individual to cast the net of dissatisfaction much wider. This raises several issues for both the complainant and the organisation itself.

   The Internet and social media sites do not absolve the individual of legal responsibility. Whilst an individual might have a genuine complaint they need to be aware of the legal framework(s) under which they make the statements. Potential breaches of the law may not be limited to one jurisdiction and an individual could face several civil law suits.

   Equally, organisations need to have a plan to react effectively and efficiently to complaints that have 'gone viral'. Even though the complainant may be in the wrong where the actual complaint is concerned, the organisation has to behave in an appropriate way as not to antagonise current and possibly future customers, as well as other stakeholders.

3. There may be customers who are 'serial complainers', taking every opportunity to raise negative issues about the brand and/

or organisation. Without careful handling, these cases can become potentially detrimental to the organisation as the complaints are disseminated more widely and are possibly distorted from the original postings.

AN ADDED DIMENSION – THE ADVOCATE WHO IS NOT A CUSTOMER

There is another dimension that we feel is often overlooked. This is where individuals become advocates even though they have not been repeat customers or, in some cases, customers at all. This may seem an anomaly, however consider these possibilities:

An individual purchases a new family car, a car which will last them several years. The whole family enjoy the various features and benefits and the overall driving experience. They are so enamoured with the vehicle that they inform family, friends, work colleagues and others (perhaps through social media). This information is then passed on to others and so the praise for the vehicle spreads. This may lead to test drives and possible purchases. In this case, however, the advocates will be unknown to the particular car company and/or distributors.

An individual who has never purchased the product and/or service yet is an advocate for the brand. This may seem unusual, however think of it from the perspective of an individual who may have a product on their 'wish list' but is unable to afford it. Their interest in the product may lead them to have a good insight into the product and its various features and benefits. A possible example is where an individual wants to own a particular sports car brand yet does not have the savings to do so. They may become more knowledgeable about the vehicle than a salesperson at the car dealership. Although not a buyer they can advocate the various features and benefits that the brand maintains, not just to friends and family but also to others through social media.

A journalist who may have the opportunity to 'sample' a product can become an advocate for the product even though they have not purchased it. Again we can think of journalists who get to test-drive various cars. They may have their personal favourites that they champion as best in their class for performance, road holding, driving experience and so on. Whilst they may not be able to afford to buy one, they become an important advocate for the brand. (See also Chapter 9.)

KEY POINTS

In this chapter we have considered the following:

1. Why building a relationship can be important to the development of organisations. The contributing factors include acquisition costs, life-time values (LTVs), profitability and issues of competition.
2. Why customers defect, in other words, why they switch from one brand to another. The reasons can be many and varied, including price, the quality of service provision, lifestyle changes and the company's lack of engagement with their customers.
3. Relationship marketing displays various characteristics: individuality, customer-focusing, interactions, being profitable, service culture, trust and commitment, rewards and recognitions.
4. Approaches to customer retention include creating and maintaining loyalty programmes, application of 'real-time' marketing tactics, employee passion and reacting to complaints.
5. Linking back to Chapter 1, the role of the advocate in building relationships between organisations and their customers.

QUESTIONS

Here is a series of questions and activities for you to undertake to aid your knowledge and understanding of the points made in this chapter.

1. Various writers have suggested that in order to gain and sustain a competitive advantage organisations must build strong relationships with their customers. Do you agree? Support your view with evidence.

2. What are the reasons why customers defect from one company to another? Can you add to the list already provided in this chapter?

3. Why do you think advocates are considered important to the long-term success of an organisation?

4. What are the challenges to retaining customers? How can these challenges be mitigated or overcome?

5. How can online-only retailers develop and maintain a marketing-oriented relationship with their customers?

6. In Chapter 7 we considered the role of 'people' in delivering service quality. Reflecting back on that chapter, the points discussed within this chapter and your own research, consider the degree to which employees influence the development of strong bonds between organisations and their customers.

FURTHER READING

Bejou, D. and Palmer, A. (Eds) (2013) *The Future of Relationship Marketing*. Oxford: Routledge.

Belanche, D., Casaló, L.V. and Guinalíu, M. (2013) The role of consumer happiness in relationship marketing. *Journal of Relationship Marketing*. Vol 12 No 2. pp. 79–94.

Egan, J. (2011) *Relationship Marketing: Exploring Relational Strategies in Marketing* (4th Edition). Harlow: Financial Times.

11
Marketing and Ethics

OBJECTIVES

By the end of this chapter you should be able to:

- Debate the possible ethical issues that marketers may encounter in their daily activities.
- Debate the role of the customer in maintaining ethical standards within marketing.
- Discuss the value of voluntary code of practice.

INTRODUCTION

In this chapter we consider the role of ethics in marketing and the types of issues that marketers may encounter. Indeed, Griseri and Seppala (2010) state that:

> ... *marketing practices seem to attract considerable criticism compared to other corporate functions. Marketing is often seen by critics as the unscrupulous side of business.*

As we will see, there are some marketing practices that do raise ethical concerns and, to some extent, underpin behaviours within a contemporary societal context. However before we examine ethics in a marketing context we need to consider what we really mean by 'ethics' and why it is important in marketing.

A question that is often posed is: 'If it is legal then it must be ethical, right?'

Well, not necessarily. Something can be acceptable under the law – however, both individuals and groups might question the ethics or morals of the action. For many years intense factory farming was perfectly legal within the UK. Chickens, for instance, were kept in cages (known as battery cages) with little room for movement (thus their natural behaviours could not be expressed, such as foraging) and fed high-protein supplements (Compassion in World Farming, 2014). Farm buildings were designed to house hundreds of these caged birds. The overall aim was to produce large volumes of eggs as the market (the consumer) demanded cheaper eggs.

From a purely business perspective this was efficient mass production on an industrial scale. Yes, the eggs were cheaper than those produced on farms that used organic methods where the chickens were free-ranged with space to roam eating natural feed. However, consumers and animal welfare groups questioned whether this practice was a cruel existence for the caged birds (Compassion in World Farming, 2014).

The farming practice was perfectly legal and an efficient means of production. However, was it ethical? Equally there was the debate whether or not factory-farmed eggs were as good (healthwise) for the consumer as those free-ranged and organically farmed. Many farms producing organic/free-ranged eggs sought to market the benefits of such farming techniques for both the animals and consumers.

However, a European Union Directive in 1999 focusing on animal welfare has significantly reduced the use of such intensive farming techniques within the EU (EU, 1999). As of 1 January 2012, conventional battery cages were banned within member states, although some caging remains permitted (EU, 1999). Could it be argued that ethical concerns for the welfare of these animals created a change in the law? Clearly, the change in legislation would have an impact upon the intensive-farming businesses, hence the long period of transition from legislation to action.

According to the welfare organisation Compassion in World Farming (2014), there remain some three billion battery-caged chickens in countries (including the USA – where it is legal in most states) outside the EU.

As we saw in Chapter 1, societal changes can influence or, indeed, change how businesses operate. Moreover, we have to consider ethics with different cultural lenses. What might be accepted as 'ethical', indeed legal in one country, may not be in another. In Victorian Britain it was normal to see children working as chimney sweeps, cleaning the thousands of chimneys of their soot and grime, working in the new industrialised factories or mining coal (Humphries, 2011).

Today, in 21st-century Britain, such actions would not only be illegal under various child protection legislation but would be considered morally reprehensible. However, in other countries children have been and currently are involved in work, producing a range of products from garments to ornaments. According to the International Labour Organization (ILO), there are some 168 million child labourers, 83 million of whom are engaged in hazardous work (ILO, 2013). Of course, not all the work these children undertake leads directly to the products that many people find in shops and on the Internet. That said, there will be a proportion of goods available that have been produced by children.

As such cases become more widely known through the spread of the Internet and social media, so has come the concerns and condemnations. Various clothing companies, for instance, were off-shoring garment production because it was more cost effective than producing within the home market. In some cases these garments were being produced by children. A combination of public attention and management concerns have led many clothing retailers to create codes of practice for their suppliers with strict sanctions if the codes are breached.

So, if an action may be deemed legal yet there is debate regarding ethicality, then how should we define ethics? There are many different views of ethics. Aristotle (384–322 BC) discussed 'living a good life', whilst John Stuart Mill (1806–1873) spoke about the rightness and wrongness of individual actions (Griseri and Groucutt, 1997). Griseri and Groucutt (1997) suggested that within a business context:

> *Ethics is the study and practice, within organisations, of the moral aspects of corporate and individual behaviour, the justifications for these, and the methods organisations use to secure and maintain morally sound behaviour.*

So we seek a moral compass that shows us the direction towards good rather than bad behaviours. There is much debate regarding whether our behaviours are created through nurture or our environment. Equally, there are individual or combined influences, and how do we perceive moral behaviour and our justification for the actions we undertake?

However, we must observe that being ethical is not always clear-cut, there are what we can call 'grey areas', as we will see in this chapter.

POTENTIAL ETHICAL PROBLEMS AND DILEMMAS

Here we examine a range of potential ethical issues.

Competitor Information

Within free market economies companies will both compete and co-operate with each other. Market knowledge can be a powerful asset and rivalry between competitors can be fierce with companies seeking to gain an advantage over each other.

Organisations can shape their marketing strategies and tactics by monitoring and understanding competitor actions. So a company can legitimately compare brand positions, pricing, advertising, promotions, levels of customer servicing, means of distribution, as well as overall business strategy. Much of this will already be in the public domain for virtually anyone to access through a company's Annual Report and Accounts as well as various media outlets.

Gathering information on rival companies is not new, and there are legitimate methods to gather competitor intelligence. However, there have been cases where companies have engaged in both illegal and unethical means of gathering such information. Such actions have included:

• Spying on competitors: This includes audio and visual surveillance of external meetings. There is also a risk that some companies may engage hackers to infiltrate a rival's networks.

- Dumpster Diving: This is where searches are made of rubbish from rival companies with the aim of finding information regarding marketing campaigns and business proposals. Today much more information is kept electronically and any paper-based material is usually shredded.

Whilst it may seem like something lifted out of *Mission Impossible* or a James Bond movie, such actions do have consequences for all concerned. Detections of actions that are deemed illegal result in heavy fines for the individuals involved (even prison terms too) and the company itself. Even where there is no criminality but the act is seen as unethical there are repercussions too. Employees may be dismissed, staff morale is affected, share prices fall, customers may boycott, and as a result the company faces a public relations battle to restore its reputation.

Consumerism

The idea of 'consumerism' will perhaps have a variety of meanings to different groups of people. On the one hand, it can be companies creating a demand for various products and services, often ones that are not essential to daily living. For others it may mean more in terms of consumer rights and protection, that the consumer requires goods and services that more closely match their needs and requirements. Within this is the right to have 'choice'. Some might say that the first is more akin to the 'production' orientation of the early to mid-20th century and that the second is more a 'societal' focus.

However, we can also link this back to Maslow's hierarchy of needs (see Chapter 2), where individuals seek greater levels of satisfaction. Griseri and Seppala (2010) refer to the work of the economist John Kenneth Galbraith, who raised concerns that marketing was creating artificial needs and that this would eventually be harmful to society. Hamilton and Denniss (2005) echo these points when they examined the increasing 'addiction' to 'over consumption', that individuals are always seeking more in terms of goods and services at the detriment of society itself.

However, with modern globalisation there has been a rise in consumerism, and this in itself has created a series of ethical issues. On the one hand, consumerism (whichever definition is followed) has led to economic growth, employment and prosperity for many – though not all. On the other hand, it could be argued, it has created demands for goods that are not essential to our everyday existence, and that it has created a 'rivalry' where we seek to have more and better things than our neighbours, even our families. That we have become a 'disposing' society, that is, we readily dispose of goods as soon as the new version is launched.

The smartphone that is working perfectly well today is disposed of tomorrow because a new version is in the stores. The 'new' version may only be a 'minor' upgrade, yet it becomes the new 'must have', the 'new fashion accessory' and at a price (this links to Roger's Diffusion Theory and 'innovators', see Chapter 2). The price is not only the investment in the new smartphone but what happens to the old one? Are the metals and components recycled? Is it refurbished and re-sold – thus having a new user whether in the UK or overseas? Or is it 'dumped' (illegal in many countries) in a landfill site where it doesn't biodegrade? Instead the various chemicals in the components leach into the soil. Some chemicals require significant concentration before they can do harm to flora and fauna, whilst others do not.

The question for consumers is really about whether or not we consider our own actions ethical or not within the context of the wider environment.

Controversial Messages

This in itself can pose a dilemma. Should companies that sell products and services become involved in controversial campaigns? During the 1990s, the Italian fashion house Benetton engaged in various advertising campaigns that didn't portray clothing but controversial subjects, such as a nun kissing a priest, a young man dying of an AIDS-related illness, refugees aboard an overcrowded ship trying to escape death and photos of US Death Row inmates (Salvemini, 2002). The company's strapline was 'United Colors of Benetton', with the underlying theme that we are all the same, we are all equal.

This type of 'shock' advertising drew attention and did, alongside the various messages, raise the profile of the company into an international brand. However, the 'Sentenced to Death' campaign, which portrayed images of inmates on Death Row at a prison in Missouri, resulted in complaints and a boycott against Benetton in the US (Salvemini, 2002). The images had reminded victim's families of what had happened, and the prison officials believed that there had been a breach of trust in gaining the images for the campaign. As Salvemimi (2002) states, the company regretted any suffering caused to the families of the victims portrayed and its intention was purely to focus on the issues of the death penalty.

The 'Death Row Campaign' would mark the end of Benetton's controversial approach to advertising. However, whilst we may consider some of the campaigns 'challenging', many did raise the issue of both gender and racial equality and the horrors of conflict.

Packaging

How much packaging is required for the products that we buy? Is the packaging either re-useable or recyclable? Could we use our own bags to reduce the use of plastic bags? These and other questions have been expressed over recent years. The growing concern is both the depletion of resources to produce the packaging and what to do with it afterwards. Technologies have assisted in developing enhanced packaging that require less materials and is biodegradable.

In Scotland all retailers charge for plastic carrier bags, whilst in other parts of the UK some retailers charge for plastic bags and others provide loyalty points for re-using bags (of any make or description).

However, it is not just about recycling but the litter that can be seen in both towns and the countryside where people dispose of packaging and the plastic bags without thought for the environmental consequences, including marine life.

One of the first places to impose a ban on plastic bags at retail outlets was Coles Bay, in Tasmania, which branded itself as *Australia's First Plastic Bag Free Town* (Freycinet Adventures, 2015). Introduced in April 2003, this area is home to a major nature reserve (Freycinet National Park), and the inhabitants sought to protect the town and reserve from plastic bags to reduce potential environmental damage (Freycinet Adventures, 2015). In the first 12 months of the ban retail outlets stopped the use of some

350,000 plastic bags (Freycinet Adventures, 2015). Recyclable paper bags are available in the local stores, and 100% unbleached cotton bags sold by Australia's Planet Ark Environmental Foundation can be purchased to carry shopping. Funds from the sale of the cotton bags go towards environmental work.

In November 2013 Tasmania introduced a state-wide ban on retailers providing plastic carrier bags to shoppers (Tasmanian Government, 2014). The aim is to reduce the number of lightweight plastic shopping bags and encourage the use of reusable bags (Tasmanian Government, 2014).

Producers, retailers and consumers alike share responsibility for the environment, thus finding ways of minimising the impact of packaging.

Privacy

A major challenge for companies and marketers alike is gaining the knowledge to better understand their customers. This is important in order to attain market share and remain viable and competitive, often within complex business environments. Yet, gaining such knowledge through legal and regulated data collection methods may pose ethical challenges. How much data should be collected? How should companies observe, especially on websites, the behaviour of individuals? Who are appropriate 'third-parties' to sell information on to? Or, in the age of social media, are we being too sensitive about our sensitive private data?

In the novel *1984*, the writer George Orwell explored a world that was both heavily regulated and invasive, where the state knew every move an individual made, every thought they possessed. Orwell was focusing on both the risks of tyrannical regimes and the possible future of humankind. Whilst many people in our world live with greater personal freedoms, companies hold increasing amounts of personal information. We accept the storage of our personal details, browsing and shopping habits to be entrusted to supercomputers located thousands of miles away. That information held in data warehouses can be categorised through data mining techniques to be the basis of communication between companies and their current and potential customers.

As Griseri and Seppala (2010) point out, every time we use a loyalty card, whether it is for a supermarket or another business, our very moves of what we buy, when we buy, how regularly we buy certain products and where we buy are tracked. Equally, credit card companies can build a picture of who we are and our patterns of spending and what we purchase. Clearly, there is the argument that such an approach assists credit card companies in tracking unusual activity and thus reducing fraud. It is a valid argument. Others might contend that it is too invasive of their privacy.

Even within legal constraints organisations, often without our knowledge, may share information with other organisations who then seek to market products or services to us. Even where there are 'opt-out' clauses and an individual accepts the sharing of information, they do not have details of the third-party vendors. It may not be until there is direct mail (via email, mobile phone text or post) that there is a possible realisation of the source. Moreover, the marketing information provided may not always be relevant to the individual receiving the message.

A UK citizen, normally protected by UK and EU privacy legislation, is not protected when accessing say a legitimate website based in the US. The website may be perfectly safe but it doesn't need to request permission to use tracking cookies, for instance. It could be argued that if it is a legal website then what is the harm in tracking the person browsing the website? Whilst it may make good business sense to track a visitor's online actions to better understand the level of effectiveness of the website, the user may feel that they are 'being watched'.

Griseri and Seppala (2010) refer to Amazon and how they seek to match recommendations with past purchases and what is held in the shopping basket. As they state, this can raise concerns in the minds of some shoppers (Griseri and Seppala, 2010). Whilst not always a successful match Amazon's aim is, through the use of technology, to make recommendations, very much in the same way as an in-store bookseller might make a recommendation if you bought a particular book. The bookseller may say, 'If you like this book by Author X, then you might like the work of Author Y', and this is very much a trait of traditional bookshops. However, this has been translated into the digital age. For some users this is an interesting, if at times slightly haphazard, approach and might steer them in the direction of another writer, composer and/or musician. However, some may view this as an invasion of their privacy as clearly their actions, their browsing, their purchases have been electronically tracked.

With the electronic storage of personal information comes increasing levels of risk. Companies may be diligent in building firewalls and security systems, however black-hat hackers seek to evade such defences to steal information. The evidence suggests that this is a constant battle between protection and attack (Risen, 2015). However, at risk is personal data and there have been numerous cases of firewall breaches and stolen passwords (Risen, 2015).

As stated earlier, with the link to social media, the concerns over privacy may be more a generational issue. Today, social media sites are often overflowing with personal information. Is it because younger people may feel more comfortable and share information, or is it a question of the risks not being fully comprehended?

Many companies more than comply with regulatory demands to protect information, and look upon it from a responsible and ethical standpoint. However, the question perhaps remains: do companies have access to too much private information? As the world becomes even more interconnected this question continues to be discussed.

Products

One of the issues that is often discussed in relation to ethics is 'intent'. Was the unethical behaviour intended? In other words, was there clear disregard for good behaviour? It could be argued that some salespeople who have employed aggressive sales tactics have taken this approach. Their concern is for their bonus rather than the well-being of their customers (see the section below on Sales Tactics).

Companies sometimes design or brand products without potentially considering the historic consequences. In 2014 the Spanish fashion retailer Zara launched a children's blue and white-striped pyjama outfit which depicted a six-pointed yellow sheriff star (with the word sheriff) on the front left-hand side (Cresci, 2014). However, when viewed in a catalogue it was difficult to see the word 'sheriff' so the yellow star had a greater prominence.

The featuring of this garment resulted in numerous complaints (Cresci, 2014). Probably for many, there is difficulty in understanding what could be possibly 'wrong' with this product – it's a young boy's pyjama outfit. However, the colours, the stripes and the yellow star (which could be interpreted as the Star of David) are reminiscent of the 'uniform' worn by Jewish prisoners in the Nazi concentration camps during the Second World War. The images from that period still resonate powerfully today.

The pyjamas were to be available in the UK and through outlets in Albania, Denmark, France, Israel and Sweden (Cresci, 2014). Following the social media comments, both Zara and the parent company, Inditex, apologised in several languages, via both social media and the mainstream press, stating:

> We honestly apologise, it was inspired by the sheriff's stars from the Classic Western films and is no longer in our stores. Nevertheless, we can understand the sensitive context and connotation that was created. We sincerely apologise if, as a result, we have offended the feelings of our customers.
>
> (Cresci, 2014; Waterfield, 2014)

Clearly in this case no harm was intended and the company reacted swiftly to both apologise and remove the garment from the stores and online. However, it does demonstrate the often-fine line along which companies operate and where they can inadvertently make an innocent error of judgement.

Pricing

As the American Marketing Association (AMA) Code of Practice (see later in this chapter) indicates, there are various pricing practices that are deemed unethical.

Price Fixing: This is normally where two or more companies agree that they will not sell their product below a certain price; in most cases the price will be virtually the same. When companies come together and agree to fix prices, this is known as a cartel. In the US and the European Union this is an illegal act as it removes the freedom of consumer choice. Equally, it can be judged unethical for the same reason, especially where the companies may advertise that the customer has choice, but they have knowingly restricted that choice.

Predatory Pricing: In many countries this is judged to be anti-competitive and thus illegal. With predatory pricing a company seeks to significantly reduce product prices so that rival companies cannot compete. The objective is to force out the competitors from the market, and when this is achieved the company raises its prices. This action seeks to create a monopolistic position where they are the only provider within the market and the customer has no choice but to purchase from them. With the competitors exiting from the market the monopoly can significantly raise prices. Countries judge this an anti-competitive move due to the fact that the customer has lost the opportunity of choice within a marketplace.

Price Gouging: This is based upon the economic principle of supply and demand. If supply of a product falls, yet demand increases then the price rises. Whilst it is a perfectly legitimate economic theory, the challenge occurs when retailers, for instance, take advantage of a particular situation. Now, within a capitalist economy the market (people) decide upon what they are prepared to pay for a product or service. However, when desperate people will tend to pay more and this is where they can be exploited.

Consider the following example. It is London, England, the weather has been fine for weeks, then suddenly there is a heavy prolonged downpour of rain just as people are leaving their offices. The workers have a choice – buy an umbrella or get soaked. The local shop sells ordinary black umbrellas (nothing fancy, nothing special). Yesterday they retailed for £2.50 (with a fair margin), now they are £8.00. The shop owner is taking advantage of the situation. Now some may say that this is good practice as the action might reap greater profits. However, are they being fair to their customers who, indeed, may remember this price increase and decide later to shop elsewhere?

'Bait-and-switch': This can also be described as a deceptive selling tactic. This is where a product is advertised, perhaps on a store window, at a particularly low price. The potential customer enters the store to look at the product, however, the salesperson states that (1) the product is now out of stock or (2) it is not very good anyway. The salesperson then states that there is another product which is much better quality but at a higher price.

The original product at the lower price may or may not have actually existed. In this case, the aim of the store is to sell the higher-priced product through deception. Where there is intention to deceive the behaviour is unethical and, in some places, probably also illegal. However, not all 'trade ups' to a higher-priced product will be unethical as long as there has been a transparent conversation with the customer and there is no false advertising to entice the customer into the store.

Promotions

In many countries marketing to children is governed by regulations, however, there remains debate as to the intensity of promotions. Prior to the Internet and mobile phones, advertising to children was directed via television and magazines (comics and 'how to' publications). According to the Yale Rudd Center (2013), in 2012 US pre-school children saw 2.8 fast food advertisements every day, whilst children aged 6–11 saw 3.2 and teenagers 4.8 advertisements.

Some countries have strict laws in terms of advertising to children. Countries such as Norway and Sweden ban advertising to children under the age of 12 (Watson, 2014). However, in the US, where the advertising industry is self-regulated, there are few legal restrictions (Watson, 2014).

According to Ramrayka (2014), in 2012 some $4.6 billion was invested by US fast-food chains in advertising to children and teenagers. According to various statistical compilations the average US child sees 16,000 30-second TV commercials annually (Statistics Brain Research Institute, 2013; Watson, 2014).

Both organisations and regulators take various points of view, as there are different sides of the argument.

Susan Linn, director for the Campaign for a Commercial Free Childhood (CCFC), stated in 2014 that:

> There's no moral, ethical, or social justification for marketing any product to children. … Advertising, in and of itself, is harmful to children. … Marketing targets emotions, not intellect. It trains children to choose products not for the actual value of the product, but because of celebrity or what's on the package. It undermines critical thinking and promotes impulse buying.
>
> (Watson, 2014)

Perhaps the question is whether or not there is a correlation between seeing an advertisement and taking action. As we examined in Chapter 9, the aim is to initiate such action as a response to needs and desires.

Ramrayka (2014) suggests that between 2010 and 2013 the number of children's meals in US fast-food outlets increased by 54%. Of course, many factors may have influenced this increase as it is unlikely that it is all a response to children seeing relevant advertisements. Judgements are also made by parents and guardians in terms of what they provide at meal times and how they advise and support the children within their care. Equally, they also provide potential role-model values.

Responsibility of the Consumer

The hotelier César Ritz (1850–1918) once stated *le client n'a jamais tort* – the 'customer is never wrong' (Nevill and Jerningham, 1908). This phrase often appears 'translated' as the 'customer is always right'.

Ritz devised a code for staff that remains in use today and that includes the line: *'If a diner complains about a dish or the wine, immediately remove it and replace it, no questions asked'* (Hotchner, 2012).

Ritz and Harry Selfridge (the founder of Selfridges, the luxury department store in London) championed the rights of the customer – actions that led to the creation of two internationally renowned and highly successful brands.

Both business and individual consumers have a responsibility in terms of ethical behaviour. Whilst the comments and actions of both Ritz and Selfridge clearly have customer service merits, it does not always mean that the customer is 'right'.

As indicated elsewhere is this chapter, UK grocery shoppers have for several years demanded lower and lower food prices. Retailers have reacted through price competition, yet how low can food prices fall? How much of the actual price is returned to those who actually produce the raw materials that comprise a large proportion of our food products, for instance, wheat, milk, cocoa and so on? One of the reasons for the introduction of Fair Trade goods was so that the growers and producers received a fair price for their labour. Whilst it is understandable for those on low incomes or who are particularly price sensitive (see Chapter 6), there are many societies that are affluent and probably can support fairer prices for goods and services.

Sorell (1994) examined the role of the customer in business ethics, and concluded that there are cases where the customer has been deemed to act unethically. He poses an example of a builder who markets their services. The builder is then asked to provide quotes and plans by a customer. The builder invests time and perhaps other resources to provide this set of plans. The customer then has the opportunity to either reject the costings/plan or discuss the options that are available. This might mean some revisions of the plans – but there is the possibility that the building work will go ahead. However, as Sorell (1994) points out, some customers may take the plans to other builders to seek a lower price, so the first builder has been disadvantaged.

Customers behave unethically if they, in turn, require an organisation to behave unethically within its own operations.

We can look at this from the point of view of a university that markets a range of programmes being offered during the next academic year. It successfully recruits students on to a one-year postgraduate programme for which they are paying £10,000 in fees plus living expenses. The university sets out the programme and what is expected of the students in order to meet the exacting standards required. In this case students are 'consumers of education', and they have rights in terms of being provided with a suitable standard of education. However, payment of fees does not automatically result in the awarding of a degree certificate; the student has to demonstrate the requisite level of knowledge, understanding and skill sets through the successful completion of the mandatory assessments.

In Chapter 7 we discussed the value of people (one of the 7Ps) and how delivering high-quality customer service adds value and can contribute to competitive advantages. There is a 'flipside' to this point, and that is the behaviour of customers towards an organisation's employees. A customer may have a legitimate complaint or concern and needs to express it. How we express that complaint or concern can be either ethical or unethical. The recipient of the complaint may just be simply that – the recipient taking the details. Yet frustration and anger on the part of the customer can exacerbate the situation rather than support a resolution. In this case it is about fairness to the person who is trying to assist the customer.

Sales Tactics

As indicated under Pricing above ('bait and switch'), various sales tactics can be deployed that many people would regard as unethical. Among these is high-pressure selling. This can occur when salespeople have 'aggressive' targets to meet to either stay in their jobs or to meet bonus expectations. The combination of 'job' and 'money' can lead some salespeople to betray the trust that many customers place in them. In such cases salespeople, in order to meet 'aggressive' targets, become themselves 'aggressive' using pressure or hard-selling approaches to their selling. There have been cases where the vulnerable have been targeted for such practices (Which? 2015).

Over the years various timeshare companies, in the US and UK, have been criticised for their approach to the selling of vacation properties. People are often invited to presentations that may include a free meal or gift. After the presentations there are meetings with the sales representations who use various techniques and tactics to persuade the customer to sign up for the rental property (Elliot, 2013). These approaches can be intense if the customer has had no previous experience of such high-pressure selling. Equally, as Elliot (2013) intimates, there may have been cases of misrepresentation of the cancellation period. This is the period by which the customer has the right to change their mind and cancel the agreement on various transactions; in many countries, such as the UK, this is a statutory right. However, the time period may vary from days to weeks.

There is the adage of *caveat emptor* ('let the buyer beware') to signify caution, however, it can be relatively easy for some people to be enticed into a false sense of security through sophisticated selling approaches. Thus there is an ethical responsibility on the part of the salesperson.

[However, is the salesperson totally to 'blame' for their behaviour? Should the marketing/sales department take some responsibility? Should the senior managers who created the 'aggressive sales environment' take some responsibility? Should the shareholders who benefit from this mode of selling also take some responsibility?]

Special Offers

Some food retailers have been criticised for various sales promotional tactics, specifically 'Buy One Get One Free', commonly called a BOGOF (BBC, 2014e). Indeed, there have been cases where supermarkets have advertised 'buy one get two free'. In principle it could be argued that this is a tactic to persuade customers to spend more, yet they are gaining value for money. However, the concerns raised are more associated with fresh food items which have a short shelf life, in other words, they need to be consumed by a certain date. Research suggests that a significant percentage of food purchased through such special offers is wasted (BBC, 2014e).

According to Recycling Now (2014):

1. Approximately 7 million tonnes of food is disposed of by UK households each year, much of which could have been consumed. However, a report by the House of Lords European Union Committee suggested that the real total could be as much as 15 million tonnes per year (House of Lords, 2014).

2. Over 12 months the average family will dispose of food costing £700.00.

3. A significant percentage of food is placed in landfill sites where it decomposes – but releases methane gas (a greenhouse gas) which can impact the environment. Wasting food also has other costs in terms of energy consumption – production, packaging and distribution.

As stated at the beginning of this chapter, there are 'grey areas'. In this particular case there are several possible issues to consider:

1. It could be argued that the supermarkets are taking a fair opportunity to promote goods which may have otherwise been left on the shelves with lapsed use-by dates. As a result this food may have become a waste product in either landfill sites or as recycled animal feed. In the latter case it can be of benefit to the farming community.

2. The onus is on the consumer to make a judgement call in terms of whether the food that they buy will be eaten by the 'use-by' date or become waste. Equally, it could be argued that if the food is not consumed by the due date, then the consumer makes it available for recycling (in several countries there are recycling facilities and collections of food waste from homes). However, the point raised above regarding greenhouses gases should also be taken into consideration.

3. That it is the responsibility of the supermarkets to take all necessary actions to prevent food wastage, and that includes how they decide upon promoting offers to consumers.

Stereotyping

This is where a company, perhaps through its advertising, will stereotype a particular group of people. We can look back at advertising from the 1950s and see the stereotyping of women as being the 'lady that stays at home and does the cleaning, washing, the bringing up of children and has dinner on the table ready for when her husband returns home'. Women were generally portrayed as those that remain the housekeeper. Moreover, if they did have a job before marrying, it was usually that of a secretary as that was the direction that most girls were channelled at school and college. Equally, it could be argued, that men were stereotyped in advertising as the 'breadwinner' who didn't engage in grocery shopping and cleaning. In these various cases, the situation today in many, though not all countries, is different.

Today household chores are often shared, and some men stay at home to raise the children whilst their highly skilled partners build careers. That is not to say that stereotyping has disappeared – it can still be seen in advertising, although perhaps more subtly than in the blatant 1950s.

CODES OF PRACTICE

In a broad marketing context there are many different types of codes of practice:

Client Company: The vast majority of SMEs and multinationals will have their own codes of conduct and practice. Increasingly these not only cover internal operations but also the relationships with suppliers, distributors and customers.

Marketing Companies: We are using this as a broad term to include marketing consultants, advertising agencies, sales agents and public relations companies. Each will have their own codes of practice, which may or may not integrate well with their client's ethical approaches.

Membership and Trade Associations: These too, whether covering marketing, public relations and so on, will also have their own codes by which members should abide (see AMA case study).

However, devising and circulating a document called a Code of Practice, Code of Conduct or Code of Ethics is only one part. This is the intent, but these codes have to be enacted in practice, and that is often the challenging aspect. Even companies that, as suggested above, have to operate by observing various codes may not always meet the required standards of behaviour. This may be for a variety of reasons from purposeful disregard through to a genuine misunderstanding.

As we have seen above, there are real concerns expressed by various groups regarding the level of marketing to children and various codes (see the AMA Code of Ethics, as an example) caution on the approach taken when marketing to children.

CASE STUDY: AMERICAN MARKETING ASSOCIATION

The American Marketing Association is (as of 2014) the world's largest professional organisation for marketers. The following pages reproduce their Code of Conduct (AMA, 2014b).

Ethical Norms and Values for Marketers

Preamble

The American Marketing Association commits itself to promoting the highest standard of professional ethical norms and values for its members (practitioners, academics and students). Norms are established standards of conduct that are expected and maintained by society and/or professional organizations. Values represent the collective conception of what communities find desirable, important and morally proper. Values also serve as the criteria for evaluating our own personal actions and the actions of others.

As marketers, we recognize that we not only serve our organizations but also act as stewards of society in creating, facilitating and executing the transactions that are part of the greater economy. In this role, marketers are expected to embrace the highest professional ethical norms and the ethical values implied by our responsibility toward multiple stakeholders (e.g., customers, employees, investors, peers, channel members, regulators and the host community).

Ethical Norms

As Marketers, we must:

1. **Do no harm.** This means consciously avoiding harmful actions or omissions by embodying high ethical standards and adhering to all applicable laws and regulations in the choices we make.

2. **Foster trust in the marketing system.** This means striving for good faith and fair dealing so as to contribute toward the efficacy of the exchange process as well as avoiding deception in product design, pricing, communication, and delivery or distribution.

3. **Embrace ethical values.** This means building relationships and enhancing consumer confidence in the integrity of marketing by affirming these core values: honesty, responsibility, fairness, respect, transparency and citizenship.

Ethical Values

Honesty – to be forthright in dealings with customers and stakeholders. To this end, we will:

- Strive to be truthful in all situations and at all times.
- Offer products of value that do what we claim in our communications.
- Stand behind our products if they fail to deliver their claimed benefits.
- Honor [*sic*] our explicit and implicit commitments and promises.

Responsibility – to accept the consequences of our marketing decisions and strategies. To this end, we will:

- Strive to serve the needs of customers.
- Avoid using coercion with all stakeholders.
- Acknowledge the social obligations to stakeholders that come with increased marketing and economic power.
- Recognize our special commitments to vulnerable market segments such as children, seniors, the economically impoverished, market illiterates and others who may be substantially disadvantaged.
- Consider environmental stewardship in our decision-making.

Fairness – to balance justly the needs of the buyer with the interests of the seller. To this end, we will:

- Represent products in a clear way in selling, advertising and other forms of communication; this includes the avoidance of false, misleading and deceptive promotion.
- Reject manipulations and sales tactics that harm customer trust.
- Refuse to engage in price fixing, predatory pricing, price gouging or 'bait-and-switch' tactics.
- Avoid knowing participation in conflicts of interest.

- Seek to protect the private information of customers, employees and partners.

Respect – to acknowledge the basic human dignity of all stakeholders. To this end, we will:

- Value individual differences and avoid stereotyping customers or depicting demographic groups (e.g., gender, race, sexual orientation) in a negative or dehumanizing way.
- Listen to the needs of customers and make all reasonable efforts to monitor and improve their satisfaction on an ongoing basis.
- Make every effort to understand and respectfully treat buyers, suppliers, intermediaries and distributors from all cultures.
- Acknowledge the contributions of others, such as consultants, employees and co-workers, to marketing endeavors [*sic*].
- Treat everyone, including our competitors, as we would wish to be treated.

Transparency – to create a spirit of openness in marketing operations. To this end, we will:

- Strive to communicate clearly with all constituencies.
- Accept constructive criticism from customers and other stakeholders.

©American Marketing Association 1 January 2013

APPROACHES TO RESOLVING AN ETHICAL DILEMMA

Figure 11.1 provides a schematic of the different ways we can approach an ethical dilemma. There is no one perfect approach and, to some extent, it depends upon our own moral compasses.

> Golden Rule: This is about individual behaviour. So it is a question of acting as you would want others to act towards you. So, within a marketing context, this could be how a salesperson acts towards a current

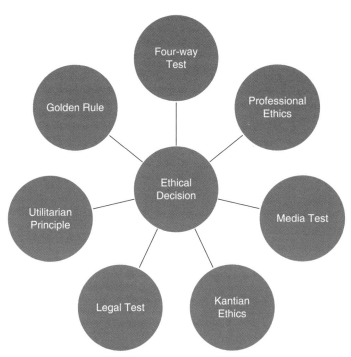

Figure 11.1 Approaches to ethical dilemmas

or potential customer. If the position was reversed and the customer was now the salesperson, how would the actual salesperson wish to be treated? Would they want honesty rather than an ethically dubious sales pitch?

Utilitarian Principle: This looks at ethics from the perspective of creating the greatest amount of good for the greatest number of people. Whilst some individuals may be disadvantaged the greater population may benefit. This still creates potential dilemmas in knowing that some people will receive less benefit as a result.

Legal Test: The test is whether or not the proposed action would be deemed legal. However, there are two points that need to be considered: (1) An action may be deemed legal, however is it ethical?

(2) Although there may be similarities, specific aspects of law vary from country to country. Therefore what would be considered legal in one country may not be in another.

Kantian Ethics: The philosopher Immanuel Kant (1724–1804) proposed universal ethical principles that underline the respect for the dignity and equality of people without claims to religion or a metaphysical concept of 'good'. Blackburn (2001) describes that as:

> When we try to stop people acting in some way, a good question is 'what if everyone did that?' ... If the answer is that something would go especially wrong if everybody did that, then we are supposed to feel badly about doing it. Perhaps, for instance, we would be claiming an exemption for ourselves that we couldn't allow other people in general.

Media Test: This is where a marketing director would ask themselves the following types of questions – 'Would I feel comfortable explaining my actions, my decisions to journalists?' 'Would I feel comfortable answering questions from journalists?' 'How would I feel if I was on television as a result of my decisions?'

Professional Ethics: We can consider this from two perspectives: (1) The views of peers within the same sector/industry/country. (2) Codes of Practice/Conduct either from a professional organisation, such as the American Marketing Association or (3) Codes of Conduct within the employing organisation.

Four-Way Test of the Things We Think, Say or Do: Herbert J. Taylor (1883–1978) was a former President of the International Rotary Club. In 1932 he wrote his 'Four-Way Test', and this was adopted, in 1943, by the International Rotary Club (Rotary, 2014).

Is it the Truth?

Is it fair to all concerned?

Will it build goodwill and better friendships?

Will it be beneficial to all concerned?

A GENERAL THOUGHT

Of course, we make decisions based upon the information that we have at a particular moment in time. As a result of additional/more accurate information what was considered ethical originally might be considered unethical later.

KEY POINTS

In this chapter we have considered the following:

1. The range of potential ethical issues or dilemmas that can impact upon both individuals and organisations. These include: gaining competitor information, consumerism, controversial messages, privacy, pricing tactics, sales and promotional tactics, and stereotyping.
2. That various organisations create codes of practice: membership and trade associations, marketing consultants, suppliers and client companies. Whilst many will be comparable with each other, some may display different approaches. This, in itself, can create a disharmony in terms of which one(s) to follow.
3. There are various approaches that can be taken to either prevent or mitigate ethical dilemmas.

QUESTIONS

Here is a series of questions and activities for you to undertake to aid your knowledge and understanding of the points made in this chapter.

1. Why do you think organisations such as the American Marketing Association have codes of ethical practice for their members? Do such codes work in practice?
2. Is the customer always right? Debate.
3. We have briefly examined some of the current ethical dilemmas or issues that both marketing teams and customers face. Research other

possible ethical dilemmas/issues in marketing. Why do you think they are ethical issues? What action do you think should be taken, and why? Discuss these points with your peers. Do they agree with you? Compare and contrast the different points of view. What are your conclusions?

4. To what extent do you think an individual's background informs their ethical behaviour within the context of marketing?

5. In Chapter 5 on Branding there is a question on the business case for tackling the counterfeiting/pirating of a brand. We now want you to examine that question from a different perspective, that of the consumer. What are the ethical issues for a customer who knowingly purchases a product that has been either counterfeited or pirated? You may want to consider the example of a tourist who buys a handbag which is marketed as genuine (but is clearly not) from a market stall in a tourist resort.

6. Refer back to Chapter 9 and consider the possible ethical implications of product placements within television programmes and movies in the context of customer perceptions.

7. Childhood obesity is a major problem in the US and increasingly so in other countries, such as the UK. Do governments have a moral responsibility to take action to reduce obesity? Or do companies that produce and/or market foods that may contribute to such obesity have an ethical responsibility to take action? Or should consumers accept their own moral responsibility for what they eat? Discuss.

FURTHER READING

Crane, A., Matten, D. and Spence, L.J. (Eds) (2014) *Corporate Social Responsibility: Readings and Cases in a Global Context* (2nd Edition). London: Routledge.

Griseri, P. and Groucutt, J. (1997) *In Search of Business Ethics. Financial Times Management Briefings*. London: FT Pitman Publishing.

Griseri, P. and Seppala, N. (2010) *Business Ethics and Corporate Social Responsibility*. Andover: South-Western Cengage Learning.

Owen, L., Lewis, C., Auty, S. and Buijzen, M. (2013) Is children's understanding of nontraditional advertising comparable to their understanding of television advertising? *Journal of Public Policy & Marketing*. Vol 32 No 2. pp. 195–206.

Raine, K.D., Lobstein, T., Landon, J., Kent, M.P., Pellerin, S., Caulfield, T. and Spence, J.C. (2013) Restricting marketing to children: Consensus on policy interventions to address obesity. *Journal of Public Health Policy*. Vol 34 No 2. pp. 239–253.

Sirgy, M.J., Grace, B.Y., Lee, D.J., Wei, S. and Huang, M.W. (2012). Does marketing activity contribute to a society's well-being? The role of economic efficiency. *Journal of Business Ethics*. Vol 107 No 2. pp. 91–102.

12

Marketing Planning and Strategy

OBJECTIVES

By the end of this chapter you should be able to:

- Explain the relationship between an organisation's overall strategy and the marketing function.
- Appreciate that in order to plan and implement a marketing strategy the organisation must possess the appropriate capabilities (resources and competences).
- Explain how frameworks such as SWOT/TOWS and Ansoff can assist organisations in the development of their marketing strategy.
- Explain the importance of a marketing audit and how it can assist in developing a marketing plan.

INTRODUCTION

This chapter aims to highlight the role of a marketing strategy (planning and the allocation of resources) in supporting the overall strategy of an organisation.

THE DIFFERENT LAYERS OF STRATEGY

It is important to have a basic understanding of organisational structures. Organisations can comprise many strategic business units (SBUs). The multinational company GE is an excellent example of this structure. The company's businesses broadly cover aviation, finance, energy, healthcare, oil and gas, mining and transportation. Figure 12.1 provides a structure that illustrates that an organisation can comprise three strategic levels – Corporate, SBU and Functional. Figure 12.2 relates that in a marketing context. Each of the SBUs (just as in the brief GE example above) illustrates different market segments.

Corporate Level

In our diagram this is the top of the organisation. Strategists often call this the Corporate Parent, with the SBUs as the 'children'. The Board at the corporate level will create the overall strategic goals of the organisation; this may even include the restructuring or divestment (selling) of SBUs.

SBUs

These can range in size from small companies to very large firms. Again, parent companies such as GE, Procter & Gamble (P&G) and Unilever control large-scale SBUs.

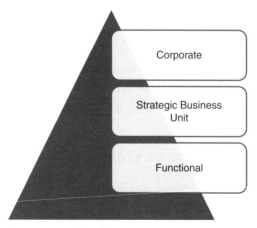

Figure 12.1 Different strategic levels

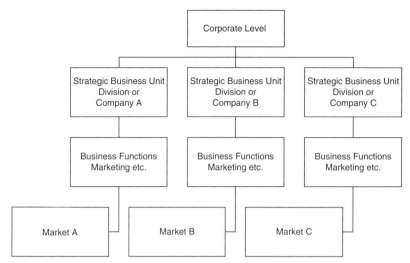

Figure 12.2 Organisational strategic levels related to the marketing function

Functional Level

This is also known as the operational level of the business. The functional level normally includes marketing, human resource management, warehousing and production.

An SBU, whether large or small, will normally have responsibility for its marketing budget. However, their marketing strategy must have some alignment to the overall corporate goals of the organisation and thus might be reflected within the corporate mission statement.

UNDERSTANDING THE INDUSTRY

Companies, unless a monopoly, do not operate in isolation, especially within a trans-national context. Therefore there is a need to understand how the industry or sector operates. Porter (1980) devised a Five Forces model to better understand how companies operate within a sector or industry context and the level of attractiveness of that sector/industry.

These Five Forces comprise Threat of New Entrants, Power of Suppliers, Power of Buyers, Substitutes and Competitive Rivalry.

As we operate within a globalised world, we often need to consider an industry within a wider context beyond purely our home sector. So, for instance, we can consider the shipbuilding industry within the UK. That will provide us with a set of parameters to work to and will reveal who is engaged within that specific market. However, in reality that is too narrow as the shipbuilding industry is global and thus the market is global. Cruise ships, for instance, are built and refitted in China, France, Germany, Italy and Sweden. The materials and components to build them come from many more countries, and equally those who order them from others, such as America and the UK. Therefore we have to consider sectors, industries and, indeed, markets from a local, regional and international dimension.

The following is a brief overview of Porter's framework.

Threat of New Entrants

This can also be considered as examining the Barriers to Entry; in other words, how easy is it to enter the sector or industry? If the barriers are low, then it is relatively easy to enter the sector with limited capital and capabilities (resources and competences). This, however, can create a situation of too many companies operating within the same marketplaces, creating saturation within the market. The result could be that prices are significantly reduced as companies compete for market share. This may well impact upon revenue streams and profitability. In some cases companies may struggle to break even and survive.

If the barriers to entry are high, then a greater level capital investment, differentiation and capabilities are required. Some of the required capabilities may be very specialist, for instance, high-tech research and development facilities.

Equally, the current competitors may individually retaliate (through marketing actions) against the new entrant.

Power of Suppliers

As we have indicated elsewhere in this book, suppliers can have different or relative levels of power. Unless they are operating within a niche market, a company supplying own-label products, for instance, to a major supermarket chain will normally have low levels of power. The supermarket (the buyer) has the greater level of power. However, a major brand will have more power as it has created a strong market presence (perhaps through marketing communications) and is demanded by customers.

Equally, suppliers may be powerful where there are few of them and they have specialist capabilities (resources and competences). Thus the industry becomes dependent upon these suppliers producing specialist products.

We also have to consider the length of the supply chain, from the raw materials through to the finished product. Throughout this 'chain' there may be some powerful suppliers and others less so. (See Chapter 8.)

Power of Buyers

As above, this will also depend upon the construction of the supply chain and the level of power of suppliers.

The power of the buyer could be high when there is a significant number of suppliers producing relatively similar (homogenous) goods. Additional supporting factors could be:

• Price competition.
• If there are low levels of emotional involvement, then switching costs may be low.

For instance, let's consider tins of ordinary sliced or plum tomatoes within UK supermarkets and discounters. There are many different varieties on offer, many at competing prices even within a single supermarket. Then consider a town where there may be various supermarkets within easy walking distance of each other. The buyer, especially if they are price sensitive and not particularly loyal to any specific brand of supermarket or tinned tomatoes, will seek out the lowest priced on offer.

Equally, where the product is scarce, is highly differentiated and/or important to the buyer, then the buyer's power will be relatively low. There will be limited choice and the power of the brand will be high. In a B2C context we can consider very specialist food products such as Sturgeon caviar. This fish product originates from Russia and Iran, and is a high-priced delicacy due to a mixture of its heritage and physical scarcity.

Within a B2B context a company may require specialist components to complete a project. For instance, consider the range and scale of components and products that goes into building a modern cruise ship. Whilst some of those components may be available from several different suppliers others may be scarce due to the specialist capabilities required to design and build them.

Substitutes

Here we can consider substitutes from two different angles: Direct and Indirect.

Direct: These are substitutes for a particular product or service. Equally, there may be situations where there are either none or very few substitutes available to meet the customer's needs. In Chapter 1 we considered an aspect of direct competition, and used an example of a couple travelling from London to Inverness in the Scottish Highlands. Let's assume that we are examining the UK's airline sector and the level of competitive rivalry. In this context let's also assume that there are two airlines that fly direct from London to Inverness. One flies from London Luton and the other from London City Airport. Equally, let's assume that there are three flights per day in each direction and the fares are comparable. Customers may decide on one rather than another based upon reputation, experiences, location of the London airports and departure/arrival times. Let's also assume that competition within the UK's airline business is intense as airlines seek greater share of the market and increased profitability. However, the couple can make substitute choices and opt for other means of travelling to Scotland.

We have reproduced the example from Chapter 1 here but without the two airline examples.

The couple want to travel from London to a hotel in the Highlands of Scotland for a vacation; this is an approximate distance of 900 km. Their options beyond the two airlines could include:

1. Driving in their own car from London to the hotel in the Highlands.
2. Being chauffeur-driven from London to the hotel in the Highlands.
3. Taking a daytime train from London's King's Cross Station to Inverness station and then hire a car to their hotel. They could also hire a taxi.

4. Taking an overnight sleeper train from London's Euston station, arriving early morning in Inverness. As in the previous example, they could hire a car or a taxi for the drive to the hotel.

5. Taking a coach from London's Victoria Coach to Inverness and then either hiring a car or taxi.

The couple will make their decision based upon certain factors. These will include price, flexibility, the level of comfort required, how easy the journey is, whether (if driving) they want to stop somewhere overnight and time commitments.

Indirect: In the example above we used the different modes of transport associated with a short vacation. If we consider the vacation as a whole, in addition to the travel expenses, there will be the cost of transport from the airport, for instance, to the hotel, the cost of the room in the hotel, dining, sightseeing and so on.

Thus there is an overall cost associated with the short vacation in the Scottish Islands. Clearly, the Scottish Tourist Board (Visit Scotland), the hotel and airline, among others, want people to visit the Highlands. However, an individual or family can spend their disposable income in many other ways. For instance, the money could be allocated to DIY activities around the home, especially if the local DIY stores are competing with each other on price and value added. In this particular example, the DIY at home becomes an indirect substitute (although a different industry) for the short vacation in the Scottish Highlands.

The challenge for the modes of transport (especially the airlines in this example), tourist board and the DIY stores is to persuade people, individuals and families that their offer is better than the others. Where consumers have options various factors may influence their choices, including price and the value added derived from the various features and benefits.

Competitive Rivalry

This is where companies within the specific sector/industry compete for relative market share. Where there is a high level of competition and products are very similar (homogenous) there may be excess capacity (too much product available) and price competition. Often the advantage of innovation is short-lived as competitors seek ways of imitating the product (without breaching trademarks and copyrights).

Equally, where there are few companies providing similar products there may be a greater level of differentiation with greater brand recognition. In such cases there may be a shortage of capacity, and that might influence new entrants into the marketplace.

Where the opportunity exists for new entrants into the sector/industry, the current companies may seek retaliatory action. It is important to note that collective retaliatory action would be deemed the actions of a cartel, and such actions are illegal under most jurisdictions. However, companies acting individually may take some form of action to maintain their market share within the sector. Such competitive actions could include price reductions, special offers and/or increased investment in marketing communications.

A market, sector and/or industry may look very attractive on paper. However, the potential new entrants must always seek to understand the different levels of risk involved in such a venture. A 'good idea' created in the Board room may not always translate successfully into a business reality.

Other Factors

The Five Forces framework was created in the 1980s. Although it remains relevant it is worthwhile considering other factors that could be linked to this framework.

• Complementors: This is where there is a link between two or more products even though they are produced by different (perhaps even competitor) companies. For example, you take a photograph on your smartphone. You can download this (via a USB connection) to your laptop. You can attach it to an email and send it to family and friends in another country. Equally, you may wish to have a physical copy of the photograph that you want to frame. You load your colour printer with photographic paper (readily available from many different types of retailers) and download the image from the laptop to the printer.

Within a short while the photograph is reproduced in the appropriate colours on the paper at the size you wanted.

When you examine this process closely several very different companies have been involved. Basically, the producers and marketers of the photographic paper, the printer and the software that drives the printing complement the actions of the manufacturer of the smartphone. Being able to print high-quality images on photographic paper is a value-added benefit of the colour printer. For many, the main purpose of the printer may be simply printing documents, even formal letters, however, the complementary benefits of printing photographs are provided.

- Co-operation: In addition to competing many companies are engaged in co-operative ventures. For instance, Companies A and B might compete in several markets but co-operate in others as this provides a mutual benefit. An example of this is Bluetooth, where various major companies have worked together, sharing knowledge, so that numerous electronic devices can communicate with each other irrespective of the brand and platforms.

- Macro Environment and Globalisation: As indicated in Chapter 1, the macro environment should not only be viewed within the narrow context of the home industry/market. As companies expand transnationally they will often encounter different industry dynamics in addition to changing macro factors. These can present new challenges, complexities and possible risks.

CAPABILITIES

Having an 'idea' is only one element in building a business. In order to develop, produce and market new products and services, organisations need to have the appropriate capabilities (resources and competences). Table 12.1 illustrates the two types of capabilities and the elements that comprise them.

Threshold Capabilities are those basic or essential capabilities required to allow the company to operate within the marketplace. For instance, if a company wanted to enter the UK supermarket business what would they need in terms of the absolute basic capabilities to enter that marketplace?

Table 12.1 Types of capabilities

Types of capability	Resources	Competences
Threshold capabilities	Threshold resources – Tangible and intangible	Threshold competences
Capabilities for competitive advantage	Distinctive (unique) resources – Tangible and intangible	Distinctive or core competences

The requirement for Threshold Capabilities will change over time as sectors/industries and market demands change. Using our mini example above, the Threshold Capabilities required to enter the UK supermarket business today are very different to those required 10 or 20 years ago. Equally, what will be required in the future could also be very different. The requirements will change over time dependent upon the macro factors, customer demands, competitors and the type of new entrants.

Moreover, we should not just focus on the home market. If a company seeks to enter a trans-national market the Threshold Capabilities required there may be very different from the home market. [There is a link here to Porter's Five Forces model and New Entrants.]

Capabilities for Competitive Advantage combine distinctive (unique) resources with distinctive or core competences. The resources are those that competitors cannot easily obtain or imitate. The distinctive competence is the ability to utilise the resources in such a way as to produce a product or service that is far superior to the competitors. Equally, it must be difficult for the competitor to obtain or imitate that ability.

Resources

There are two main types of resources – Tangible and Intangible.

- Tangible: These can be described as physical assets of an organisation. These could include facilities, plant (equipment), human resources and finance.

- Intangible: These are described as non-physical assets of an organisation. These could include reputation and intellectual capital (patents, brands, systems or processes, knowledge and skills).

Tangible and Intangible resources should not be considered as totally separate areas. There can be clear linkage between the two, for instance, between human resources, knowledge/skills and reputation, and equally between facilities and reputation. There can be various permutations.

As indicated elsewhere in this chapter, a company's management might have a 'bright idea' for a product and how to market that product. However, does the organisation have the resources and competences to take that 'bright idea' and turn it into a reality?

PRODUCT LIFE CYCLE

As with human life a product or a brand has a life cycle, which in some cases are short and in others quite long. This is often represented as a graph; here we show a stereotypical graph with explanatory notes (Figure 12.3).

Figure 12.3 illustrates a generalised product life cycle. As we saw in Chapter 5, some corporate brands have had a market presence for a significant period of time. Many highlighted within that chapter will probably continue, in one form or another, for a considerable period of time in the future. Equally some of their products will display longevity whilst others will not. The following provides a 'snapshot' of a stereotypical product life cycle, however, it will provide you with an understanding of some of the decisions and actions that could be implemented.

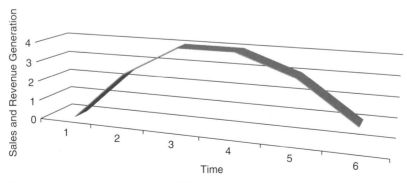

Figure 12.3 A generalised product life cycle

Introduction (1)

This is the point where the product is introduced to the market. The length of this phase will depend upon the type of product, pricing, overall market demand and level of competition. Depending upon the type of product there may have been significant research and development costs. The company will seek to gain, where possible, a return on the R&D investment within a relatively short time frame. To achieve this they may engage in a significant spend on marketing communications. Depending upon demand, the company may be able to gain an increased share of the market. This may be the case in high-tech markets where Innovators and Early Adopters (see Chapter 2) are particularly important.

Growth (2–3)

This is the growth phase. There may be competition within the marketplace – yet demand is strong. The length of the overall growth phase will depend upon the type of product, pricing and market demand. The company will continue to market the product through the use of marketing communications tactics. Equally, the company should be gaining returns on their investment. During this phase the product should be a profitable venture for the company.

Maturity (4)

This is where there is reduced level of growth leading to no growth and a steady state. There may be more competitors within the marketplace offering enhanced features and benefits that cannot be matched by this particular product. Equally, the product may be entering obsolescence as a result of changing technologies. The company may continue to invest in marketing communications but at a much reduced rate than previously. The aim here is to maintain its market share even though there is no growth. The product will still be generating revenue and profit.

Decline (5)

There is declining demand for the product. This may be due to a combination of market forces including new competitors within the market offering better products and aftersales support. Overall the competition may be too fierce to compete.

Some products can be 're-energised', perhaps through add-ons or new ingredients in a food-related product. Such action may also provide the opportunity to enter new markets.

Equally, a decline in one market could provide the impetus (if not already taken) to seek out new markets in new territories. A product may be in decline in one market but have significant growth potential in another, indeed even becoming the market leader.

Death (6)

The company decides to end sales of the product. This can mean (1) Ending production, which could result in the closure of manufacturing plants, if there are no alternative uses possible for those plants. For example, if the company is a confectionery manufacturer, then the production facilities could be used to manufacture another confectionery product. There may be some costs incurred in adapting the plant, however these costs can be recouped from the sales of the new product. However, if the company seeks to close the plant (with associated redundancies) there will be costs incurred. (2) Divestment: selling the product and the manufacturing facilities to another company. The buyer may be able to rejuvenate the product and/or use the production facilities to manufacture other products.

ANSOFF'S GROWTH MATRIX

Strategist Igor Ansoff developed a simple framework to illustrate possible strategic directions (Table 12.2).

Consolidation – Market Penetration: This is where the company either seeks to hold its position within the market with the product on offer or to build increased market share. The organisation can seek to increase usage from current customers and/or gain new customers within their current market. The organisation may deploy a range of tactics including price competition, special promotional offers (such as buy one get one

Table 12.2 Ansoff's growth matrix

	Present product/services	New product/services
Present markets	Consolidation – Market penetration	Product/Service development
New markets	Market development	Diversification

Source: Based on Ansoff, 1973

free). Equally, the organisation can seek to expand the range of uses for their product, for instance, encouraging adults to use baby shampoo, baby oil and talcum powder for themselves. Another example could be advertisers suggesting that a breakfast cereal can be eaten at any time of the day or night – not just for breakfast.

Product/Service Development: This is where the company launches a new product or service within their current market. An example would be a detergent manufacturer launching a new range of fabric stain removers to work alongside their bio and non-bio detergents, thus aiming at the current users of their detergents.

Market Development: Where the company seeks new regional and trans-national markets for current products or services.

Diversification: This is where the company moves out of its current product/service offers and markets into new spheres of activity. There are different levels of business risks involved in diversification. A company can reduce the risk by entering into related areas, where the product/service/market has some relationship to the products/service/markets that already exist within the company's portfolio.

- Forward Integration: A company may adopt a forward integration approach which links to their outputs, for instance, the transport and distribution of their own products rather than outsourcing to other companies.

- Backward Integration: In a backward integration approach, the company develops links to inputs. For example, a company producing tinned vegetables may acquire/develop farms and thus grow many of the vegetables themselves rather than buying them from other farms. In such a case the company can market the produce as fresh from their own farms to their own canning factory.

- Horizontal Integration: This is where a company seeks additional activities that are directly related to their existing activities, either from a competitive or complementary perspective. For instance, car companies acquiring other car companies that have strong market share in markets that they do not. So a Chinese car manufacturer may acquire a European car manufacturer in order to develop their presence within Europe.

A higher-risk approach is for a company to enter unrelated markets. In unrelated diversification the company expands into businesses and markets in which it traditionally has no experience. This may be a number of reasons, including:

- The products and/or services which it has traditionally offered are in decline. As the products/service/markets are no longer viable, the company must seek alternatives in order to survive. Thus seeking out an alternative business operation.
- The markets in which the company operate are saturated and there may be little or no opportunity for market development elsewhere.
- The product may no longer be legally viable and thus banned by the home government. The ban may not currently exist in other countries and thus production would have to be moved to another country. This may not be a financially viable option, thus the company may seek diversification in order to remain in business.

SWOT

Figure 12.4 is the schematic that is often used to illustrate the Strengths, Weaknesses, Opportunities and Threats (SWOT) that have both organisational and industry significance.

Internal Factors

These are factors that are specifically internal to the organisation. The organisation's management must undertake a SWOT with clear objectivity. It is often easier to inflate a company's strengths and dismiss the

Figure 12.4 SWOT schematic

weaknesses. However, this is more likely to lead to failure within the marketplace.

- Strengths: These are the strengths that drive the organisation forward. These could include: specific capabilities, highly efficient economies of scale, effective financial management – good revenue generation and cash flow management.

- Weaknesses: These are the specific problems or issues that reduce the potential effectiveness (and success) of the organisation. These could include indecisive management – lack of focus, poor inventory control leading to high inventory levels – thus high warehousing costs or poorly trained sales staff equating to poor revenue generation within store. In our experience many students discuss the end results of a company's weaknesses when they need to focus on the root causes of the weaknesses.

External Factors

These are factors that are external to the organisation and ones where the organisation will have little or no control over. A good starting point for examining possible sector/industry-based are the macro factors (see Chapter 1).

- Opportunities: These are the opportunities that exist (or may soon exist) within the marketplace (local, national, regional and/or trans-nationally).

For instance, changing legislation can open up markets. An example is the deregulation of air travel in Europe, America, India and the Far East. This has provided the opportunity for new entrants into a marketplace that was dominated by national carriers (often called legacy airlines). This external opportunity provided the incentive for the creation of the many low-cost airlines that we see today, including Southwest (USA), easyJet (UK), AirAsia (Malaysia) and SpiceJet (India).

- Threats: These are the threats that exist (or may soon exist) within the marketplace (local, national, regional and/or trans-nationally). For example, increased regulation within the sector/industry; changing consumer tastes (the healthy eating lobby); economic cycles – the onslaught of a recession/depression risks an increase in unemployment levels and thus reduces disposable incomes. Changing physical environments may be a threat, for instance, a severe drought in one region of the world could result in the shortage of a particular crop, thus increasing costs and prices for products made from that crop.

A SWOT provides an organisation with a 'snapshot' of where it is in relation to both internal and external factors. However, it will need to undertake further analysis to understand the relationship between these various factors; this is where TOWS (Figure 12.5) is useful (Weihrich, 1982).

SO Options: This focuses on the relationship between the internal factor – Strengths – and the external – Opportunities. The question for the organisation is: Does it have the internal strengths (for example, capabilities) to take advantage of the opportunities that are now being presented within the marketplace?

WO Options: This focuses on the relationship between the internal factor – Weaknesses – and the external – Opportunities. In this particular situation what internal weaknesses are reducing/preventing the organisation from taking advantage of the opportunities being presented within the marketplace? Such an examination should encourage the organisation to seek the means to overcome the weaknesses. Of course, taking advantage of the market opportunities may be time-dependent and competitors may be able to react more effectively and efficiently due to their internal strengths.

Figure 12.5 TOWS framework

ST Options: This focuses on the relationship between the internal factors – Strength – and the external – Threats. In this case, the organisation has the strengths (for example, capabilities) to either overcome or avoid the potential/real threats, such as increased competition.

WT Options: This focuses on the relationship between the internal factor – Weaknesses – and the external – Threats. In this case the organisation will need to consider how the identified organisational weaknesses will expose the company to the external threats. For example, assume that the Board of Directors of a company in Country A has decided to focus all its production and marketing efforts into selling into Country B. The Board has committed the company to a strategy that might provide high returns but also could incur a high level of risks. Let's assume that diplomatic relations between Countries A and B begin, over time, to falter to the point where ambassadors are removed. Country A then seeks to impose unilateral sanctions on goods being sold by companies in Country A to Country B. This means that the profitable market once held by the company has disappeared because the company's inherent weakness was the Board's decision-making abilities where they committed the company to one overseas market. Unless a company can react effectively, to find new markets, such a strategy could result in bankruptcy.

MARKETING AUDIT

A marketing audit is a means of collecting and analysing information from a variety of sources both internally and externally to the organisation. This can be viewed as a strategic approach to marketing planning.

Some of the models and frameworks that we have already examined will have been used to collect information. The audit allows us to bring together that information to help inform both decision-making and the implementation of a marketing plan.

The audit allows an organisation to:

1. Understand its various internal strengths and weaknesses along with external opportunities and threats.
2. Understand its capabilities (resources and competences) and what additional capabilities it may require to develop and implement a successful marketing plan.
3. Develop a marketing strategy that meets the objectives as set out in the organisation's corporate objectives.

The following overarching themes are based upon the work of Kotler, Gregor and Rogers (1977). This helps to provide us with a template.

Environmental Audit

This is an analysis of both the micro and macro environments (see Chapter 1). These will need to be examined from both a home and overseas perspective. Moreover, the dynamics of the macro environment will have to be taken into consideration.

It is here too that the organisation would seek to examine the competition, from the perspective of the current incumbents and potential new entrants. Within this analysis an organisation would examine the competitor's strategies and tactics, especially in relation to what are the differentiators between the various competitors.

An organisation may also use Scenario Analysis in an attempt to identify certain options that may be available to them over the short, medium and longer terms.

Marketing Strategy Audit

This covers two key areas: Objectives and the Marketing Strategy. These need to synchronise with the overall strategy of the organisation. The marketing team might seek to answer the following questions:

- What are the overall corporate objectives?
- What overarching strategy should we develop to meet those objectives?
- What should be our objectives and why?
- What is the timescale for undertaking the strategy?
- What resources will be required to undertake the marketing strategy?
- What will be the tactics deployed to implement the strategy?
- How will these tactics be deployed?
- How will the degree of success of the strategy be measured?

Marketing Organisational Audit

This will normally consider the structure and functional efficiency of the marketing department. This will link into resources (as discussed earlier in this chapter). However, we should not purely consider what happens within the marketing department. It should also include how efficient the interface is between the marketing department and other functional units within the organisation as well as external providers (for instance, advertising agencies). Normally the two key internal units will be the operations and finance departments – operations in relation to the production of the goods or service, and finance from the perspective of budgetary monitoring and control.

Marketing Systems Audit

Technology has greatly aided the gathering, storage and the analysis of data. Organisations will either maintain their own data warehousing and data mining or outsource it to specialist companies. As stated elsewhere in this text, information can be stored and updated every time we use our loyalty and credit cards, search an online site (adding to our favourites) or complete a purchase. This information helps to build a profile of us, what types of products or services we like (or would like), frequency of purchasing and our credit ratings. With developments in both computer hardware and software, companies will seek to enhance their understanding of us as a customer. For companies to remain viable, especially within (or potentially) highly competitive markets, they have to have efficient and effective means of processing data.

Marketing Productivity Audit

Marketing teams need to consider the level of profitability for each product and/or service being offered. In some cases an organisation may market one product at a break-even price because it encourages the customer to purchase other products at a much higher price. An example of this action can be B2B stationery suppliers.

Marketing Mix Audit

Previous chapters have discussed the key characteristics of products, price, promotion, placement (distribution), people, processes and physical evidence (physicality). The audit would need to consider, among other factors, their viability (or contribution) and their interrelationships.

Market Research and Forecasting

These are ongoing processes and generally underpin many of the actions stated above. As stated earlier, an organisation may seek to create and examine different scenarios in order to consider options and subsequent actions. For instance, if there is the potential for a long-term drought in certain regions of the world where coffee plants grow, what impact will that have on the price of coffee beans? What is the customer prepared to pay for their instant or ground coffee? What should the coffee shops of London, Paris, New York, Sydney and Seattle, for instance, charge? These are just a few of the questions that might be considered.

Summary

By 'auditing' the marketing team will have a better understanding of the environment in which they operate and the capabilities currently available to them. Moreover, it provides the opportunity to undertake a gap analysis. This is the gap between the capabilities that they have and those that they really need to be competitive within the marketplace. The audit also assists the marketing team in preparing a marketing plan.

MARKETING PLANS

We can describe a marketing plan as a document that details the requirements for a company's marketing activities over the short, medium and longer term. In other words, it is a blueprint that provides direction. As with any plan there needs to be some degree of flexibility, especially when operating within a globalised, often unpredictable, world.

A useful method of looking at a marketing plan and the key components of that plan is by using the SMART mnemonic. This initiates questions that need to be answered in order to create a functional plan.

S – SPECIFIC: This is where the marketing team explain what they are seeking to achieve in as specific detail as possible. What is the plan to achieve and why? What capabilities will be required (including budget)? There needs to be 'fine' detail to the plan so that actions and outcomes can be controlled and measured. Plans need to be based upon sound logic.

M – MEASURABLE: This is where criteria or indicators are established to measure both progress and final outcomes. As stated above, a plan needs to be flexible, so it is important to analyse the plan whilst it is in progress. This provides the team with the opportunities to adjust the plan as it develops, as and when necessary.

A – ACHIEVABLE: The question for the marketing team is whether or not what they are proposing is actually achievable within the time frame and budget. This will include identifying the capabilities (resources and competences) necessary to operationalise the plan. Sometimes plans can be overly ambitious, turning out to be unrealistic with resultant negative consequences. Equally, a perfectly achievable plan may become unrealistic due to unforeseen external factors, such as political instability.

R – RELEVANT: Is the plan relevant to the marketing objectives and therefore the organisation's overall aims and objectives? Is the plan relevant to the environment, whether nationally, regionally or trans-nationally, in which it operates?

T – TIMESCALE: This is the overall timescale designated to operate the plan, for example, over three years. A plan is often subdivided into activities that will have their own separate timescales within that three-year period. The aim should be to instigate actions that can be achieved within the allocated time frame.

Core Strategy – Marketing Objectives

These objectives need to be action-oriented and quantifiable, for example, increasing market share of Brand A by X% with a profit margin of Z% over Y years.

There needs to be a clear rationale provided for each of the objectives.

Target Markets

This links back to Chapter 4 and STP. The organisation must seek to target the right customer group within the appropriate segment of the population. Failure to do so will lead to wasted resources and failure to meet both the marketing and corporate objectives.

Marketing Research

As stated in Chapter 3, marketing research helps organisations gain a greater understanding of their current and potential future customer base. Market research equally aids an organisation in understanding current and changing market trends. The research will also indicate the current position of the organisation's products and services, which, in turn, may influence the setting of the marketing objectives.

Outcome of the Marketing Audit

The marketing audit will provide the team with both internal and external information that will help in devising and operationalising the tactical aspects of the plan. The audit should also highlight actual and potential weaknesses that need to be addressed. These weaknesses, unless mitigated, could hamper the successful operationalisation of the plan.

Moreover, it should highlight any additional capabilities required to fulfil the marketing objectives.

Assumptions

Whether stated or not, there are normally assumptions 'built' into a plan. Those assumptions can include economic stability based upon past and current predictions. However, as was witnessed in 2008, the US and UK banking crises unravelled over a relatively short time frame, with many economists and financial observers being caught unawares (Greenspan, 2013). The crisis in the US and UK spread trans-nationally, leading to many countries suffering a period of recession and austerity measures (UK and Greece are two cases).

Key Tactics

The marketing team need to articulate what actions will be taken using the various elements of the marketing mix. For instance, to gain additional market share a company may add more product within the package for the same price (for example, eight chocolate bars for the price of six). Alternatively, a company may reduce its prices in order to be more competitive within the market and thus potentially gain more market share. In both these cases they may be supported by a co-ordinated and high-profile marketing communications campaign.

Budget

Whilst a marketing department will have an overall budget (including staffing and facilities costs) it should allocate a 'ring-fenced' proportion for the marketing plan. This is then subdivided and apportioned to specific actions and activities, for example, the marketing communications plan.

Implementation Programme

This examines how and when the plan will be implemented. Key points include:

Who is to implement the plan? Is the right team in place? Do they understand the processes? Is there linkage across the organisation? Could they use cross-functional teams for implementation? When is the plan being 'rolled-out?' Will it be 'rolled-out' in stages? Who will monitor and adjust the plan accordingly?

Performance Measurements and Evaluation

The performance of the plan has to be monitored, on a regular basis, against key indicators and the overall marketing objectives. Where subsequent changes are made throughout the life of the plan, then they too need to be re-evaluated on an ongoing basis.

WHY PLANS FAIL

It is likely that the majority of marketing plans undergo some form of adjustment within their life span for a myriad of reasons. However, it is equally clear that many marketing plans fail to meet their aims and objectives. Potential reasons include the following:

Poorly Articulated Plans

One of the challenges of developing and writing a marketing plan is articulating, in a clear and concise manner, what the plan is about and what people need to do. Without clarity and direction, it can be difficult to effectively instigate the plan.

Lack of Understanding of the Market

Perhaps no market research has been undertaken: Not all organisations undertake market research, some because they cannot afford the investment and others because they do not believe it to be viable. However, it is necessary to have some understanding of how the market operates in order to attempt to meet the set objectives. Otherwise how does the company know that it is even targeting the right customer group?

Lack of Understanding of Changing Market Conditions

As has been indicated throughout this text, organisations need to have an awareness of changing market conditions. This applies to trans-national markets as well as the home market.

Inability to React to Changing Circumstances

Environmental scanning (see Chapter 2) helps management to (1) generally be aware of changes within the micro and macro environments, and (2) to use their capabilities to react to the unfolding changes. If companies are neither monitoring nor have the necessary capabilities to react, then their plan can become inflexible. The organisation will be outperformed by more agile competitors (both incumbent and new).

Unrealistic Targets

Sometimes plans are too ambitious and are virtually impossible to fulfil, especially in terms of the organisation's overall direction and capabilities. It may look 'impressive' on paper but cannot be delivered in reality.

Lack of Control Mechanisms and Monitoring Systems

(These do not have to be complex!) There may be cases where (1) there are no systems in place to monitor the plan, or (2) the systems that are in place are insufficient or ineffective for the task. In both cases, the marketing team will be unlikely to gauge the effectiveness of the plan until either plan-end or something serious impacts the plan during its life. Both situations could compromise the overall effectiveness of the plan.

Insufficient Budget(s)

This can occur in several ways: (1) Being over-ambitious. This could be a marketing team not being selective in their choice of actions to meet budgetary restrictions. (2) The team, along with the finance department, not undertaking detailed costings in order to prepare the marketing plan budget. This results in insufficient funds to meet all the activities that are linked to the objectives. (3) Not building into the marketing plan budget a contingency fund for unforeseen circumstances. (4) The allocated budget being insufficient to meet the demands of the senior management team and their objectives (this also links, in part, to (1) above).

Poorly Trained or Insufficient Number of Staff

As stated in Chapter 7, people are potentially an organisation's most important resource. Members of the team may invest significant energy and enthusiasm into the plan, however if they are not trained they are unlikely to deliver to the required standard. Moreover, whilst enthusiasm must be championed, used inappropriately could actually be damaging to the aims and objectives of the plan. Equally, there is the need to have a sufficient number of staff to be able to deliver the plan to the required standard. Whilst reducing staffing loads may, in the short term, reduce costs, in the longer term it may be counterproductive if the marketing plan cannot be implemented efficiently and effectively.

Lack of Leadership, Direction and Support from Senior Management

Plans need to be both directed and supported by the senior management team. Whilst this may not require day-to-day engagement, it will require interventions, as and when necessary. These interventions may include: (1) Suggestions and providing focus. (2) Providing necessary capabilities, especially resources.

Equally, senior managers need to provide the various teams involved with encouragement and moral support. However, when senior management either lacks engagement or is too interventionist, plans may become dysfunctional. Whilst a plan may be implemented it may lack the necessary focus, thus not meeting the necessary business objectives.

KEY POINTS

In this chapter we have considered the following:

1. The different layers of strategy: corporate, business (often associated with Strategic Business Units) and functional (the activity level including finance, operations and marketing).
2. The importance of understanding the industry or sector in which the company operates. This is particularly important in terms of understanding the relative strengths of suppliers and buyers, the level of competitive rivalry and whether or not new competitors have the opportunity to enter the marketplace. Equally, as well as competing, companies can co-operate with rivals within certain business sectors as this can be mutually beneficial.
3. For companies to enter a market and compete successfully within that market they need the requisite capabilities (resources and competences). What is important to note is that the required basic capabilities to enter a market will change over time, mainly through changing competitive dynamics and customer demands.
4. The product life cycle comprises five/six key components: introduction, growth, maturity, decline, rejuvenation (in some cases only) and death. Reflect back to Chapter 5 (Branding) and the longevity of some internationally recognisable brands.
5. Ansoff's Growth Matrix provides both strategists and marketers with a means of illustrating actions in relation to products/ services and markets.
6. SWOT and TOWS matrices are mechanisms for bringing together both internal and external factors to assist decision-making within diverse and competitive environments. Where a company operates internationally, they will undertake such analysis for each of their markets.
7. The marketing audit develops out of many of the approaches stated above, and includes the analysis of the environment

in which the organisation operates, organisational structure, systems and the integration and operation of the marketing mix.

8. Marketing plans need to be SMART in their development, structure and implementation.

9. The key components of a marketing plan are: objectives, target markets, findings from marketing research, outcome of the marketing audit, assumptions, tactics, budget, implementation, performance measurements and review.

10. However, for a variety of reasons, not all marketing plans are successful. The reasons include lack of understanding of market dynamics, insufficient budget, lack of senior management leadership and direction, and poorly trained staff.

QUESTIONS

Here is a series of questions and activities for you to undertake to aid your knowledge and understanding of the points made in this chapter.

1. As we have seen from this and previous chapters, a large proportion of markets are highly dynamic and competitive. What are the potential challenges for marketers developing plans within this context? Can these challenges be overcome, and, if so, how?

2. Why do you think, within a marketing context, that it is important for a company to understand and regularly review its capabilities (resources and competences)?

3. Why do marketing plans fail, and how can the causes of such failure be mitigated or overcome?

4. Why is it important, from a marketing perspective, to understand the relative power of suppliers within a market? Equally, why is it important to understand the relative power of buyers within a market? What can marketing teams learn from this knowledge?

FURTHER READING

Brennan, R., Baines, P. and Garneau, P. (2007) *Contemporary Strategic Marketing* (2nd Edition). London: Palgrave Macmillan.

McDonald, M. and Wilson, H. (2011) *Marketing Plans: How to Prepare Them, How to Use Them*. Chichester: John Wiley & Sons.

References

Aaker, J.L. (1997) Dimensions of Brand Personality. *Journal of Marketing Research*. August Vol 34 No 3. pp: 347–356.

ACA (2014) History of the ACA. Aircraft Carrier Alliance. www.aircraft carrieralliance.co.uk/about

Alexander, R. (2012) Which is the world's biggest employer? BBC News Online. 20 March.

AMA (2014a) Definitions of Marketing. American Marketing Association. www.ama.org/AboutAMA/Pages/Definition-of-Marketing

AMA (2014b) Statement of Ethics. American Marketing Association. www.ama.org/AboutAMA/Pages/Statement-of-Ethics.

Ansoff, I. (1987) *Corporate Strategy*. Harmondsworth: Penguin Books.

Antunes, A. (2013) A look at Brazil's booming (yet closeted) multi-billion pink dollar gay market. Forbes magazine online. 6 July 2013.

Baker, C. (2015) Dairy industry in the UK: statistics. Standard Note: SN/SG/2721. Social & General Statistical Section. House of Commons Library. 29 January 2015.

Bamford, V. (2014) Sugar Puffs renamed Honey Monster Puffs as Halo cuts sugar from recipe and name. The Grocer 16 October 2014.

BBC (2013) Huge survey reveals seven social classes in the UK. BBC News Online 3 April 2013.

BBC (2014a) Iceland volcano: Aviation risk level from Bardarbunga lowered. BBC Online 24 August 2014.

BBC (2014b) Queen to name new aircraft carrier HMS Queen Elizabeth. BBC News Online 22 February 2014.

BBC (2014c) Supermarket price war sees cost of milk go down. BBC News Online 7 March 2014.

BBC (2014d) Alcohol floor price announced for England and Wales. BBC News Online 4 February 2014.

BBC (2014e) Supermarket 'bogof' deals criticised over food waste. BBC News Online 6 April 2014.

BBC (2014f) Costa Concordia Disaster. (This is a collection of BBC news and feature reports that provides background to the Costa Concordia incident). www.bbc.co.uk/news/world-europe-16646686

Bell, C.R. and Zemke, R. (1987) Service breakdown: The road to recovery. *Management Review*. Vol 76. No 10. pp: 32–35.

Berfield, S. and Baigorri, M. (2013) Zara's fast-fashion edge. Bloomberg Business Week Online. 14 November.

BIS (2010) Pricing Practice Guide. Department of Business, Innovation and Skills. UK Government. November.

Blackburn, S. (2001) *Being Good: An Introduction to Ethics*. Oxford: Oxford University Press.

Bloomberg (2014) Bloomberg Business: Inditex Business ITX Snapshot. www.bloomberg.com/research/stocks/snapshot/snapshot.asp? ticker=ITX:SM

Blomqvist, R. Dahl, J. and Haeger, T. (1993) *Relationsmarknadsföring: strategi och metod i servicekonkurrens (Relationship Marketing Strategy and Methods for Service Operations)*. Gothenburg: IHM Publishing.

Boerlu, H. (2013) Houston issues ticket to a Mini Cooper parked on a wall. www.bmwblog.com

Booms, B.H. and Bitner, M. J. (1981) Marketing strategies and organisation structures for service firms in Donnely, J.H. and George, W.R. (eds). *Marketing of Services*. Chicago: American Marketing Association.

Bowie, D. and Buttle, F. (2004) *Hospitality Marketing: An Introduction*. Oxford: Elsevier Butterworth-Heinemann.

Briggs, A.D.M., Mytton, O.T., Kehlbacher, A., Taffin, R., Rayner, M. and Scarborough, P. (2013) Overall and income specific effect on prevalence of overweight and obesity of 20% sugar sweetened drink tax in UK:

econometric and comparative assessment modelling study. Research paper 31. *British Medical Journal*. Vol 347 October.

Burn-Callander, R. (2011) £6bn: The amount that the 'pink pound' contributes every year to the UK economy. *Management Today* 2 November 2011.

Butler, S. (2012) Zara's owners bucks the economic gloom to outgrow Spain's retail banks. *The Observer* 3 June.

Buttle, F. (1990) Where do we go with relationship marketing? In Buttle, F. (ed.) *Relationship Marketing: Theory and Practice*. London: Paul Chapman Publishing.

CAP (2014) Advertising Standards Authority Codes. Committee for Advertising Practice. www.cap.org.uk/advertising-codes

CCS (2014) Overview of the Crown Commercial Service, a UK Government department. www.gov.uk/government/organisations/crown-commercial-service/about

CIM (2010) Cost of customer acquisition vs customer retention. Fact File. The Chartered Institute of Marketing.

Compassion in World Farming (2014) Welfare issues for egg-laying hens. http://www.ciwf.org.uk/farm-animals/chickens/egg-laying-hens/welfare-issues/

Cracknell, R. (2010) The ageing population: The UK's ageing population has considerable consequences for public services. Value for Money in Public Services. Key Issues for the New Parliament 2010, House of Commons Library Service.

Cresci, E. (2014) Zara removes striped pyjamas with yellow star following online outrage. *The Guardian Online* 27 August 2014.

CSCMP (2014) About Us – Definitions. Council of Supply Chain Management Professionals. www.cscmp.org.

DairyCo (2014) Dairy sales and consumption. www.diary.co.uk

Davidson, D. (1997) *Even More Offensive Marketing*. London: Penguin.

DEFRA (2014) United Kingdom Milk Prices & Composition of Milk January 2014. Report by the Department for Environment, Food and Rural Affairs, UK Government 27 February 2014.

De Pelsmacker, P. De., Geuens, M. and Bergh, J.V. den, (2010) *Marketing Communications: A European Perspective*. Harlow: Financial Times/ Prentice Hall.

DeSouza, G. (1999) Designing a customer retention plan. *Journal of Business Strategy*. Vol 13 No 2 pp: 24–28.

Elliot, C. (2013) The Navigator: The high pressure of time share sales. *The Washington Post* 4 April 2013.

Engel, J.E., Blackwell, R.D. and Miniard, P.W. (1990) *Consumer Behavior*. Dryden Press.

EU (1999). Minimum standards for the protection of laying hens. European Union Council Directive 1999/74/EC.

Freycinet Adventures (2014) Visitor information for Freycinet and Coles Bay. www.freycinetadventures.com.au/freycinet/overview/

Gilligan, C. and Wilson, R.M.S. (2003) *Strategic Marketing Planning*. Oxford: Butterworth-Heinemann.

Ginn, J. Stone, M. and Ekinci, Y. (2010) Customer retention management in a recession. *Journal of Direct and Digital Marketing*. Vol 12, No 2 October – December. pp: 115–127.

Greenspan, A. (2013) No one saw it coming: Why the financial crisis took economists by surprise. Foreign Affairs. November/December.

Griseri, P. and Seppala, N. (2010) *Business Ethics and Corporate Social Responsibility*. Andover: South-Western Cengage Learning.

Grönroos, C. (2000) *Service Management and Marketing: A Customer Relationship Approach*. (2nd Edition) Chichester: Wiley.

Grönroos, C. (2004) The relationship marketing process: communication, interaction, dialogue, value. *Journal of Business and Industrial Marketing*. Vol 19 No 2. pp: 99–113.

Groucutt, J. (2005) *Foundations of Marketing*. Basingstoke: Palgrave Macmillan.

Groucutt, J., Leadley, P. and Forsyth, P. (2004) *Marketing: Essential Principles*, New Realities. London: Kogan Page.

Groucutt, J. and Griseri, P. (2004) *Mastering e-Business*. Basingstoke: Palgrave Macmillan.

Halo Foods (2014) Overview of the company. Halo foods is owned by the Raisio Group. www.glistenltd.com/Halo_Foods/About_Halo_Foods/About_Halo_Foods www.raisio.com/en/en.

Hamilton, C. and Denniss, R. (2005) *Affluenza: When Too Much is Never Enough*. Sydney: Allen & Unwin.

Hardy, T. (2012) Reaching gay consumers: beyond the 'pink pound'. *Marketing Magazine*. 9 November 2012.

Heinz (2014) Company background. www.heinz.com/our-company/about-heinz

Hines, T and Bruce, M. (2007) *Fashion Marketing: Contemporary Issues*. (2nd Edition) Oxford: Butterworth-Heinemann.

Hotchner, A. E. (2012) A legend as big as the Ritz. Vanity Fair, July 2012.

House of Lords (2014) Counting the cost of food waste: EU food waste prevention. House of Lords European Union Committee. 10th Report of Sessions 2013–14. Paper HL154. The Stationery Office.

Humphries, J. (2011) *Childhood and Child Labour in the British Industrial Revolution*. (Cambridge Series in Economic History). Cambridge: Cambridge University Press.

ILO (2013) Marking progress against child labour: Global estimates and trends 2000–2012. International Labour Office, International Programme on the Elimination of Child Labour (IPEC) – Geneva: International Labour Organisation.

Interbrand (2014a) Best global brands. www.bestglobalbrands.com/2014/ranking/

Interbrand (2014b) Four ages of branding. www.bestglobalbrands.com/2014/featured/the-four-ages-of-branding/

IPO (2014) IP Crime Report 2012–2014. Crime Group, Intellectual Property Office. (This is a UK Government Department.)

Jobber, D. (2004) *Principles and Practice of Marketing* (4th Edition). Maidenhead: McGraw-Hill.

Kahle, L., Poulos, B. and Sukhdial, A. (1988) Changes in Social Values in the United States during the past decade. *Journal of Advertising Research*. Vol 28 No 1. February–March. pp: 35–41.

Keller, K.L. (2001) Building customer-based brand equity. *Marketing Management* July/August, pp: 15–19.

Kotler, P. and Keller, K.L. (2009) *A Framework for Marketing Management*. (4th Edition). London: Prentice Hall/Pearson Education International.

Kotler, P., Gregor, W. and Rogers, W. (1977) The marketing audit comes of age. *Sloan Management Review*, Vol 18. No 2 Winter. pp: 25–43.

Lauterborn, R. (1990) New marketing litany. Four P's passe, C-words take over. Forum, Advertising Age. 10 October. p: 26.

Laczniak, G.R. and Murphy, P.E. (1991) Fostering ethical marketing decisions. *Journal of Business Ethics*. Vol 10. No 4. pp: 259–271.

Leisure Database (2015) The 2014 State of the UK Fitness Industry Report. The Leisure Database Company.

LME (2014) About Us – Corporate Overview. London Metal Exchange. www.lme.com/about-us

Lo, J.L.W., Rabenasolo, B. and Jolly-Desodt, A-M. (2004) Leveraging speed as a competitive advantage: A case study of an international fashion chain and its competitors. Conference Paper. Sixth Framework Programme, Fashion Net International Conference 28th–29th September.

Luker, S. (2012) Burson-Marsteller called in to cover Costa Concordia disaster. PR Week. 16 January.

Maslow, A.H. (1943) Theory of Human Motivation. *Psychology Review*. Vol 50 No 4 July. pp: 370–396.

McBride (2015) McBride Annual Report and Accounts 2014.

Media Week (2014) Newspaper ABCs *i* is the only title to gain circulation in 2013. Media Week 22 January 2014. (NB: the *i* is a national UK newspaper.)

Menkes, S. (2000) Fashion house move to tighten brand control: A licence to kill. *New York Times* 4 July 2000.

Mihm, B. (2010) Fast fashion in a flat world: Global sourcing strategies. *International Business & Economics Research Journal*. Vol 9 No 6. June. pp: 55–63.

Mondelēz (2014) Fact Sheet 2014: Unleashing a Global Snacking Powerhouse. Mondelēz International.

Montgomery, A. (2014) Smith & Milton re-brand Honey Monster. Design Week. 20 October 2014.

Morgan, E. and Dent, M. (2010) *The Economic Burden of Obesity*. Oxford: National Obesity Observatory.

Nevill, R. and Jerningham, C.E. (1908) *Piccadilly and Pall Mall: Manners, Morals and Man*. London: Duckworth. (Reprinted 2011 through Ulan Press.)

Ofcom (2014) The Broadcasting Code. Independent regulator and competition authority for the UK communication industries. www.stakeholders. ofcom.org.uk/broadcasting/broadcast-codes/broadcast-code/

Ogunyemi, T. (2014) The growth of UK Afro-Caribbean hair care and beauty market. Think Ethnic www.thinkethnic.com 7 October 2014.

Ozimek, J. (2010) The disloyalty ladder – two rungs further down. *Journal of Direct and Digital Marketing*. Vol 11 No 3. January–March. pp: 207–218.

Porter, M.E. (1980) *Competitive Strategy*. New York: Free Press.

PRSA (2012) Statement on public relations – definitions. Public Relations Society of America. www.prsa.org

P2PFA (2014) About P2P Finance. Peer-to-Peer Finance Association. www. p2pfa.info/about-p2p-finance

Ramrayka, L. (2014) Brands continue to target fast food at kids. *The Guardian Online*. 25 February 2014.

Recycling Now (2014) Food waste. Recycle Now Online. Recycling Now is a recycling campaign for England which is funded by the UK government and managed by WRAP and used by over 80% of English local authorities. WRAP is a private not for profit organisation funded by the UK government to work with businesses, local authorities and communities to reduce waste.

Reddy, M. and Terblanche, N. (2005) How not to extend your luxury brand. *Harvard Business Review*. December 2005.

Reevoo (2014) Overview of the organisation and its rating system. www. reevoo.com/about-us/

Reichheld, F.F. (1993) Loyalty based management. *Harvard Business Review*. March–April. pp: 64–73.

Reichheld, F.F. and Sasser, E.W. Jr. (1990) Zero defections: Quality comes to services. *Harvard Business Review*. Vol 69 (Sept–Oct). pp: 105–111.

Risen, T. (2015) New agency to aid battle against hackers. *US News Online*. 10 February 2015.

Rogers, E.M. (1983) *Diffusion of Innovations*. 3rd Edition. New York: Free Press.

Rotary (2014) The four way test. Rotary International. www.rotary.org/myrotary/en/learning-reference/about-rotary/guiding-principles

Ruddick, G. (2010) Kraft buys Cadbury for £11.9bn: A Q&A. *The Telegraph Online*. 19 January.

Rushe, D. (2012) iPhone 5: Apple sells 5 million in first 3 days. *The Guardian* 24 September 2012.

Salvemini, L.P. (2002) *United Colors: The Benetton Campaigns*. London: Scriptums Editions.

Schiffman, L.G., Kanuk, L.L. and Hansen, H. (2012) *Consumer Behaviour: A European Outlook*. (2nd Edition). Harlow: Financial Times/Prentice Hall.

Schramm, W. (1955) *The Process and Effects of Mass Communications*. Urbana, Il: University of Illinois Press.

Shannon, C.E. (1948) A mathematical theory of communication. *Bell System Technical Journal* Vol 27 (July and October) pp: 379–423 and 623–656.

Siltanen, R. (2014) Yes, a super bowl ad really is worth $4 million. *Forbes Magazine*, 29 January 2014.

Smithers, R. (2014) Organic food and drink sales rise after years of decline. *The Guardian* 13 March 2014.

Soil Association (2014) Organic Market Report 2014. Soil Association.

Sorell, T. (1994) Is the customer always right? *Journal of Business Ethics*. Vol 13 November. pp: 913–918.

Spary, S. (2014) Sugar Puffs ditches name and brings back Honey Monster in rebrand. *Marketing* 20 October 2014.

Statistics Brain Research Institute (2013) Television watching statistics (verified 7 December 2013) www.statisticbrain.com/television-watching-statistics/

Sull, D. (2009) Competing through organisational agility. *McKinsey Quarterly*. December.

Tasmanian Government (2014) About Tasmania's plastic bag ban. Department of Primary Industries, Parks, Water and Environment. Tasmanian Government www.plasticbags.tas.gov

Telegraph (2015) The world's largest container ship arrives at the port of Felixstowe. *The Telegraph Online* 7 January 2015.

Tesco (2014) About Us – Corporate Background. Tesco plc. www.tescoplc.com

Tfl (2014) Transport for London. This PDF provides details of the different advertising formats used on London buses, metro trains and at the bus stations and underground stations. www.tfl.gov.uk/cdn/static/cms/documents/tfl-advertising-standard.pdf

Tfl (2015) Facts and Figures – London Underground. Transport for London www.tfl.gov.uk/corporate/about

The Body Shop (2014) Corporate overview. Body Shop International. http://www.thebodyshop.co.uk/services/aboutus.aspx

TripAdvisor (2014) About TripAdvisor. http://www.tripadvisor.co.uk/PressCenter-c6-About_Us.html

Unilever (2014a) Dove: Overview. http://www.unilever.com/brands-in-action/detail/Dove/292077

Unilever (2014b) Brands in Action – Cif. www.unilever.com/brands-in-action

Wall, M. (2014) Big Data: Are you ready for lift-off? *BBC News Online* 4 March.

Waterfield, B. (2014) Zara apologies for striped 'Holocaust' pyjamas with yellow star. *The Telegraph Online* 27 August 2014.

Watson, B. (2014) The tricky business of advertising to children. *The Guardian*, 24 February 2014.

Weihrich, H. (1982) The TOWS matrix – a tool for situational analysis. *Long Range Planning* April Vol 15 No 2. pp: 54–66.

Which? (2015) Stairlifts pressure-selling exposed by Which? Four in 10 stairlift customers report bad practice. *Which? Magazine Online* 23 January 2015.

Whyatt, C. (2014) The true cost of aircraft carrier HMS Queen Elizabeth. *BBC News Online* 4 July.

Yale Rudd Center (2013) Fast Food Facts: Food Advertising to Children and Teens Score 2013: Measuring Progress in Nutrition and Marketing to Children and Teens. Yale Rudd Center for Food Policy and Obesity.

Yao, J. (2015) New trend in online sales of insurance products. *China Economic Net*. 24 January 2015.

INDEX

301